THE FUNCTION OF
"CHINA"
IN
MARX, LENIN, AND MAO

THE FUNCTION OF
"CHINA"
IN
MARX, LENIN, AND MAO

by

Donald M. Lowe

UNIVERSITY OF CALIFORNIA PRESS
BERKELEY AND LOS ANGELES, 1966

University of California Press
Berkeley and Los Angeles, California
Cambridge University Press
London, England

TO MY PARENTS

Acknowledgments

I wish to thank Professors Reinhard Bendix and N. V. Raisanovsky for the kind encouragement they gave to an earlier draft version of this study. As will be evident in the following pages, I owe most to my teacher, Professor J. R. Levenson. In addition, Professor F. I. Kaplan painstakingly provided me with the sort of criticism which only a very good friend can give. Naturally, none of them are responsible for the guilt of omission and commission, which must be present in any work of synthesis and interpretation.

The interlibrary loan service at both Duquesne University and the University of California, Riverside, has been most helpful. And I am especially indebted to the generous advice of Mr. Ts'eng Hsien-lin of the Hoover Institute and Library.

During various stages of the study, the following provided financial support: the Ford Foundation, through its Foreign Area Training Fellowship, supported the initial stage of the research; Duquesne University provided for the typing of an early draft; a Faculty Fellowship from President Clark Kerr of the University of California enabled me to revise that draft; and the Academic Senate of the University of California, Riverside, financed the typing of the revised manuscript.

D. M. L.

Riverside, Calif.
November, 1965

Contents

Introduction

How did Marx, Lenin, and Mao see China? And how can we explain the differences in their views?

This is a study in the historical significance of the Marxian, Leninist, and Maoist ideas of China.* It is neither a general study of the adaptation of Marxism to non-Western societies, nor a theoretical study of the Marxist controversy regarding the nature of the Oriental society. The historian's emphasis is different from that of the social scientist or philosopher. A historian seeks an answer to the question regarding any phenomenon: "How did it come about?" He answers it in terms of the specific antecedents of that phenomenon. He is more interested in the how-possibly question, with its implication of once-upon-a-time, than in the why-necessarily question with its implication of typology.[1] The answer to the former question depends on the specific context of that phenomenon.

Obviously, there have been changes in the Marxist, that is, Marxian-Leninist-Maoist, ideas of China. But a historical study of the changes in the Marxist ideas of China has to be composed of several parts. To begin with, there is the need to relate the Marxist ideas of China to the development of Marxist thought in general. Certainly, no historian can accept the Marxist claim of unchanging orthodoxy. Yet change within orthodoxy is a far different proposition from change uninhibited by any claim to intellectual orthodoxy. Marxist change has to be accomplished within the perspective of the unity of theory and practice. Marx, Lenin, and Mao have all harped upon this unity, although each of them had a different interpretation of it. The question is: "What is the relation of the

* By Marxian I mean the thought of Marx and Engels. By Marxist I mean the entire span of thinking within the Marxian framework.

changing ideas of China to the changing Marxist correlation of theory and practice?"

Further, both the Marxist ideas of China and the main body of Marxist thought have to be historically related to their situational contexts. By relating Marxism and its idea of China to the nineteenth-century West European intellectual situation, Leninism and its idea of China to the early twentieth-century Russian intellectual situation, and Maoism and its idea of China to the twentieth-century Chinese intellectual situation, we hope to derive the historical significance of the changing Marxist ideas of China. The question has become: "How did such changes in the Marxist ideas of China occur?"

Finally, the answer to the question "how" depends upon the correlation of available historical data with a relevant methodological hypothesis. There is no perspective knowledge without presuppositions.[2] The problem is not how to approach an unorganized body of historical material with as blank a Lockean mind as possible, but to seek a hypothesis relevant to the question posed and the material available. Such a hypothesis will have to be applicable to the three differing contexts of the three ideas of "China."

Let us begin the quest.

Marxists speak of the unity of theory and practice. Theory is universal in pretension, involving the long-range validity of historical materialism, whereas practice is specific in preoccupation, involving the short-range objective of revolutionary action. The unity of the two implies a necessary adjustment between thought and action.

But behind Marxist intellectual consciousness lurks the tension between reason and society. Reason is universal in expectation, whereas society is specific. The tension between universal reason and social reality is the background for the Marxist unity of theory and practice. Marxist consideration of theory emphasizes the universalist demand of reason, whereas Marxist consideration of practice emphasizes the particularist demand of social reality. The Marxist unity of theory and practice presupposes the ultimate primacy of reason over society.

The phenomenon of tension between reason and society is

Western in origin. But with the progression of Marxism from the West to originally non-Western but now westernizing societies, the tension between Western-oriented reason and Western society becomes the tension between Western-oriented reason and a westernizing society.* Marxism now requires the unity of a Western-oriented rational theory and a non-Western-oriented revolutionary practice. In the process both theory and practice are transformed.

We have three sets of dichotomies: First, theory and practice; then, reason and society; and, finally, Western rational theory and westernizing society. Each dichotomy includes the conflict between the concern for the universal and the concern for the particular. The concern for the universal is standardized by the Western model of reason; the concern for the particular is oriented toward the specific revolutionary practice in different situations. The Marxist consciousness with its insistence on the unity of theory and practice is an attempt to resolve this tension. Consciousness becomes potentially more plausible as it is transposed from the Western to a westernizing situation. The plausibility depends on the ability of the consciousness to justify specific practice in universal Western terms and to insist that Western values are relevant to a westernizing situation. The motivation behind the transferred consciousness is the westernized intellectual's need to seek the Western equivalence of his own society.

The historical significance of the Marxist ideas of China depends upon the correlation of the changing ideas of China with the changing Marxist unity of theory and practice in different, changing

* The phenomenon of westernization/modernization eventually includes all levels of the transformation of a hitherto non-Western/premodern society. It is a complex continuum. The word "modernization" implies a model of technical efficiency, whereas the word "westernization" implies a model of Western rational values. Of course, the two concepts are interrelated, and it is almost impossible to separate the two models. Since in this work we are more concerned with the interaction of Western values and non-Western traditions in a westernizing/modernizing situation, I shall use the word "westernization." However, I wish to emphasize that to be westernized can never be the same as being Western. From the West come the stimulation, the challenge, and the pressure for a post-traditional type of change. But a westernizing society does *not* change in the direction of the Western model. For a further discussion, see below, p. 45.

situations.[3] The hypothesis to be employed in the study of these changing relations is that *a continuing, yet transforming, tension exists between the concern for the universal and the concern for the particular, from one intellectual situation to another.* With this in view, I shall spin a web, which I hope is the historian's.[4]

Chapter One

Marx

Eighteenth- and nineteenth-century European ideas of China provided the background for an understanding of the Marxian idea of China. These European ideas of China may be interesting in themselves. But their interest is always limited for us by the awareness that they were ancillary to the main intellectual preoccupations of contemporary Europe. Throughout this period, Europeans tended to see China as a prototype of unchanging despotism. Yet the image of China as Oriental despotism had different implications from the eighteenth to the nineteenth century. The historical significance of this change depends on the change in contemporary European intellectual preoccupations.

From Leibniz's *Novissima Sinica* (1699) to Voltaire's *Essay on the Customs and the Spirit of the Nations* (1756), the "unchanging Oriental despotism of China" was held in high esteem. According to Leibniz, China was superior to Christian Europe both in politics and in ethics.[1] And, according to Voltaire, the Chinese were superior not only because of the antiquity of their civilization, but also because of the uniformity and stability of their laws.[2] The climax of European admiration for static China came with François Quesnay's *Despotism of China* (1766): "This state is the most beautiful in the world, and the most densely populated, and the most flourishing kingdom known." [3] China, he says, is a stable despotism based upon natural law. "Thus, everything is permanent in the government of that empire, like the immutable general and fundamental law, upon which it is firmly, intelligently established." [4]

Yet from Montesquieu through Herder to Hegel, the evaluation of China's Oriental despotism was different. In *The Spirit of the Laws* (1748) Montesquieu considered China the prototype of a society pervaded by the spirit of fear.[5] He showed how the nature

of her climate, the condition of her economy, the origins of her
conquering dynasty, the character of her people all conspired to
promote that polity. Neither honor nor virtue could motivate
his Chinese society. In his *Outlines of a Philosophy of the History
of Man* (1784–1791), Herder conceived of China as an agrarian
society dominated by a paternalist state; that state inhibited the
proper development of the rational and emotional capacity of the
people; therefore ancient China remained stationary, like an old
ruin on the verge of the world.[6] Hegel, in his *Philosophy of
History* (1830–1831), stated that China was at the initial stage in
the realization of freedom; she had never advanced beyond the
stage of freedom for the emperor alone; therefore in China the
emperor commanded and the people complied without reflection
or will. This, according to Hegel, accounted for the unchanging
despotic character of Chinese society.[7] The unfavorable evaluation
of China culminated in the mid-nineteenth-century idea of China
as the prototype of a slavish, reactionary, static society.[8]

The change in the evaluation of Oriental despotism in China was
directly related to a change in the European sources of information
concerning China. From the seventeenth to the nineteenth century,
the two main sources for European information on China were
missionaries and merchants. The missionary, especially the Jesuit,
source prevailed during the first half of this period. But during
the second half, with the decline of missionary activities and the
rise of commerce, the mercantile source predominated.[9] The
scholarly, sympathetic missionaries came into contact with the
court society of the Confucian scholars, and sent back to Europe glowing accounts of the China they saw.[10] On the other
hand, the more practical European traders, in search of wealth and
adventure, came into contact with the merchants and compradores
of the South Chinese ports. Inevitably, their reports emphasized
the nonidyllic aspects of that country.[11]

Indirectly, this change in the evaluation was related to a change
in the position of China vis-à-vis contemporary Europe. The
Ch'ing China of the seventeenth and eighteenth centuries was at
the height of its prosperity and power, and could easily impress a
contemporary European observer. However, in the late eighteenth
and nineteenth centuries, the economic and technological trans-

formation of Western Europe plus the gradual decline of the Ch'ing dynasty had altered this relationship. European observers in the late eighteenth- and nineteenth-century China were not as favorably impressed.

But the historical significance of the changing evaluation of static, despotic China lies in the changing functional role of this idea within European intellectual preoccupations, from the eighteenth to the nineteenth century. Favorable, yet static China fulfilled a different role in eighteenth-century Europe than unfavorable, still static China in late eighteenth- and nineteenth-century Europe.

Reason in the philosophy of the Enlightenment was at once universal in its expectation and particular in its preoccupation. The universal demand of reason rested on the success of seventeenth-century mathematical-mechanist science, and on the Cartesian expectation that this logical-scientific model of knowledge should be applicable to humanistic-historical studies. The understanding of history was limited by the rational model of nature. Yet the *philosophes* of the eighteenth century had one particular preoccupation: to use universal reason to attack the absolutist-aristocratic-ecclesiastical bases of the *ancien régime*. The tension between universal demand and particularist preoccupation was reflected in the idea of progress, which represented the application of reason to history. On the one hand, the rational idea of progress projected the vision of universal history with a single cosmic design; and this was the process in which reason emerged empirically and became comprehensible to itself.[12] On the other, the idea of progress focused on the emergence of rationalism in Europe since the fifteenth century.[13]

In such an intellectual situation, the favorable estimate of static China merely reinforced the predicament of the idea of progress. The *philosophes* were particularly concerned with criticizing the *ancien régime* and they used China as a polemical model. However, China, as well as classical antiquity and the noble savage, obstructed the realization of a truly progressive, linear scheme of historical development. Static China illustrated the uniformity of natural law. But static China and the specific expectation of rational progress in Europe since the fifteenth century could not be integrated into a single scheme of universal history. At this level, the idea of China throws light upon the theoretical problem of Cartesian historiography.

This problem was best exemplified by the efforts of Voltaire. He first projected the idea of a philosophy of history, as the self-consciousness of the reason immanent in universal history. Yet in his attempts at universal history, Voltaire was unable to universalize rational progress, nor was he able to explain, in terms of his own rational presupposition, the ups (rationality) and downs (irrationality) of his history. The ideal of universal history implied a coherent, dynamic process. But Voltaire's reason was modeled upon uniformed, mechanistic nature. The difficulty was, therefore, a Cartesian legacy.[14] Static China pointed to the eighteenth-century *mésalliance* between uniformed nature and historical process.

The development of the idea of history from Montesquieu through Herder to Hegel increasingly clarified the distinction between uniformed nature and historical process. This resulted in the autonomy of the idea of history from the idea of nature.* Montesquieu viewed each of his typologies, whether despotic, republican, or monarchical, as functionally coherent. He did not explicitly state a linear progression, although he did imply that a monarchy was superior to a republic, and a republic superior to despotism. Herder's vision of humanity was the totality of unique, individual nationalities. His romantic vision rejected the uniformity of nature. Finally, Hegel transformed the totality into an immanent process in which reason progressively realized itself. He worked out the implications of Voltaire's idea of universal history; and he succeeded in discarding Voltaire's concept of nature.[15]

The particular preoccupation with Europe demanded that the new process of history lead up to contemporary Europe as the final, culminating chapter in the history of the world. On the other hand, the rational process of universal history assumed not only that the important histories of the world are arranged into a single linear scheme of progress, but that an immanent "cause"

---

* Of course, this development merely confirmed the genius of Vico, who was alone in his Anti-Cartesian stand during the early eighteenth century.

exists within the entire historical process from one stage to another and that "cause" be resident in each stage. This is the demand of immanent, universal reason. As Hegel insisted: "Reason . . . is substance, as well as infinite power; its own infinite material underlying all the natural and spiritual life which it originates, as also the infinite form, that which sets this material in motion. On the one hand, Reason is the substance of the universe. . . . On the other hand, it is the infinite energy of the universe. . . ." [16]

The contemporary European idea of an inferior, static China pointed to the tension between European preoccupation and universal history. Stagnant, unprogressive China could be the initial stage of any European's universal history. It would reinforce the preoccupation with linear history leading to present-day Europe. But a static China prevented the complete realization of an immanent process of universal history. This problem was brought out most clearly in Hegel's philosophy of history, because he tried to work out the implications of universal history more conscientiously than anyone before him.

Universal history, according to Hegel, "shows the development of the consciousness of freedom on the part of the Spirit [that is, subjective Reason], and of the consequent realization of that freedom. This development implies a gradation—a series of increasingly adequate expressions or manifestations of freedom, which result from its idea." [17] The unit of history is a nation, and the state is the objective realization of the national spirit. Universal history is the progressive objectification of the self-conscious spirit, freedom, in the state. In Oriental despotism only one is free, the emperor. In ancient Greece some are free, the citizens. But in the German state freedom is legalized for all. [18] The significance of this scheme is not that Hegel strained facts to fit his theory, but that, unlike Voltaire, Montesquieu, or even Herder, he did produce a linear scheme of universal history. However, in terms of his own presupposition, Hegel did not succeed in realizing a truly immanent process of universal history. He conceived of Oriental history as being static, unchanging. If that is the case, nothing in the Oriental stage can explain the development of universal history to the next stage, namely the Greek. Of course, Hegel could always appeal to the cunning of reason. But that is a *deus ex machina,* which failed to conform to his own presupposition of immanent, universal reason.

Inferior, static China assisted Hegel in the construction of a linear universal history, yet prevented him from realizing universal history as a truly immanent process. The Hegelian idea of China thus typified the unresolved tension between European preoccupation and universal process in Hegel. This is the background for an understanding of the Marxian idea of China.

THE ORIENTAL PHASE OF HISTORICAL MATERIALISM

Historical materialism, the Marxian scheme of history, is another version of the rational process. George Lichtheim had the following to say about the process of history in Marx:

> For his own purpose it was essential that the pattern of events should display the kind of internal logic where each successive stage is seen to arise as a matter of necessity, and not just of fact. Thus processes such as the development of feudalism out of primitive tribalism, or the growth of bourgeois society within the feudal system, had to be related to changes inherent in the logic of the anterior stage.[19]

Lichtheim's characterization of the immanent rationalism of Marxian history fits exactly the immanent rationalism of Hegelian history. In this respect, we cannot overemphasize the Hegelian legacy of the young Marx, and behind Hegel the descent from Voltaire.[20]

Rationality is the ordering of values in terms of a projected universal logical model. Within such an order, reason and universality are coterminous. On the other hand, history is a particularist order dependent on the actual development of a specific society and its culture. Of course, rationality and historicity interact upon each other. The rational model must be colored by its historical frame of reference; and the historical order is in turn modified by its rational value. Nevertheless, each represents a distinct field of concentration.

Eighteenth- and nineteenth-century Europe was in transition from the estate society of status to the class society of wealth. In the painful process of transition from tradition to value, thinkers appealed to universal reason for a possible solution. To put it grossly, there was un underlying tension between universal reason and European society. Voltaire was a *philosophe* within the French Cartesian tradition. He assumed the tension between reason and society and was preoccupied with the rational critique of the *ancien régime*. His philosophy of history was subsidiary to that purpose. Hegel, an academic rationalist in the estate society of the Germanies, compensated for the actual failings of his own social environment by insisting on the greater reality of his constructed world of dialectical reason. His universal history sought to justify the equivalence between the real and the rational.

Marx saw in industrializing western Europe the culmination of social alienation and depersonalization. Yet his Hegelian heritage led him to assume the ultimate equivalence between the real and the rational. He expected the resurrection of the Hegelian rational utopia from the ashes of his critique of existing socioeconomic contradictions in western Europe. It would be the triumph of reason over society. Herein lies the significance of the Marxian unity of theory (the rational process of historical materialism) and practice (the specific preoccupation with revolution). Historical materialism provided a generalized rational justification for the specific revolutionary expectation in industrial Europe, whereas the preoccupation with European revolution provided the *telos* for the historical materialist process.

Nevertheless, there is an inevitable tension between the concern for a rational order of universal history and the specific pre-occupation with European revolution. During the decades of the forties and fifties, Marx was concerned with a scheme for universal history. After that, he became more preoccupied with the phenomenon of European society; and his early Hegelian concern for universal history faded into the background. In his *Economic and Philosophic Manuscripts of 1844*, Marx saw the history of man between primitive community and ultimate communism as a history of self-alienation; and private property was the objectifica-tion of the alienated labor of man.[21] Although Marx succeeded here in turning Hegel's dialectical concept of subject-object relation into socioeconomic categories of thought, the reasoning was philosophical rather than historical. In *The German Ideology*

(1845–1846), Marx and Engels saw world history as consisting of four forms of property ownership: The first form was tribal ownership.[22] This was the stage of primitive production, characterized by hunting, fishing, animal husbandry, and the beginnings of agriculture. The second form was the ancient communal and state ownership; here a slight trace of private property had already developed; the division of labor was quite advanced, as evidenced by the differentiation between town and countryside.[23] The third form was feudal ownership, characterized by small-scale primitive cultivation of land using serf labor, and by small-capital handicraft industry using the labor of apprentices and journeymen.[24] From feudalism emerged the fourth form of ownership, large-scale private capital. This was the era of manufacture, characterized by the command of large capital over wage labor, the subordination of countryside to the town, and the world-wide tendency of commerce.[25]

In *Manifesto of the Communist Party* (1848), Marx and Engels defined the history of all pre-Communist societies as the history of class struggle. Class struggle is the social manifestation of the contradiction inherent in a particular mode of production. Through class struggle this contradiction in production is resolved, and society advances to its next historical stage. In the ancient world there was the struggle between patricians and knights as exploiters, and plebeians and slaves as the exploited. During the Middle Ages, the struggle was between feudal lords and peasant serfs, and between guildmasters and apprentices or journeymen. In the modern capitalist era, the struggle has been simplified to that between the bourgeoisie and the proletariat.[26]

By 1859, Marx had somewhat revised this scheme of history. In that year, in the preface to *A Contribution to the Critique of Political Economy*, he wrote: "In broad outlines we can designate the Asiatic, the ancient, the feudal, and the modern bourgeois methods of production as so many epochs in the progress of the economic formation of society."[27] This statement has to be explained by Marx's 1857–1858 manuscript concerning pre-capitalist economic formation, entitled *Outline of Critique of Political Economy*. There, he considered the Asiatic, the ancient, the Germanic, and the feudal forms as all being precapitalist, in the sense that none of them possessed the two necessary ingredients of capitalism, namely free labor and detachment of the worker from the land.[28] Of all these forms, the Asiatic form persisted because in it the individual worker never became independent of the community, where the circle of production was self-sustained, involving the unity of agriculture and craft manufacture.[29] Therefore, the 1859 phrase, "the progress of the economic formation of society," has to be interpreted in the sense of progressive development away from the self-enclosed village community in the direction of free labor and detachment of the worker from the land. This was not inevitably a historical sequence, although it was true that in Europe the ancient form led to the feudal form, which in turn led to the bourgeois form.

After the fifties, Marx was no longer concerned with any scheme of world history. In *Capital*, when speaking of the family as an institution, he said: "It is, of course, just as absurd to hold the Teutonic-Christian form of the family to be absolute and final as it would be to apply that character to the ancient Roman, the ancient Greek, or the Eastern forms which, moreover, taken together form a series in historical development." [30]

But he never elucidated what he meant here. And in 1877, in reply to an article by N. K. Mikhailovskii, Marx wrote: "For him it is absolutely necessary to change my sketch . . . into an historico-philosophical theory of a Universal Progress, fatally imposed on all peoples, regardless of the historical circumstances in which they find themselves. . . . But I must beg his pardon. This is to do me both too much honor and too much discredit." [31]

But this was written in polemics against Mikhailovskii, to obtain the support of the Russian populists. Therefore, on such an occasion, Marx especially condoned the populists' argument of an exceptional course of development for Russia. It does not refute the existence of his interest in historical process, some twenty years earlier.

Many years later, under the influence of L. H. Morgan, Engels further elaborated the primitive stage of Marxian history. In *The Origin of the Family, Private Property and the State* (1884), Engels divided human development into three major epochs: savagery, barbarism, and civilization.[32] Civilization was the proper subject of history, the former two being stages of prehistoric culture. During the later stage of barbarism, there was "the further division of labor between agriculture and handicrafts, hence the production of a continually increasing portion of the products of labor directly for exchange, so that exchange between individual producers assumes the importance of a vital social function." [33] Civilization consolidated and intensified the division of labor, particularly by sharpening the opposition between town and countryside. It added a further division by creating a merchant class—a class which would concern itself exclusively with the function of commodity exchange.[34] Presumably, the Asiatic, the ancient, the feudal, and the bourgeois forms all fall within the epoch of civilization.[35]

√Marx and Engels were not much interested in Asia. Yet in their various attempts to structure a universal process of history, they had to take that vast area into account. Later in their preoccupation with the dynamics of European society they also touched upon Asia. What did they have to say specifically about Oriental society and the Asiatic mode of production?

Before 1848, Marx and Engels showed little knowledge of Asia. Being students of Hegel and close associates of the Young Hegelians, they were undoubtedly under the influence of the prevailing German idea of Asia as being stagnant and unprogressive. After the failure of the revolutions of 1848, when Marx took up residence in London, he began to study the writings of the classical economists. Through his reading of Adam Smith, Richard Jones, and J. S. Mill, he became acquainted with their views of Asia.[36] Smith had commented on the stationary, unprogressive nature of Chinese economy, where the national wealth was mostly derived from agriculture and manufacture, with foreign commerce much neglected.[37] Jones' contribution was his study of ryot rent in India and his thesis that in Asia the sovereign owned all the land.[38] The younger Mill further elaborated the study of ryot rent, and the dominant role of government in the construction of public water works. He emphasized the bureaucratic character of Oriental despotism.[39] In their June, 1853 correspondence, Marx and Engels were pleased about their recent discovery of *Voyages de François Bernier.*[40] This popular late seventeenth-century travel account of India reconfirmed for Marx and Engels the views of Smith, Jones, and Mill on Asia.[41]

But Marx and Engels never systematized their concept of the Asiatic mode of production. From the various disconnected statements and off-hand remarks, we can point to three versions in three different periods. The first version emerged in June, 1853, when Marx and Engels were stimulated by their discovery of Bernier's travel account. The second version can be extracted from the various volumes of *Capital*. And the third version is to be found in Engels' *Anti-Dühring* (1878). However, each version will have to be reconstructed.

The first version of their Asiatic mode of production can be found in the June, 1853 correspondence between Marx and Engels, as well as in the article by Marx, "The British Rule in India," for the June 25, 1853, issue of *The New York Daily Tribune*. In their correspondence, Marx and Engels agreed that the absence of private landownership was the key to an understanding of Asiatic society.[42] Engels, in his letter of June 6, attributed this lack of private property in Asia to the nature of its climate and soil. "Artificial irrigation is the primary condition for agriculture here and this is a matter for either the communes, the provinces, or the central government." [43] Thus public water works became an important function for an Asiatic government and often were the basis for the rise and fall of Oriental empires. In his letter of June 14, Marx explained that the stationary character of the Indian economy could be attributed to "two mutually dependent circumstances: (1) the public works were the business of the central government; (2) besides these, the whole empire was divided into villages, each possessing a completely separate organization and forming a little world in itself." [44] Referring to this self-enclosed village community, Marx said: "I do not think we can imagine a more solid foundation for the stagnation of Asiatic despotism." [45]

In "The British Rule in India," Marx used the ideas derived from his correspondence with Engels. He divided the function of the Oriental government into finance, war, and public works, and said: "This prime necessity of an economic and common use of water . . . led in the Orient . . . to the interference of the central government. Hence an economic function devolved upon all Asiatic governments, that of providing public works." [46] The government's responsibility for water works plus the dispersion of population over a vast territory gave rise early in India to a peculiar system of self-enclosed village community. [47] This system restricted the social and economic development of the population and perpetuated Oriental despotism. [48] In short, Marx and Engels inferred that land and water works were the keys to the communal economy of Asia, and control of land through the monopoly over water works was the key to Oriental despotism.

The second version of the Asiatic mode of production, when reconstructed from the various volumes of *Capital*, appears as follows: [49] Communal labor and property were a spontaneous form of primitive economic organization, which could be found at the dawn of all civilizations. [50] This communal labor was based upon the common ownership of the means of production and was characterized by relations of dominance and servitude. [51] Reciprocal interdependence, the prerequisite for any commodity exchange, did not exist in a primitive communal society. The exchange of commodities, therefore, must begin along the borders of such communities, and gradually extend to within each community. [52] The primitive community had a natural economy, where little of the agricultural produce entered into the process of exchange circulation, and where domestic handicraft existed along with this agriculture. [53] As an example Marx cited the ancient village community of India. "The simplicity of . . . these self-sufficing communities . . . supplies the key to the secret of the unchangeableness of Asiatic societies." [54] In such a primitive community rent payment in kind was the only source of surplus value. The state arbitrarily extorted an enormous amount of rent payment. This kept the peasantry at the subsistent level. [55] The state alone commanded surplus value, which was consumed either in magnificent display or in public works. Thus increase in production did not lead to capital accumulation, that prerequisite for a commodity-exchange economy. [56]

Capital contains a revealing passage concerning the relation of the Asiatic mode to the other modes of production:

In the ancient Asiatic and other ancient modes of production, we find that the conversion of products into commodities, and therefore the conversion of men into producers of commodities, holds a subordinate place, which, however, increases in importance as the primitive communities approach nearer and nearer to their dissolution. . . . They can arise and exist only when the development of the productive power of labor has not yet risen beyond a low stage, and when, therefore, the social relations . . . are correspondingly narrow.[57]

In other words, Marx in *Capital* conceived of economic development as increase in the circulation of commodity exchange. The ancient mode of production was a limited advance over the primitive mode. But in the ancient mode commodity production was still overshadowed by production for consumption. The Asiatic mode of production was a variant of the ancient mode. It was a persistent form of the ancient mode because the presence of Oriental despotism, through its consumption of surplus value, prevented any further growth in the production for commodity exchange.

Though resembling the 1853 version, the *Capital* version of the Asiatic mode of production varied in emphasis from the former. In 1853 Marx and Engels were still under the influence of Smith, Jones, Mill, and Bernier. Consequently, in their 1853 version they emphasized the phenomena of self-enclosed village communities and of governmental control of water works. These two fundamental factors explained for them the persistence of Oriental despotism. The approach was that of political economy. The *Capital* version revealed a decreasing influence in the political economists' concept of Asia. As a critic of the capitalist system of production for commodity circulation, Marx now emphasized the lack of commodity exchange in Asia. The *Capital* version singled out the phenomena of self-enclosed village communities and of state consumption of surplus value. These two fundamental factors explained the stagnation of Oriental economy, because the lack of capital accumulation prevented the development of production for commodity exchange. The *Capital* version de-emphasized the absence of private property and the necessity of water works. In *Capital* Marx cited the irrigation works in India as examples of early human industry to control nature, and as one of the material bases for state power. But he did not pursue the argument further.[58] The reasoning behind the *Capital* version was consistently economic and more cogent than that behind the 1853 version.

In the third—or *Anti-Dühring*—version Engels envisaged natural communal economy as the basis for the Asiatic mode of production. In ancient India "direct social production and direct distribution exclude all exchange of commodities, therefore also the transformation of the products into commodities." [59] Ancient India, said Engels, had both communal ownership and state ownership of land. Eventually, these primitive communes developed into small-peasant villages.[60] Engels identified the communal phase of Asia with the primitive mode of production, and the village phase with the ancient mode of production. The latter was characterized by the combination of small peasants and slave laborers.[61] In the *Anti-Dühring* version, public water works did not seem so important. Engels described the need for water works as merely one of the socioeconomic bases for the rise of state power.[62] He had nothing to say about Oriental despotism.

In conformity with the prevailing nineteenth-century European idea of the Orient, Marx and Engels attempted three versions of the stagnation of Asia. The 1853 version used self-enclosed village community and the state water works to explain the persistence of the political phenomenon of Oriental despotism. The *Capital* version used the self-enclosed village community and the state consumption of surplus value to explain the economic phenomenon of underdevelopment in commodity exchange. The *Anti-Dühring* version emphasized the self-enclosed village community, but pointed to the eventual transition from communal landownership to small-peasant landownershp. The shift in argument away from state water works and Oriental despotism, I believe, has to be explained basically by the change in approach from that of political economy to that of economics. Therefore, the political-economic approach indicated the interaction between Oriental despotism and Asiatic economy, and the economic approach explained the Asiatic mode of production in purely economic terms.

THE MARXIAN IDEA OF CHINA

In discussing the several versions of the Asiatic mode of production, we have not mentioned China because Marx and Engels used India as the model in their construction of the Asiatic mode. In addition, Smith, Jones, Mill, and Bernier also based their views of Asia on Indian data. When they talked about Asia, they all had in mind India rather than China. This creates the problem of determining whether the Marxian idea of China and the Marxian concept of the Asiatic mode of production are equivalent.

During the initial period of their collaboration, up to 1848, Marx and Engels made few references to China. In *Condition of the Working Class in England in 1844* (1845), Engels mentioned China as a market for English manufacture and the new American manufacture.[63] In *The German Ideology* (1845–1846), Marx and Engels spoke of the impact of industrial capitalism in transforming the world, including China, into a single market for its manufacture.[64] Engels discussed again the relation of China to Europe in *Principles of Communism* (1847): For thousands of years China and India had made no progress, but now English manufacture had converted the world into a single market, thus affecting native work habits; hence isolated, unchanging China also had to move toward an economic revolution.[65] In a London speech of November 30, 1847, Engels repeated: "Lately we have seen how China, which for more than a thousand years had defied progress and historical development, is being revolutionized by English machineries and drawn into [the mainstream of European] civilization." [66]

In all these early references China was mentioned in connection with the impact of European industrial capitalism. Marx and Engels seemed to be interested in China only insofar as she could be related to the central phenomenon of European capitalism. For the sake of clarity, we shall consider the Marxian idea of China under three headings: Their account of China's role in the world market for European manufacture; their view of Chinese society and her contemporary situation; and their forecast of prospective change for China.

China's role in the world market for European manufacture

In *Manifesto of the Communist Party* Marx and Engels pointed out that the Indian and Chinese markets accelerated the development of commerce, navigation, and industry in bourgeois Europe; but the market kept on expanding and the demand rising, so that eventually manufacture could not suffice, and manufacturing capital was transformed into industrial capital; the relation between bourgeois capitalism and overseas market was extremely intimate, each contributing to the development of the other.[67] In *The German Ideology* Marx and Engels had anticipated much of what was said in the *Manifesto*. But China was not specifically mentioned.[68]

Behind the thesis of the intimate relation between the Chinese market and European manufacture, we detect the Marxian hope that the Chinese market would accelerate the coming of the European economic crisis. In a letter to Marx dated January 6, 1852, Engels remarked that the English cotton industry had consumed more raw cotton in 1851 than in 1850. But since little was exported to the Continent, it must be the Indian and Chinese markets which consumed the surplus and kept the English cotton industry going.[69] As revealed in a letter by Marx to Weydemeyer dated April 30, 1852, both he and Engels believed that the overseas market alone postponed the immediate occurrence of an economic crisis in England.[70] But they claimed that the benefit of the Indian and Chinese markets was more immediate than lasting. Later that year, on August 21, Engels wrote joyously to Marx that the English exporters to India and China had so overstocked their markets that at the latest the long expected crisis would occur within a month or two![71] Somehow the crisis failed to materialize. In an article for the June 14, 1853, issue of *The New York Daily Tribune*, Marx predicted that the Taiping rebellion in China would lead to an economic crisis in England, since the rebellion would inevitably bring about a disruption of the Chinese market.[72] Therefore Marx could proclaim that the rebellion "will throw the spark into the overloaded mine of the long-prepared general crisis, which, spreading abroad, will be closely followed by political revolutions on the continent." [73] In the period immediately after 1848 when their memory of the revolution was still very much alive, each minor incident rekindled the expectation of another revolution in Marx and Engels.

The commercial crisis of 1857 once more aroused the revolutionary expectation of Marx and Engels. They returned to the role of China in the world market. In the September 20, 1858, issue of the *Tribune*, Marx stated his belief that the treaty of Nanking (1842) did not bring about an increase of European exports to China, but rather precipitated the commercial crisis of 1847. The potentiality of the Chinese market was very limited, far smaller than European expectations. Therefore Marx hoped that "by raising dreams of an inexhaustible market and by fostering speculations, the present treaty [of Tientsin (1858)] may help in preparing a new crisis." [74] In the next article for the same newspaper, September 25, 1858, Marx presented yet another argument for the role of China in precipitating an European crisis: Since the finances of the British government in India depended on the sale of illegal opium to China, if the Chinese government were to tolerate poppy cultivation and to legalize the opium trade, the British government would automatically be confronted with a serious financial crisis.[75] In an October 5, 1858, article Marx repeated his belief that "the consuming and paying powers of the [Chinese] have been greatly overestimated." [76] Engels, in an October 7, 1858, letter to Marx, predicted that the expectation of the Indian and Chinese markets would lead to overproduction in England, and a revival of credit and exchange by the following spring.[77] Marx, in his reply of October 8, countered with the argument that such an expectation was misleading, since the export to China had remained stationary.[78] In the October 15, 1858 issue of the *Tribune*, Marx reiterated his belief that the Chinese would soon legalize poppy cultivation and levy duty on the import of opium, and that this would inevitably create a financial crisis in England.[79] In "The British Cotton Trade," for the October 14, 1861, issue of the *Tribune*, Marx wrote that the U. S. Civil War had disrupted the American demand for British cotton goods, while raising the prices for raw cotton. This increased the export of cotton goods to India and China, which in turn drove down the prices of cotton goods in those countries. The result was that declining prices of cotton goods could not keep pace with the rising cost of raw cotton.[80] Thus Marx envisaged the capitalist's dilemma! Marx reported to Engels on March 3, 1862, that according to the latest Board of Trade statistics English export to China had fallen.[81] Three days later, in another letter to Engels, Marx concluded that the 1861 English export to China was much less than the 1859 figure.[82] This would naturally affect the prosperity of the English economy. But finally on December 9, 1869, Engels had to admit to Marx that "China with its gradual market expansion seems about to save again the cotton trade at least for a short time." [83]

In *Capital*, Marx emphasized the close interaction between the bourgeois mode of production and the world market. Each stimulated the other. But with a declining rate of profit, if only to maintain the same profit return, capitalist production must ever expand and required an ever-expanding market. "Thus arose the system of mass consignments, by virtue of advances, to India and China, and this soon developed into a system of consignments purely for the sake of getting advances. . . . This had to lead inevitably to an overcrowding of the markets and to a crash." [84]

The Marxian thesis of the contradiction between an ever-expanding production system and a slowly extending market kept Engels, in 1886, still predicting the proximity of an economic crisis for England.[85] However by 1892, in the face of apparent economic prosperity, Engels had to admit that capitalism had had a revival. This had been brought about by many unforeseen circumstances. Among them, Engels included the ability of the Chinese market to absorb increasingly more English goods.[86] In a letter to Danielson dated September 22, 1892, he asserted: "The last new market which could bring on a temporary revival of prosperity by its being thrown open to English commerce is China. Therefore English capital insists upon constructing Chinese railways." [87]

Marx and Engels approached China's role in the world market for European manufacture through their preoccupations with the capitalist system and with the coming European revolution. In their analysis of European capitalism they pointed out the importance of the world market, whereas from the viewpoint of their revolutionary preoccupation they predicted that a contradictory relation between production and market would lead inevitably to a crisis. The contemporary European idea of static China suited much better their revolutionary preoccupation than their economic critique, that is, a relatively static Chinese market would precipitate the contradiction between dynamic production and slowly expanding market. By the late nineteenth century, with a decline in revolutionary preoccupation, Engels also abandoned the static, unchanging aspect of the Chinese market.

Chinese society and her contemporary situation

Aside from occasional mentionings, Marx and Engels wrote seventeen articles on China in the 1850's for the *Tribune* and one article in 1862 for *Die Presse*. Of the articles for the *Tribune*, the first, written in June, 1853, discussed internal conditions in China, the remaining sixteen, written between 1857 and 1860, the commercial and diplomatic relations of China to Britain. The 1862 article for *Die Presse* was on the Taiping rebellion.

In 1850 Marx had described China as "the oldest and most unshakeable empire of the world. But the increasing population of that country has long made social relations oppressive for the majority of the people." [88] There is more information in the June 14, 1853, article by Marx for the *Tribune*, "Revolution in China and in Europe": The emperor was considered to be the father of all Chinese, and his mandarins sustained this paternal authority in their respective districts. This paternal authority was the only moral link embracing the vast machinery of the Chinese state.[89] An isolationist policy was adopted by the conquering Manchu dynasty in order to maintain this authority.[90] "Complete isolation was the prime condition of the preservation of old China." China thus resembled "a mummy carefully preserved in a hermetically sealed coffin." [91] In later *Tribune* articles, Engels, on June 5, 1857, described China as "the rotting semi-civilization of the oldest state in the world." [92] And Marx, on September 20, 1858, described her as "a giant empire . . . vegetating in the teeth of time, insulated by the forced exclusion of general intercourse, and thus continuing to dupe itself with delusion of Celestial perfection."[93] On September 25, 1858, Marx repeated that China had a patriarchal constitution sustained by its mandarin bureaucrats.[94] In the July 7, 1862, article for *Die Presse* Marx concluded that China was a typical Oriental empire, exhibiting an immutability in social substructure and restless changes in the personnel of political superstructure.[95]

As for her economy, Marx, in the October 5, 1858, and December 3, 1859, *Tribune* articles and in his October 8, 1858, letter to Engels, described China as a society based on a combination of small-scale agriculture and domestic manufacture.[96] This agriculture was carried on intensively, like gardening.[97] China's economic stability was marked by the absence of new wants and by the preference for traditional costumes.[98] The people were depressed by burdensome and harassing taxes.[99] In such an immobile economy the credit system remained underdeveloped, although legal-tender paper was used at an early date.[100]

When they reported on contemporary China, Marx and Engels appeared better informed and less doctrinaire. In a January 31, 1850, review article, Marx wrote that, with the opening of the treaty ports, cheap British and American goods had inundated the Chinese market and had thus subjected the Chinese handicraft industry to the competition of machinery industry; this had brought on a social crisis in that country, which had long been suffering from overpopulation. "Taxes," Marx wrote, "ceased to come in, the state reached the brink of bankruptcy, the population sank totally into pauperism and broke out into rebellion. . . . The country came to the verge of ruin, and is already threatened with a mighty revolution."[101] Marx had learned from an account by C. Gutzlaff, a returned German missionary, that there was a group of rebels in China who advocated socialist ownership of land. This excited Marx's imagination.[102]

The most detailed comment on contemporary China, occasioned by news of renewed Taiping outbreaks, appeared in "Revolution in China and in Europe," in the *Tribune* of June 14, 1853. Here Marx wrote that "the occasion of this outbreak has unquestionably been afforded by the English canon forcing upon China that soporific drug called opium."[103] The opium war of 1839–1842, he continued, had disrupted the authority of the Manchu dynasty, had ended China's isolation, and made her a part of the world market. Up to 1830 the balance of trade had been in favor of the Chinese. But since 1833 the export of silver had become an increasing drain on the Chinese economy. This unfavorable balance of trade had been due entirely to the illegal opium trade. Besides, the illegal trade tended to demoralize and corrupt the Chinese mandarin officials in the south. Simultaneously, the import of English cotton goods had also risen since 1833. This had placed Chinese spinners and weavers under severe competition. The excessive consumption of opium, the drain of precious metals, the disruption of domestic handicraft industry, the demoralization of public administration, and the need to pay tribute indemnity after the war—all had contributed to an increasing strain upon the Chinese society. Such had been the origin of the Taiping rebellion which Marx attributed ultimately to the market effect of industrial capitalism.

In the January 23, 1857, *Tribune* article, Marx commented on the lorcha *Arrow* incident which brought on the second Anglo-Chinese war, that "the British are in the wrong in the whole proceeding." [104] This, said Marx, was a case of the British invading a peaceful country without prior declaration of war; the first Chinese war was condoned by the other powers, because of the prospect of opening trade relations with China; but this economic bait could no longer be dangled before the other powers now, because the immediate result of the second Chinese war would be to cut off Canton from the tea-growing region—a development which could not benefit the Eastern trading nations.

In another article for the same paper, on April 7, 1857, Marx feared that with the closing of maritime trade as a result of the second Anglo-Chinese war, Europe would have to depend upon the overland trade route under Russian monopoly; this, he said, would work to the advantage of no one, except the reactionary Russian autocracy.[105] Marx's sympathy was clearly on the side of the Chinese, during the war of 1856–1860. "The Chinese have at least ninety-nine injuries to complain of, to one on the part of the English." [106]

Engels, in the article "Persia-China" for the June 5, 1857, issue of the *Tribune*, believed that he detected the rise of anti-foreign nationalism in southern China, as a result of the second

war. "One thing is certain, that the death-hour of Old China is
rapidly drawing nigh. Civil war has already divided the South
from the North." [107] In the September 25, 1858, article for the
same paper, Marx repeated that the inability of the Chinese
government to suppress the opium trade had led to its smuggling,
and the ensuing corruption which accompanied that smuggling
had demoralized the government officials and destroyed the
bulwark of the patriarchal constitution of old China. [108] The
legalization of the opium trade by the treaty of Tientsin (1858)
represented for Marx the failure of the authority of the Chinese
government. [109]

In the July 7, 1862, issue of *Die Presse*, Marx returned to the
Taiping rebellion: The movement had from the beginning a
religious complexion, he said, but that was a feature common to
all Oriental movements; the immediate causes for the Taiping
rebellion were the pressure of Western industrial capitalism on
native Chinese society. However, Marx now felt that the rebellion
had degenerated into senseless slaughter. [110] "It is the result of
petrified social life." [111] In 1850 Marx was enthusiastic about the
Taiping rebellion, mainly because he sympathized with its so-
called socialist project of landownership. By 1853 he considered
the rebellion a result of the impact of industrial capitalism upon a
hitherto stable Asiatic economy and society. He welcomed it only
insofar as this rebellion might be the spark to light a European
conflagration. Finally in 1862 Marx condemned the rebellion,
because of its semireligious garb and senseless destruction.

Marx and Engels, in describing Chinese society, began with the
contemporary European idea of a static China. She was an
unchanging political empire superimposed upon a stagnant economy of small-scale agriculture and domestic handicraft industry.
But as Marx and Engels approached the nineteenth century, they
abandoned the prototype of a static China. As China drew closer
to the phenomenon of Western capitalism, she seemed to lose her
stability. Through the theoretical perspective of a dynamic
Western economy, Marx and Engels saw a changing, rather than
static, China.*

* I am maintaining a distinction between the changes of a nineteenth-
century China under the pressure of the industrial West and the idea of a

Forecast of prospective change for China

Marx and Engels saw in the Taiping rebellion the effect of industrial capitalism upon a hitherto changeless old China. Already in the *Communist Manifesto* they had pointed out that the bourgeoisie would draw all nations into the current of European civilization. With the threat of cheap commodities, the bourgeoisie would compel all other societies to adopt the capitalist mode of production. In this way, "it has made barbarian and semi-barbarian countries dependent on the civilized ones, nations of peasants on nations of bourgeoisie, the East on the West." [112]

Marx in a letter to Engels dated October 8, 1858, hinted at the prospective change for Asiatic society: The bourgeoisie of the mid-nineteenth century was experiencing another sixteenth century, that is, the phenomenon of a world market which in the sixteenth century had brought about the growth of manufacturing capitalism. The world market of the mid-nineteenth century had two effects—in Europe it was accelerating the prospect of a socialist revolution, and elsewhere it was bringing about the bourgeois mode of production.[113] Under the impact of industrial capitalism the Asiatic mode of production could not long survive.

In Volumes II and III of *Capital* Marx predicted that the capitalist mode of production would have a disintegrating effect upon all older modes. And "wherever it takes roots, there it destroys all forms of commodity production which are either based on the self-employment of the producers, or mainly on the sale of surplus product. The production of commodity is first made general and then transformed by degree into the capitalist mode of commodity production." [114] But this transformation would be slow, due to the obstacles presented by the internal solidarity of precapitalist modes of production. "The great economy and saving in time resulting from the direct connection of agriculture and manufacture offer [in China] the most dogged resistance to the

changing China as seen in the theoretical perspective of a dynamic Western economic model. In this study, I attempt to show how the actual changes of nineteenth- and twentieth-century China are seen in the changing Marxist perspective of tension between concern for universal theory and concern for specific practice.

products of great industries, whose prices are everywhere perforated by the dead expenses of their process of circulation." [115] In Volume I of *Capital* Marx indicated another possible effect of industrial capitalism upon Asia: "By ruining handicraft production in other countries, machinery forcibly converts them into fields for the supplying of its raw materials. . . . A new and international division of labor . . . springs up, and converts one part of the globe into a chiefly agricultural field of production, for supplying the other part which remains a chiefly industrial field." [116]

Engels, in a September 12, 1882, letter to Kautsky, wrote that when the time came the victorious European proletariat would lead the colonial countries speedily to independence. These countries would naturally follow the European lead. "Economic needs alone will be responsible for this. . . . One thing alone is certain: the victorious proletariat can force no blessing of any sort on any foreign nation, without undermining its own victory." [117] What Engels meant was that these countries must first undergo the capitalist mode of production. The transition of non-European countries from their traditional mode of production to the capitalist mode and then to the socialist mode could not be shortened.

In a September 22, 1892, letter to Danielson, Engels discussed to some extent the prospective change of China: British capitalist prosperity depended on the world market, hence the British interest in rail construction in China. But the railways would upset the entire basis of small-scale agriculture and domestic industry in China. Millions of Chinese would become hopelessly unemployed. The consequence would be a wholesale migration of Chinese coolie labor abroad, bringing about a lower standard of living throughout the world.[118] In a letter to Kautsky dated September 23, 1894, and in another to Sörge dated November 10, 1894, Engels reiterated this alarmist view: The introduction of railway, steam engine, electricity, and large-scale industry into China would disrupt the old system of small-scale agriculture and domestic manufacture, and force millions of unemployed to migrate overseas. There would then follow a disastrous competition of labor in Europe and America! [119]

With the collapse of the idea of a static China, Marx and Engels had to forecast the type of change to come in China. If static China was an exception to the universal process of historical materialism, changing China was now seen in the light of the dynamic industrial West. China under the impact of industrial capitalism would bypass the feudal mode of production, but would have to follow the capitalist and then the socialist footpath of the advanced West. Ultimately the goal would be the same. China's change would be a testimony to the dynamics of European capitalism, rather than the universality of historical materialism.

In this connection it may be worthwhile to mention the Marxian analysis of the prospective changes in Russian society. Marx and Engels had always considered Russia "semi-Asiatic in her condition, manners, traditions, and institutions." [120] This was because of her primitive communal property. However, as Marx pointed out in *A Contribution to the Critique of Political Economy* (1859), this communal property was merely a variation of the primitive form common to other peoples.[121] Ever since the revolutions of 1848, Marx and Engels had been hostile toward Russia, because they considered her the bastion of political reaction in Europe. Though semi-Asiatic, Russia was intimately interwoven with European development. As late as 1873, Engels wrote that "no revolution in western Europe can be definitely and finally victorious as long as the present Russian state exists at its side." [122] Since the seventies, because of their newly acquired reputation within the Russian populist circle, Marx and Engels were compelled to forecast the future course of development in Russia. But no matter how much concession they might give to the populists' argument for an exceptional, noncapitalist course of development in Russia toward the socialist goal, they consistently qualified such a tactical concession. They said that, on the basis of her indigenous forces, Russia must go through the regular course of economic development, and any exception must depend not upon Russian uniqueness but upon the dynamics of the West's march toward socialism.[123]

AN EVALUATION

Marx and Engels inherited the idea of static China from their European contemporaries and predecessors. This idea was contained in their early concern for universal history. Later they approached the study of China through their preoccupation with the European capitalist system. China was still static; but she had now become a part of the world market. In that role she contributed toward the contradiction between an ever-expanding capitalist production system and a slowly extending world market. But in the interaction between production and market they saw an hitherto static China being transformed by the dynamics of the capitalist system. Pre-nineteenth-century China was a combination of small-scale agriculture and domestic handicraft industry, imposed by Oriental despotism. But nineteenth-century European economic forces destroyed the stability of both Chinese politics and Chinese economy. Out of this turmoil Marx and Engels foresaw China eventually adopting the capitalist mode of production, and *then* advancing toward communism. They began with the idea of a static, unchanging China; they ended with the idea that China was static before the nineteenth century, but was changing under Western economic pressures in the nineteenth century.

Since the Asiatic mode of production was based upon Indian data, what was the relation of the idea of static pre-nineteenth-century China to the Asiatic mode? The 1853 version of the Asiatic mode emphasized the self-enclosed village community and state water works as the basis for Oriental despotism. The *Capital* version used the self-enclosed village community and state consumption of surplus value to explain the lack of commodity circulation in Asia. The *Anti-Dühring* version agreed with the *Capital* version, but in addition pointed to the eventual emergence of small-peasant landownership from communal landownership. The idea of a static pre-nineteenth-century China as being based upon small-scale agriculture and domestic industry fitted well with the *Capital* and *Anti-Dühring* versions of the Asiatic mode of production. It did not agree with the 1853 version. When describing pre-nineteenth-century China, Marx and Engels never mentioned communal landownership or state water works, the two characteristics favored by the 1853 version. This in spite of the fact that Marx had written an extensive article on China, "The Revolution in China and in Europe," in 1853. We have to conclude, therefore, that the Marxian idea of a static China had a minimal relation with the 1853 version of the Asiatic mode of production; and though agreeing with the two later versions it did not exactly coincide with them.

According to the *Capital* and *Anti-Dühring* versions, the Asiatic mode of production emerged from the primitive communal mode to become a stagnant variant of the ancient mode. These two later versions attributed the stagnation to the lack of commodity circulation in Asia. The explanation was strictly economic. On the other hand, the 1853 version saw the stagnation as resulting from the interaction between self-enclosed communal economy and Oriental despotism. The phenomenon of state water works was the vital link between economics and politics. From the 1853 version to the two later versions, the argument shifted from political economy to economics. Nevertheless, all three versions represent a major failure of historical materialism as universal history. The Asiatic mode was the sole exception that prevented historical materialism from becoming a linear process of universal history. In addition, Asiatic stagnation argued against the immanent economic "causation" underlying historical materialism. Because of the Asiatic mode of production, historical materialism never became universal history. It was an unsystematized combination of a European process of history and the conventional idea of the static East.

As a variant of the Asiatic mode, the idea of an unchanging pre-nineteenth-century China also illustrated the theoretical failure of historical materialism. Yet the idea of a changing nineteenth-century China did not improve the theoretical consistency of historical materialism. Marx and Engels saw nineteenth-century China as being inherently static until change was introduced by an external "cause." There was no immanent economic dynamics for change within Chinese society. The "cause" was superimposed by the capitalist West. It was an admission of Western economic dynamics, not an argument for the immanent universality of the Marxian historical process. Moreover, the change introduced into nineteenth-century China did not argue away the blot of her pre-nineteenth-century stagnation.

Against the background of late eighteenth- and nineteenth-century European ideas of China, Marx and Engels introduced some changes into their idea of China. Contemporary European ideas of China were a combination of stagnant economy and Oriental despotism. The Marxian idea of pre-nineteenth-century China generally retained that combination. Yet the Marxian idea of changing nineteenth-century China was new. The question here is the relevancy of these ideas of China to the historicity of China. The idea of static China was significant within the context of European intellectual preoccupations. Yet as a perspective to view China, it distorted what we believe to be the truth of Chinese historical reality. Traditional, dynastic China did not undergo the changes familiar to Europe. Chinese society has been so different from European society that historians now regard the Europe-oriented morphology of change as not applicable to China. They regard each historical phenomenon as specific and unable to remain stationary, and historical understanding as depending on the specificity and intrinsic factors within that phenomenon. If that is true, then the Marxian idea of changing nineteenth-century China was a partial improvement. Marx and Engels saw a changing China because they could finally detect familiar Europe-oriented changes. Immediately, this was justifiable because European forces contributed a great deal toward the nineteenth-century changes of China. But Marx and Engels failed to understand that prospective changes in China, resulting from the interaction of indigenous traditions and Western forces, could not follow the European footpath. This is a problem in Western-valued perspective, which is currently being considered from different angles by both Chinese Marxists and some Western social scientists.[124]

But the historically significant change from the Hegelian to the Marxian idea of China depends upon the changing functions of this idea within the Hegelian historical process and within the Marxian unity of theory and practice. The Hegelian idea of static China occupied the initial stage of an immanent process of universal history. It typified the tension between universal process and European preoccupation. Marx and Engels inherited this tension from Hegel. Their idea of a static China typified that inheritance. However, the Marxian idea of a changing nineteenth-century China was related to their preoccupation with the dynamics of a

West seemingly in the stage of transition from capitalism to socialism. The Voltairean-Hegelian concern for a rational universal process was contained by the specific Marxian preoccupation with revolutionary practice in Europe. The theory of historical materialism became the rational justification for that utopian expectation. Thus the Marxian idea of China illustrated the shifting emphasis of Marx and Engels away from universal theory to specific practice.

Chapter Two

The Russian Situation

THE RUSSIAN INTELLIGENTSIA

Leninism did not develop logically from Marxism. It was a historical development constituting the transplantation of Western Marxism to Russia. We must therefore seek its explanation in the interaction between Marxist thought and Russian society. This search leads us to that unique phenomenon, the Russian intelligentsia.[1]

The Russian intelligentsia was neither an economic class nor a social stratum. It was a Western-educated, yet socially heterogeneous group with a common intellectual preoccupation. In the words of A. Koyré, the intelligentsia was characterized by its consciousness of the contrast between Russia and the West. And in this consciousness it was torn between the two, not able to be fully committed to either.[2]

Without investigating how westernized Russia was, we may safely assume that Russia and western Europe were not identical. Each society had tensions and cohesions of its own. But no society can develop autochthonously, as Oswald Spengler thought it could. Extraneous elements alter the development of any society. In modern times Russia has been increasingly exposed to influences from the West. The westernization of Russia has been a complex phenomenon of different strata of Russian society reacting and developing under the influence of various Western forces. The stimulation, the challenge, the pressure came from the West. But the result was a Russia neither in the image of the old pre-Western Russia, nor in the image of the new Western model. Becoming westernized is not the same as being Western.

Nineteenth-century Russia represents yet another intermediary stage in the continuing interaction between Russia and the West. The least westernized stratum of Russian society was the peasant masses. Peasant economy in the nineteenth century was affected by the international grain market; and as far back as the seventeenth century contact with the Greek "West" had brought about a religious schism within the orthodox peasantry. During the seventeenth and eighteenth centuries, the autocratic leadership over Russian society enabled the tsars to assume the initiative in the westernization of Russia. It resulted in the semi-Western, semi-Russian *chinovnik* bureaucracy of the nineteenth century. Semibureaucratized tsardom, itself an anomaly, was caught between the diplomatic-military competition with Western states in the international arena and the mobilization of Russian resources at home. But the state-initiated westernization had backfired in the late eighteenth and nineteenth centuries, leading to unforeseen, antistatist consequences. This is noticeable in the changing orientation of the Russian nobility, the *dvorianstvo*. Unlike the hereditary aristocracy of the West which could be traced back to feudal origins, the eighteenth-century *dvorianstvo* lacked estate solidarity of its own. It was a service-owing gentry nobility, catering to the autocratic state. At the time of Peter the Great, because of his demand for westernization, the gentry nobility had to submit to Western education. In the second half of the eighteenth century, the nobility desired Western education. Lacking a style of its own, the nobility became a successful imitator of the West. It was the most westernized, least Russian segment of Russian society. Russia was torn by a semibureaucratized autocracy, Frenchified nobility, and schismatic peasantry. Westernization did not heal but rather further accentuate the tensions of Russian society.

The westernization of the *dvorianstvo* went further than that of any other segment of schismatic Russia. The heart of the *dvorianstvo* was open to the West, although its feet were closely planted upon the Russian serfs. Because of its westernization, it felt apart from the Russian masses; yet it was a Russian gentry dependent socially and economically upon the Russian peasantry. It looked toward the West; yet coming from Russia it could never be truly at home in the West. The westernization of the *dvorianstvo* promoted its social alienation.

The Russian intelligentsia originally emerged from the westernized *dvorianstvo*, being its most Western-educated segment. An increase in Western education seemed inevitably to lead to an increase in the sense of alienation, so that social alienation became conscious intellectual alienation. Russia was the center of the intelligentsia's concern, whereas the West provided for the universal norm. The tension was one between the particularist demand of Russia and the universal demand of Western values. True to its own situation the intelligentsia was preoccupied with the dichotomy between Russia and the West.[3]

The concepts of elite and masses, of consciousness and spontaneity, of theory and practice were various intellectualized formulas used by members of the Russian intelligentsia to express their different understanding of the fundamental tension in Russian society: It was a tension between Western-educated elite and Russian masses, between Westernized consciousness and Russian spontaneity, and between Western theory and Russian oriented practice. The words "elite," "consciousness," and "theory" were Western-oriented, whereas the words "masses," "spontaneity," and "practice" were Russian-oriented. Each dichotomic concept reflected the underlying tension between Western values and Russian particularism. The history of the Russian intelligentsia in the nineteenth century revealed a progressive development, through these concepts, to arrive at a *realistic* correlation between these two conflicting sets of demands.*

To understand Lenin's correlation of Marxian thought (one version of Western rational value) and Russian society, we shall review briefly three successive types of the nineteenth-century Russian intelligentsia, and see how the tension between Western values and Russian particularism developed through them. These are: the *dvoriane* intellectuals from approximately 1825 to 1848; the populist intellectuals in the 1860's and 1870's; and the Russian Marxist intellectuals in the 1880's and 1890's.

The dvoriane *intellectuals*

Although drawn mostly from the gentry nobility, the *dvoriane* intellectuals as the bearers of intellectual alienation differed from

---

* Realistic, in the sense that such correlation must come to terms with the underlying tension between the demand of Western values and the demand of Russian society.

the majority of the *dvorianstvo*. In their role as the mediators between Western thought and Russian society, the intellectuals, against the tendency of the majority, sought to meet the conflicting demands of Russia and the West. This distinctive characteristic can be traced back to the eighteenth century.[4]

At that time, against the passive acceptance of French culture by the majority of the gentry nobility, the intellectuals consciously tried to redress the balance by seeking the demands of Russia. Under the pressure of Western values, some tried to idealize the Russian national character or the Russian peasantry;[5] others to discover Russia in her past and history.[6] Another indication of the desire to redress the balance between Russia and the West was the adoption of a critical attitude toward the West. In that way the demand of Western values could hopefully be contained.[7] Most typical of the intellectual's dilemma, N. I. Novikov (1744–1818), the Freemason publicist, rejected equally the uncritical acceptance of the West and the glorification of Russia's past. He advocated the combining of the best in the West with one's love for Russia.[8]

After the outbreak of the French Revolution, both tsarist autocracy and gentry nobility, realizing the social basis of their respective interests, gradually turned conservative.[9] In opposition to that and true to their intellectual commitment, the intellectuals became more radical. This radicalism culminated in the Decembrist Revolution of 1825, the work of mostly young *dvoriane* officers stimulated by Russian patriotism and Western political ideas. The failure of the Decembrist Revolution set the stage for an understanding of the orientation of the *dvoriane* intellectuals in 1825–1848.

Because of the Decembrist Revolution Nicholas I (1825–1855) became extremely suspicious of both the *dvoriantsvo* and intellectual westernization. He now depended more on his *chinovnik* bureaucracy than on his nobility, which widened the gulf separating the bureaucracy and the nobility.[10] For the intellectuals the 1825 revolution became an antistatist inspiration. But its failure also testified to the inefficacy of an exclusively elitist approach to political revolution.[11] However, there was no immediate further political repercussion.

Under the rigid censorship and police regimentation of Nicholas

I, the intellectuals tended to shy away from politics. The Decembrists' program of constitutional politics and abolition of serfdom was shelved. The intellectuals seemed divorced from the social and political issues of contemporary Russia. Their activities tended to center on the universities, the literary journals, and the semisecret discussion circles (*kruzhki*). They were intellectually influenced by two sources: the French utopian socialism of Fourier and St. Simon,[12] and the German idealist philosophy, with Schelling and Schiller in the thirties and Hegel in the forties.[13] But underneath the commitment to French and German ideas was the commitment to Russia. Herzen in his autobiography reconstructed this ambivalent atmosphere of the intellectuals: "What impressed them was the complete contradiction of the *words* they were taught with the realities of life around them." [14] Through the French and German intellectual vocabulary they searched for Russian identity. The tension between these two commitments manifested itself in the preoccupation with the dichotomy of Russia and the West.[15]

Peter Chaadaev (1793–1856), in one of his *Letters on the Philosophy of History* written during 1829–1831, expressed succinctly this sense of intellectual alienation: "We have never moved in concert with other peoples; we do not belong to any of the great families of mankind. We are not part of the Occident, nor are we part of the Orient; and we don't have the traditions of the one or of the other. . . . We live in the most narrow present, without a past or a future, in the midst of a flat calm." [16]

Russia was becalmed precisely because of Chaadaev's inability to reconcile his love for Russia with his consciousness of Western values. And according to Ovsianiko-Kulikovskii, in his *History of the Russian Intelligentsia*, this Chaadaev theme of the tension between Russia and the West was typical of all intellectuals of the period.[17] V. G. Belinsky (1811–1848) in his *Literary Reveries* of 1834, after reviewing the history of Russian literature, complained that Russia had no literature. But he placed his hope in the future enlightenment of the true spirit of the Russian people. The West would provide the enlightenment, but the genius was native. "Then shall we have *our own* literature, then shall we be the rivals and not imitators of the Europeans." [18]

In the thirties when the Westerners and Slavophiles were not yet split into two camps, both were nurtured on German philosophy. And both were committed to love for Russia. In the forties both continued to believe in the future of Russia. The Slavophiles were not ignorant of Western values; nor were the Westerners lacking in love for Russia. But their versions of Russia's future destiny differed. The Westerners believed in a Western destiny for Russia. They assumed the relevancy of Western values for Russia. On the other hand, the Slavophiles projected a non-Western future for Russia. They denied the Russian relevancy of Western values, and instead relied on some idealized Russian traditions, such as the orthodox religion and the Russian sense of unitary community (*sobornost*). They saw the dichotomy between Russia and the West as an unbridgeable gulf separating "we" and "they." K. Aksakov (1817–1860) typically emphasized this gulf when he said: "All European states are formed through conquest. Enmity is their fundamental principle. . . . The Russian state, on the contrary, was founded . . . by a voluntary invitation of the government. . . . Thus in the foundation of the Western state: violence, slavery, and hostility. In the foundation of the Russian state: free will, liberty, and peace." [19]

And, as his brother I. Aksakov (1823–1886) pointed out, underlying the dichotomy between Russia and the West was "the antagonism of the two opposite spiritual principles of enlightenment." [20] It was the antagonism between the orthodoxy and *sobornost* of Russia and the rationalism and individualism of the West.

Alexander Herzen (1812–1870) poignantly described the psychology of the Russian intellectuals, at the beginning of his *Dilettantism in Science* (1842–1843):

> We live on the borderland of two worlds: hence the constraint and uneasiness which weighs upon thinking people. The old convictions and former conceptions are shaken, but still dear to our hearts. The new ideas, great and all-embracing as they may be, have not yet borne fruit. . . . But people given to meditation suffer and seek to reconcile the differences at all cost. Man cannot live in internal discord, with the cornerstone of his moral basis missing.[21]

Even for the pre-1848 Herzen, supposedly a Westerner, beneath the commitment to Western ideas there was the commitment to Russia. In a letter to an old friend, written in 1838, Herzen proclaimed his unbounded faith in the future progress of Russia.[22] In this period before 1848 he believed that Russia had no real history of her own, but Peter's westernization had brought humanizing development to Russia. "With us the Petrine period is brought to an end. . . . After our time a period of organic, substantial and at the same time human growth will begin for Russia. Then her role in the fate of Europe will not be purely negative . . . but positive." [23] Russia's future would reside in a common destiny with the West. However, after the failure of the revolutions of 1848, a disillusioned Herzen admitted: "Those standards which a study of Western civilization has set up in our minds can find neither room nor substitutes for the peculiar and individual properties of Russian national life" (*Kolokol*, 1859).[24] His faith in the future of Russia now depended on emphasizing the distinction between Russia and the West. It was revealed in his distrust of Western democracy, his desire for dedicated revolutionaries, and his belief in the future of the Russian commune (*obshchina*), and in the autonomous development of Russian socialism. These ideas became the foundation of populism in the sixties and seventies.[25]

Politically repressed and socially isolated, the *dvoriane* intellectuals of 1825–1848 lived in their own world of ideas, imported from France and Germany. Yet in spite of that, the intellectuals revealed a consistent commitment to Russia and were preoccupied with the dichotomy between Russia and the West. The Westerners' commitment to a westernized future for Russia presupposed the compatibility of Russia and Western values. Their easing of the tension between Russian society and Western values brought with it a denial of the particularity of Russia. The Slavophiles' idealization of Russian tradition emphasized the incompatibility between Western values and Russia. But their separation of Russia and the West denied the real challenge of Western values. Both positions, in different manners, de-emphasized the underlying tension between the demand of Russia and the demand of Western values. In addition, both were operating in the realm of ideas exclusively, unlike their Decembrist predecessors and their populist descendants.

The populist intellectuals

In the sixties and seventies both the general atmosphere of Russian society as well as the orientation of the intellectuals had changed. The reign of Alexander II (1855–1881), which opened with Russia's defeat in the Crimea and then proceeded to the emancipation of serfdom, is characterized by movement and reform, different from the reign of Nicholas I. But the intelligentsia had changed too. Besides the *dvoriane* intellectuals, there were in the forties the *raznochintsy* intellectuals.[26] These were intellectuals of non-*dvoriane* and nonbureaucratic origins. They were the university-trained sons of the clergy, the merchants, and other lower classes, who could neither return to the occupations of their fathers nor find sufficient employment in the bureaucracy.[27] They therefore added their own *déclassé* orientation to the intellectual alienation of the *dvoriane* intellectuals. On the whole, the *raznochintsy* intellectuals tended to be more radical than the *dvoriane* intellectuals. The former, though in the minority, provided the initiative for the intellectual orientation of the sixties and seventies.[28]

In this period the intellectuals were more self-conscious than before and desired to break out of their isolation. As an indication of the former, this was the period when the word "intelligentsia" first appeared in the Russian language.[29] As an indication of the latter, this period saw the transformation of the *kruzhki* into broad agitational movements.[30] For this changed orientation, both the new atmosphere of Alexander's Russia and the new social composition of the intelligentsia must to some extent be responsible. The preoccupation with the dichotomy between Russia and the West was therefore displaced by the preoccupation with the relation between the conscious elite and the spontaneous masses. As F. Venturi pointed out, "for the next twenty years the revolutionary movement was to have two simultaneous aims: a difficult journey of exploration into the real life of the Russian people and an attempt to organize [the radical intellectual] minority."[31]

The preoccupation with Russia and the West reflected the theoretical concern of isolated intellectuals who felt themselves torn between their Western education and their Russian roots. The emphasis on the relation between elite and masses, a reaction against the previous preoccupation, was a somewhat more practical concern with the problem of change in nineteenth-century schismatic Russia. The tsarist government with its vested autocratic interests could not be expected to support change; and the Decembrist Revolution demonstrated the failure of an exclusively elitist approach to change. Therefore the formula of the unity of elite and masses emerged as the basis for the revolutionary transformation of Russia. The elite on the basis of its positivist scientific education would be conscious of the direction of change; the masses would spontaneously command the necessary elemental force for change. The unity of elite and masses implied a correlation between westernized consciousness and Russian spontaneity. Behind the formula of elite and masses loomed once more the tension between the universal demand of Western values and the particularist demand of Russia.

D. Pisarev (1840–1868) turned against the philosophical polemics of the earlier generation. He based himself upon the cult of scientific nihilism. The intellectuals, he said, had been talking nonsense: "We have an urgent need for a positive basis for research, for factual material out of which to forge ourselves an outlook and convictions as firm and solid as steel. We will look round at living nature instead of half-closing our eyes or obstinately scrutinizing letters, words and phrases." [32]

Science was the great equalizer. It enabled Pisarev to get away from the ideological controversy of the relation between Russia and the West, and claim that Russian civilization was in "no way better or worse than any other." [33] The need was to look at Russian "reality." Pisarev's appeal was to science and reality.

N. A. Dobroliubov (1836–1861) in his review of Turgenev's novel *On the Eve*, in 1860, commented on the heroine Helena's desire to perform good deeds, to end the suffering of her fellow men: "She expresses that vague longing for something, that almost unconscious but irresistible desire for a new way of life, for a new type of people, which the whole Russian society, and not only its so-called educated section, now feels." [34]

This was the new elite of activists. On the other hand, Dobroliubov idealized the Russian peasantry. In "Features for the Characterization of the Russian Common People" (1860) he claimed that the Russian peasantry had always had strength and goodness. However, serfdom had distorted the basic characteristics of the Russian people. [35] The elite did not impart anything new to the masses, because the latter already had the necessary traits for free development. Education was the link between the conscious elite and the spontaneous masses, since "the object of education . . . is to stimulate and clear up in the mind that which has long lived in the soul, but has lived spontaneously, unconsciously." [36]

Dobroliubov had asked: "But where are the men among us who are capable of action?" [37] The novel *What Is to Be Done?* by N. G. Chernyshevsky (1828–1889), which appeared in 1863, was the answer. It was a novel about "the new people." Positivist science could teach them that their personal interests were identical with the common good. They could therefore live and work harmoniously in their new scientific environment. There would be none of that old world of superstition and antagonism: "In our day it is no longer the same; the number of these human beings grows continually, and from year to year the increase is perceptible. . . . In time they will be the majority. In time, even, they will be the totality: then all will be well in the world." [38]

The utopian optimism of the novel suited exactly the expectation of the intellectuals of the sixties and seventies. *What Is to Be Done?* inspired an entire generation of radicals.

The populist program of the sixties represented a theoretical correlation of the tension between Western values and Russian particularism. Populism (*narodnichestvo*) denied a unique destiny for Russia. It accepted a common socialist goal for both Russia and the West. Its socialism was the French version taught by St. Simon, Fourier, and Proudhon. Yet populism placed an enormous emphasis on the communal tradition of Russia. Although destined for a common Western goal, Russia was different. Her communal

tradition had preserved among the Russian peasantry the spirit of
co-operation, quite unspoiled by capitalist competition. On this
basis Russia could have an autonomous development toward
socialism. Because of her communal tradition, she could skip the
industrial, capitalist phase. The acceptance of the Western goal
of socialism was tempered by the prospect of an accelerated
Russian development based upon her idealized tradition. The
underlying assumption of the populist program was the equivalence
between the socialist consciousness of the Western-educated elite
and the communal spontaneity of the Russian peasantry. Assuming
this equivalence, the unity of the elite and the masses would realize
the populist program of a unique Russian path to the Western
socialist goal.

The populist movement of the seventies was the crucial testing
of the ideological program of the sixties. Would there be the
automatic unity between the elite and the masses, as all good
populists had come to believe? In the 1873–1874 movement "to
the people" (*v narod*) enthusiastic young students and radicals
went into the Russian countryside, to live and agitate among the
masses. They expected to arouse the peasantry into a mass movement for change. But the Russian peasantry was not interested in
the ideological program of the young intellectuals. The failure of
the movement to the people destroyed the plausibility of the
automatic unity between the elite and the masses. By 1879 the
populist movement split into the Black Partition (*Chernyi Peredel*)
and the People's Will (*Narodnaia Volia*). The Black Partition
tried to maintain the ideological unity of conscious elite and
spontaneous masses. It insisted that the time was not yet ripe.
Therefore in the interim it worked for the program of equalitarian
partition of the black-soil land. The People's Will dropped the
expectation of mass spontaneity and emphasized instead the ter-
rorist activities of the conscious elite. But behind the failure of
the populist program was the collapse of the equivalence between
the elite's westernized consciousness and the peasants' Russian
spontaneity. Once more the Russian intelligentsia was faced with
its dilemma.

The Russian Marxist intellectuals *

Since the sixties the pace of change inside Russia had accelerated. Much of this change was the necessary governmental and social adjustments to the end of serfdom for the peasant majority. But the process of Russia's industrialization also quickened, so that by the 1890's industrial production in Russia was increasing at the rate of approximately 8 percent per annum.[39] Nevertheless, the emergence of Russian Marxism during the last two decades of the century cannot be understood against this broad background. It has rather to be explained against the immediate background of the populist movement.[40]

Populism had provided a comprehensive outlook for the radical intellectuals. It was a program for Russia's transformation which took cognizance simultaneously of the universal demand of Western values and the particularist demand of Russia. But by the late seventies, with the chasm between the conscious elite and the spontaneous masses, the populist outlook no longer had such comprehensive plausibility. Thus Russian Marxism emerged as another approach to the old dilemma.

More specifically it was G. V. Plekhanov (1856–1918) who in 1880–1882, "troubled by the failure of Chernyi Peredel and plagued by . . . doubts concerning the vitality of the peasant commune," turned from populism to Marxism.[41] In 1883 he led in the founding of the first Russian Marxist organization, called the Emancipation of Labor Group. For the next twenty years he dominated with his intellectual leadership the Russian Marxist revolutionary movement.

Plekhanov was aware of this populist background. His earliest Marxist writings were undertaken within the framework of anti-populist controversy. In "Socialism and the Political Struggle" (1883), his first Marxist work, he complained against the populists' "amazing conclusion that Russia's economic backwardness was a most reliable ally to the revolution." [42] In "Our Differences"

* We shall not mention the significant rise of both professional and *zemstvo* liberalism and *Vekhi* conservatism in the 1890's and 1900's, because, though important for the development of the Russian intelligentsia, they are not parts of the background for an understanding of Leninism.

(1884), his most important Marxist work of the period, he devoted much attention to criticizing all those, from Herzen to L. Tikhomirov, who emphasized the non-Western village community of Russia: "It is difficult for an intelligent Russian to get away from the influence of the 'West.' By declaring the more advanced theories of Europe to be 'inapplicable' to his own country, the Russian social figure does not save his exceptionalism, but only transfers his sympathy from a serious model to a caricature." [43]

With the breakdown of his belief in a Russian populist path to the Western socialist goal, Plekhanov once more felt the universal demand of Western values. The new faith for him was Marxism, universally applicable for all societies. He said: "Marx's general philosophical and historical views stand in exactly the same relation to modern Western Europe as to Greece and Rome, India and Egypt. They embrace the entire history of humanity [including] Russia." [44]

If Marxist economic analysis were universally applicable, then Marxist revolutionary expectation would also be valid. But, before he could maintain his revolutionary expectation for Russia, a Russian Marxist revolutionary must re-view Russia in familiar Marxist garb. Russia in universal Marxist perspective acquired Western characteristics. As the basis for his Marxist faith, Plekhanov insisted that Russia *since 1861* had become capitalistic: "We only want to point out the indisputable facts which show beyond refutation the transitory situation of our national economy. . . . Capitalism is going its way: it is ousting independent producers from their shaky positions and creating an army of workers in Russia by the same tested methods as it has already practised 'in the West.' " [45]

Her village community had been gradually disrupted by the money economy. Russia was already Western. The only peculiarity Plekhanov admitted was that capitalism's "uninterrupted advance from 'West' to East is taking place with constantly increasing speed." [46] Therefore Russian capitalism would fade away before it would have had time to blossom completely. Russian capitalism would not last as long as English capitalism. The question was not whether Russia could escape capitalism, but what would be the pace of her capitalist development.

For Plekhanov, since Russia was already capitalistic, she would have in her nascent proletariat the basis of a genuine Western consciousness. In "A New Champion of Autocracy, or Mr. L. Tikhomirov's Grief" (1889), he said: "In the working class a *people* in the European sense of the word is now being created in Russia. . . . Thus the inexorable course of historical development solves all those contradictions which in our country are characteristic of the position of . . . "intelligentsia.". . . It is among the proletariat that the Russian revolutionaries will find that support of the *"people"* which they have not had until recently." [47]

Here was another version of the new people which Dobroliubov and Chernyshevsky had sought in the sixties. And with it the old problem of the relation between westernized consciousness and Russian spontaneity seemed to have disappeared.

In his second draft program for the Russian Social Democrats, 1887, Plekhanov said: "The principal means for the political struggle of the workers' groups against absolutism . . . is agitation among the working class and the further spread of socialist ideas and revolutionary organizations among that class." [48] His primary emphasis was the strengthening of the Russian working class, and that meant "the clarity of its political consciousness, its cohesion and degree of organization." [49] The Russian Marxists, according to Plekhanov, had to play their revolutionary role in union with the working-class movement. He criticized the Blanquist tendency of the People's Will: "The Social-Democrat wants the worker *himself to make* his revolution; the Blanquist demands that the worker should *support* the revolution which has been begun and led for him and in his name by others. . . . This difference is of immense practical importance; it is precisely what explains the hostile attitude of the Social-Democrats to the conspiratorial fantasies of the Blanquists." [50]

Against later tendencies in the Russian Marxist movement, Plekhanov was consistently faithful to this approach.[51]

For a post-1825 radical, the prospect for the transformation of Russia depended upon the unity of the elite and the masses. Behind the unity of the westernized elite and the Russian masses was the need to reconcile the demand of Western values with the demand of Russia. The populists assumed the automatic unity of populist elite and peasant masses in a non-Western Russia. Their program was a unique Russian path to the Western socialist goal. But the events of the seventies showed that the unity of populist elite and peasant masses did not exist. On the other hand, Plekhanov assumed the automatic unity of the Russian Marxist elite and the proletarian masses in capitalist Russia. He accepted the demand of Western Marxist values; and in reaction against the populists he emphasized Russia's equivalence to the West. But what about the demand of Russia?

The Russia of the 1890's, with the acceleration of her industrial development and the commercialization of her agriculture, certainly did not conform to the populists' image of a non-Western society. Yet westernizing Russia, with her precapitalist traditions now in transformation, did not conform to the Western model of Marx and Engels either. Besides, some events in that decade had begun to jeopardize Plekhanov's assumption of the automatic unity between Russian Marxist elite and proletarian masses: The strikes of Russian workers in the mid-nineties revealed a fundamental split between the economic orientation of the trade unionists and the political orientation of the Plekhanovites. The latter seemed to be merely an adjunct of the strike movement.[52] The tail could not wag the dog. The Economists, aware of this trend, advocated that "the task of Social Democrats lies in carrying out continuous agitation among factory workers on the basis of their everyday petty needs and demands." [53] In the late nineties the Economists succeeded in capturing control of the Russian Social Democratic Union, so that in 1900 Plekhanov withdrew his Emancipation of Labor Group from the Union.[54]

Where was the automatic unity of elite and masses, upon which Plekhanov had based his expectation of a Marxist-oriented transformation for Russia? Because of his excessive dependence on Marxist theory, Plekhanov could not maintain a distinction between the conscious elite and the spontaneous masses. Yet there was a real schism between the Marxist elite and the proletariat in contemporary Russia. Plekhanov was unable to accede to the particularist demand of Russia. The Plekhanovites by the late nineties were in danger of being isolated from the real agitation of the nascent Russian proletarian movement. This was exactly Plekhanov's complaint against the Blanquist tendency of the populists, in the eighties! Yet, Economist agitation was no guarantee for a Marxist revolution in Russia. What was to be done, from the perspective of a Russian Marxist revolutionary?

THE PROBLEM OF RUSSIA'S EQUIVALENCE TO THE WEST

Behind westernization loomed the challenge of Western rational values. Such values are secular rather than ritual, legal rather than symbolic. Their arguments are based more upon function than upon precedence. They are transcendent and universal in claim. On the other hand, non-Western traditions are precedented forms of value. They cannot be universally valid, but are relative to a continuously familiar situation. They promote a cyclical perspective which contains persistent, repetitive problems. The problems arising from a fast-changing, unfamiliar situation must sooner or later be seen as new problems. The interdependence between non-Western traditions and a slow-changing, familiar situation differs basically from the interaction between Western rational values and a fast-changing situation.*

The confrontation between Western values and native traditions implies the prior breakdown of a non-Western situation. Here traditions have lost their familiar pre-Western environment and become attenuated traditions-through-transformation. They, as the embodiment of the pre-Western specificity of that society, still affect the existing westernizing situation, and continue to command some allegiance. On the other hand, Western values based on the universal-logical model seemingly can claim comprehension of the new unfamiliar situation. Yet, transplanted Western values are not the same as Western values in the West. This is the inevitable difficulty, which may or may not be obvious to the intellectuals, themselves caught in the westernizing predicament.

* All descriptive words used in this paragraph, such as secular, ritual, legal, symbolic, precedented, familiar, changing, new, and persistent, are comparative in meaning. No value can be strictly secular, legal, functional; nor any tradition entirely ritual, symbolic, precedented. Nevertheless, Max Weber's insight regarding the distinction between rational and traditional authorities is most rewarding.[55]

Within the westernized consciousness of the Russian intelligentsia Western rational values furnished the universal norm. Yet no matter how westernized, these intellectuals still felt the psychological pull of Russia. Depending upon their perspectives, the demand of Russia might emerge as a recognition of the Russian situation or as idealization of Russian traditions. This was the tension in the intelligentsia's role as mediator between Western thought and Russia. Rationality and historicity are two disparate orderings of reality. Their reconciliation would hopefully be effected, if the Russian intellectual could claim somewhere, somehow, sometime the equivalence of Russia to the West.* Therefore the solution to the problem of Russia's equivalence was the key to the reconciliation between Western values and Russian particularism.

The crucial problem of Russia's equivalence to the West could be "resolved" in three ways: (1) Acceptance of the demand of Western rational values, to the neglect of the demand of Russia; (2) acceptance of the demand of Russia, by denying the demand of Western rational values; and (3) correlation of the demand of Western values with the demand of Russia.

The Westerners of the thirties and forties, such as Belinsky and the pre-1848 Herzen, projected Russia's Western equivalence into the future. A Russia westernized in the image of a Western model would be compatible with the West. In order to do that, the Westerners had to exaggerate the universal validity of Western values and its Russian relevancy. In a world of universal ideas, they could not make exceptions for Russian particularism. Russia was negative; she acquired positive characteristic only to the extent that she became westernized. In addition, they could not maintain a distinction between the Western model and westernization. The Westerners lived in a world of abstract ideas. Their reasoning was indicative of their position as westernized intellectuals nurtured by French and German ideas, isolated from the rest of Russian

---

* Strictly speaking, the equivalence of Russia and the West, even if possible, will not eliminate the tension between rationality and historicity, since intellectuals in the West also felt the tension between universal value and historical particularism. However, from a westernizing perspective, the tension between Western values and non-Western particularism is greater than the tension between Western values and Western particularism.

society. But how long could a Russian intellectual iconoclastically maintain his faith in the West, without acknowledging any tie with Russia? It was psychologically difficult to do. Certainly Herzen even from abroad could not, after 1848.

The Slavophiles in the thirties and forties denied Russia's equivalence to the West, past, present, or future. They felt the demand of Russia, which they idealized as the traditions of orthodoxy, *sobornost*, and commune; and they had a sense of the distinction between westernization and the Western model. But ultimately they questioned the universal validity of Western values and especially its Russian relevancy. The quest was not for the validity of values but rather for its historical appropriateness. Therefore, it would be Western values for the West, and Russian traditions for Russia. But by emphasizing the appropriateness of the Russian traditions for Russia, the Slavophiles exaggerated the prospect for traditions to persist in transformation. They had to deny the subversion of native traditions by Western values. The Slavophiles in their idealization of Russia were just as distant from the westernization of Russia as were the Westerners.

The populists in the sixties and seventies posited Russia's eventual equivalence to the West, after a non-Western development. Western socialism was the universal goal. But, according to the populists, Russia with her communal tradition could attain socialism by bypassing the capitalist stage of development. There was after all some positive value to Russian particularism. The populists' program was a reconciliation of the demand of Western socialism with the demand of communal Russia. The assumption was the equivalence between the socialist consciousness of the westernized elite and the communal spontaneity of the Russian peasantry. But socialism was a projected Western value goal, whereas communalism was an idealized Russian tradition. If the two could really be equivalent, then whence the tension between Russia and the West? Being less isolated than the *dvoriane* intellectuals of the thirties and forties, the populists sought the Western equivalence of Russia in practice as well as in theory. The failure of the unity of the elite and the masses in 1873–1874 ruined both populist theory and practice.

The Plekhanovite Russian Marxists in the eighties and nineties emerged on the basis of the failure of the populist program. They insisted on Russia's capitalist equivalence to the West. Once more, like the Westerners, they depended on the universal validity of Western values and its Russian relevancy. This time it was the Western value of Marxism which enabled Plekhanov to maintain his belief in a unity of the Russian Marxist elite and the proletarian masses. But that was all Plekhanov succeeded in salvaging. He de-emphasized the difference between westernizing Russia and the Western model. The failure to maintain such distinction meant an inability to accede to the particularist demand of Russia; and belief in the unity of elite and masses without sensitivity to the demand of Russia could not be the basis for an effective revolutionary program.

As the nineteenth century proceeded, the ivory-tower atmosphere of the Westerners and Slavophiles changed to the revolutionary concern of the populists and Plekhanovites, and the populist idealization of communal Russia to the Plekhanovite idealization of capitalist Russia. The continuing westernization of Russia accentuated the schism and tension in society, and made the problem of westernization more difficult to ignore. In addition, the changing social composition of the intelligentsia increased its radical orientation. And the intelligentsia's consciousness of its own past—from the failure of the Decembrist elite, through the isolation of the Westerner-Slovophile elite, to the populist formulation of the unity of elite and masses, and the Russian Marxist reformulation of the same—contributed to the increasing self-consciousness its own role in changing Russian society.

Thus the easing of the tension between Western values and Russian particularism became not merely a problem of the psychological-intellectual reconstitution of the intelligentsia, but also one of the practical transformation (that is, conscious westernization) of Russian society. In other words, the problem of Russia's equivalence to the West would have to be solved both in theory and in practice. This was the burden of Russian history for Lenin.

RUSSIAN IDEAS OF CHINA

In nineteenth-century Russia the prevailing idea of China was that of a static, inferior society; it was akin to the contemporary

European idea of China. But a small minority of Russian intellectuals differed from this view. Russian ideas of China were ancillary to the intellectuals' preoccupation with the dichotomy between Russia and the West. The historical significance of a particular idea of China is to be sought in that intellectual's interpretation of the relation of Russia to the West. Within the preoccupation of the Russian intelligentsia, what was the relation of China to the tension between Western values and Russia?

Chaadaev felt the pressure of Western values on Russia. His refusal to acknowledge any positive characteristic in Russia left him desolate. He claimed that his memory of Russia included neither a charming recollection nor a gracious image. "Alone of all the peoples in the world, we have not given anything to the world, and we have not learned anything from the world." [56] For Chaadaev, the world had always been divided into two principles, the Orient and the West, corresponding to two dynamic forces in nature. The Orient with its solitary meditation first spread enlightenment over the world. This was followed by the dynamic, active West. "But in the Orient, the docile minds, who were prostrated before the authority of time, exhausted themselves in their absolute submission to a venerated principle, and one day, imprisoned in their immovable syntheses, they fell asleep, without any inkling of the new fates in store for them." [57] Since value resided in the West and Russia was negative, in Chaadaev's mind the Orient would persist in her stagnation. In his love for Russia he sought her eventual westernization. Therefore, he insisted "the history of the Orient has nothing in common with the history of our country." [58]

East is East, and Russia *will be* West, and never the twain shall meet: such was the attitude of the Westerners. As they saw it, the stagnation of China persisted. There was neither interest nor reason to change it. But, to the extent that Russia was not Western, from the Westerners' viewpoint, the idea of stagnant China could be used as a model for Russia's past. Belinsky, in his *Literary Reveries*, pointed out that the customs of a nation would be characteristic of its originality: "Look at China: there a mass of people confess several different faiths; the highest social estate, the mandarins, confess none, and perform religious rites merely for the sake of a decorum; but what unity and community of customs they have, what independence, what specific and peculiar character! How tenaciously they cling to them!" [59] Elsewhere, he referred to China as an obsolete nation that had outlived its life and was leading a mechanical existence like a corpse; [60] national conceit and susceptibility was a purely Chinese sentiment; [61] in rotten China there were no upstarts, all were bribe takers in conformity with the general depravity; [62] the vices of the Chinese were bound up with their spirit.[63] But Belinsky used this image of the stagnant East to view Russia's non-Western past. He felt that Russia, before Peter the great, differed from Asia yet had Asiatic traits. "Generally, Russia was Asia, but in a different character." [64] From a Westerner's perspective, where value resided in the West and the hope prevailed that Russia would eventually be Western, the Russian past and Asia were compressed into the negative category of non-West.

Herzen, before 1848, had a typical Westerner's view of stagnant China. In 1844 he complained that the East lacked in science; it was so diffused that it could not arrive at any self-understanding:

> Asia is a land of disharmony and contrasts. It has no sense of moderation in anything. . . . The life of the peoples of the East consisted of either the ferment of terrible upheavals or the stagnant calm of monotonous repetition. The Easterner had no sense of dignity: he was either a cringing slave or an unrestrained despot. His thought was, likewise, either too modest or too arrogant. . . . The religious and gnostic life of Asians alternates between feverish restlessness and dead stillness. . . . The East could never impart an adequate form to its thought because it had never reasoned out its contents but only dreamed about it in various images.[65]

After 1848, because of his disenchantment with the West, Herzen became somewhat more receptive toward the East. He now believed that the East, with its people exploited by the West, would be the focus of world revolution; and he even claimed that the Eastern and Mongol elements in Russia had preserved her village commune from Western destruction.[66] However, Herzen had too great a commitment to the uniqueness of communal Russia, to be able to equate Russia with the East. From a perspective that saw Russia in terms of her uniqueness, she could be neither Eastern nor Western. Therefore he claimed, "we have no more

real link with the modern world than we have with China." [67]
China was static. "On the contrary, Russia is an Empire still in its
youth." [68]

The Slavophiles, against the pressure of Western values, sought
compensatory values in the idealization of Russian traditions.
Emphasizing unique Russia as the antithesis to the West, the
Slavophiles were as little interested in the stagnant East as the
Westerners. A. S. Khomiakov (1804–1860) in his *Notes on
Universal History*, the most important work of Slavophile historiography, saw the Iranian spirit of freedom and the Kushite
spirit of necessity as two principles continuously in opposition
through history. Both Europe and Asia represented the triumph
of the Kushite principle, whereas it was the Slavs' mission to
maintain in purity the Iranian principle. With this dichotomy,
Khomiakov preserved the prevailing idea of stagnant Asia. "Meek,
petrified, half-dead" China was, according to him, the result of a
combination of Oriental despotism and ascetic Buddhism.[69] When
the Slavophiles talked about the East, they usually meant the
orthodox East, in opposition to the Catholic West. Asia was hazy
in the distant background.

Unique Russia as the orthodox East, under pressure from the
West, could possibly feel closer to Asia. Therefore, Dostoevskii
(1821–1881) answered the question "What is Asia to us?" in the
following manner: "Russia is not only in Europe but also in
Asia; . . . the Russian is not only a European but also an Asiatic.
Moreover, Asia, perhaps, holds out greater promises to us than
Europe. In our future destinies Asia is, perhaps, our main outlet!" [70]
On the other hand, unique Russia out of a sense of Christian
solidarity would prefer Europe to Asia. Hence K. Leontiev
(1831–1891) believed that Russia, being neither Western nor
Eastern, had the mission to save the West from the East, in the
impending conflict between the two.[71] But for others who lacked
a sense of the orthodox uniqueness of Russia, in opposition to the
West, Russia could very well become Eastern. This approach
rejected the prevailing idea of the stagnant East. Instead it idealized
the East. Such was the position of Tolstoy (1828–1910) and of the
romantic Easterners of the late nineteenth century, the *Vostoch-
niki*.[72] Each tried to discover in Asia ideals antithetical to the West.

To them, the East was a source for values, in opposition to the pressure of Western values.

Chernyshevsky, as a populist intellectual, accepted both the uniqueness of communal Russia and the Western values of science and socialism. He was preoccupied with the correlation of unique Russia and Western universal value. Such was his approach to the problem of Russia's equivalence to the West. In accordance with this perspective he accepted the prevailing idea of the static, inferior East. In his *Essay on the Scientific Conception of Certain Problems of World History*, Chernyshevsky considered China to be an old, decaying society. "Chinese history shows no stagnation, but a series of declines of civilization due to the oppression of barbarian invasion and conquest. After every decline the Chinese recovered . . . only to sink again under the blow of barbarians." [73] His novel *What Is to Be Done?* abounds with remarks concerning Chinese decadence. For instance: ". . . the most savage European is very gentle, the most cowardly very courageous, the most epicurean very moral [when] compared with the Chinese." [74] The East was not relevant to Chernyshevsky's preoccupation with unique Russia and Western values.

Plekhanov inherited his idea of Asia from both Western Marxism and his own Russian background. His intellectual perspective required the acceptance of Western Marxism and the insistence on Russia's equivalence to the West. If value resided in the West and Russia was already Western, why should he be interested in revising the prevailing idea of an inferior Asia? Therefore his approach to the idea of the East was similar to that of the Westerners of the thirties and forties.

For Plekhanov, the East represented a combination of economic stagnation and political despotism. Asia's economy was that of a self-sufficient village community lacking monetary and commodity circulation. He mentioned water works [75] but they were not important. Instead, he followed Marx's *Capital* version of the Asiatic mode of production. In "Our Differences" he quoted from *Capital* to emphasize that the simple organization of the village communal economy was the key to the unchangeableness of Asia.[76] Asiatic politics was that of a centralized despotism, with little prospect for free, progressive development.[77] There was naturally interaction between political despotism and communal economy.

In his emphasis on Russia's equivalence to the West, Plekhanov broke with the populists' insistence on the uniqueness of Russia. From his universal Marxist perspective no country could be unique. Yet pre-1861 Russia was not Western. Therefore he used the model of a stagnant Asia to view that Russian past. Pre-Western Russia was Asiatic. In this respect his view was similar to that of Belinsky. According to Plekhanov, "The old Muscovite Russia was noted for her completely Asiatic character. This strikes one in the economic life of the country, in all its usages and the whole system of state administration. Muscovy was a kind of China, situated not in Asia but in Europe." [78] Peter the Great in his westernization merely strengthened the Asiatic dominance of state over society. Plekhanov equated the Russian commune with the village community of Asia.[79] Not until the emergence of capitalism during the second half of the nineteenth century did Russia become truly Western. "With [the proletariat's] appearance the very character of Russian culture is changing: our old *Asiatic* economic life disappearing, giving place to a new, *European* one." [80] If he insisted that pre-1861 Russia was Asiatic, he was equally adamant in maintaining that post-1861 Russia was already Western. The description of post-1861 Russia as "a kind of European China" was "utterly false," he insisted.[81] From Plekhanov's rigid Marxist perspective, the world was clearly demarcated into East and West, and his Russia must be entirely one or entirely the other.

Chapter Three

Lenin

Lenin was a Russian Marxist revolutionary. He was inspired by the Western values of Marxism, and wanted to bring about a Marxist-oriented revolution in Russia. But Marxian theory did not logically point to a Russian revolution; nor did the prospect of a Russian revolution easily fit into a Marxian scheme. Throughout his career Lenin tenaciously pursued the necessary correlation of Western theory and Russian practice. And in the process he had to revise both. This tenacity to correlate theory and practice distinguished him from the Plekhanovite Marxists and the Russian populists. From the former, he inherited his Marxist faith; from the latter he derived his concern with the unity of conscious elite and spontaneous masses. But the correlation of universal Marxist faith with specific Russian revolutionary practice was his own.

The Leninist unity of Western-oriented theory and Russian-oriented practice was yet another solution to the perennial problem of Russia's equivalence to the West. Only when one could claim Russia as the equivalent of the West, would the tension between the demands of Western values and of Russia be eased. From the viewpoint of his central preoccupation with Russia's Western equivalence, Lenin's intellectual career can be divided into four major periods: From 1893 to approximately 1899; from 1899 to the outbreak of World War I in 1914; from 1914 to the Bolshevik victory in 1917; and from 1917 to his death in 1924.

From 1893 to approximately 1899

During this initial period Lenin followed Plekhanov in insisting on the universal validity of Marxism and in denying the uniqueness of Russia; this was the basis for their conversion to the Marxist faith. Therefore Lenin emphasized that Russia was economically already the equivalent of the capitalist West. In his earliest manuscript, "New Economic Development in Peasant Life" (1893), Lenin pointed out that agriculture in south Russia was commercially prosperous, largely exploiting hired labor.[1] He was interested in seeking a commercial capitalist basis for post-Emancipation Russian agriculture. Therefore not only did Russia have capitalist industries, but even her agriculture was undertaken along capitalist lines.[2] In "What the 'Friends of the People' Are and How They Fight the Social Democrats" (1894), he agreed with Plekhanov that "Russia *has entered* the capitalist path." [3] Therefore the populists' belief in a noncapitalist path for Russia was already disproved by her recent economic development. And in "The Heritage We Renounce" (1897) he criticized the populists for their "belief in the exceptional character of the Russian economic system in general, and of the peasantry, with its village community, artel, etc., in particular." [4] His concern was to emphasize Russia's capitalist equivalence to the West.

Capitalism was the great transformer. If Russia had become capitalist since 1861, what was she before that? On the one hand, Lenin referred to pre-Emancipation Russia as being *semifeudal;* on the other hand, he sometimes used such Russian words as *barshchina* and *krepostnost* to describe her pre-1861 agricultural serfdom.[5] In this initial period, he never clarified whether pre-1861 Russia was explicitly Western (in the feudal sense) or Asiatic (in the communal sense). In *The Development of Capitalism in Russia* (1899), he said that "the precapitalist countryside constituted (from the economic viewpoint) a network of small local markets which linked up tiny groups of small producers, severed from each other by their separate farms, by the innumerable medieval barriers between them, and by the remnants of medieval dependence." [6] This, he continued, had been destroyed by the advent of large-scale industry in post-1861 Russia.[7] However, he admitted that Russian capitalism was complicated by such factors as "servile institutions, absolutism, the social estate system, and the bureaucracy." [8] Hence in "The Tasks of the Russian Social Democrats" (1897) he spoke of "autocratic and semi-Asiatic Russia." [9] Nevertheless, in terms of her fundamental economic tendency, Russia was a part of the capitalist West. This was one of the very few times during the 1893–1899 period when Lenin used the word "Asiatic" to describe tsarist Russia. After 1899, when he no longer emphasized Russia's Western equivalence, Lenin stressed the Asiatic character of tsarist Russia more.[10]

The emphasis on Russia's capitalist equivalence to the West implied the acceptance of the universal validity of Western Marxian theory and the denial of Russian uniqueness. It facilitated the adoption of Western Marxian strategy for the Russian Marxist movement. Therefore the Lenin of 1893–1899 insisted that the fundamental program of the Russian Social Democrats was the class struggle of the proletariat against the capitalists and the landowners.[11] It was a strictly orthodox Marxian program. There was no inkling of any revolutionary prospect in Russia besides that of the nascent proletariat. Nor was there any sophistication concerning the relation between the Social Democrats and the Russian proletariat.

But a strictly orthodox Marxian program was no guarantee that a Marxist-oriented revolution could be realized in Russia. The strikes of the mid-nineties pointed out the isolation of the Plekhanovite elite from the proletarian masses. Temperamentally, Lenin as a revolutionary could never accept the Economists' position, which called for agitation in terms of the spontaneous grievances of the proletariat. To maintain his position as a Russian Marxist revolutionary, Lenin had to correlate Western Marxian theory with the specific revolutionary prospect in Russia. This meant abandoning the Plekhanovite insistence on Russia's equivalence to the West, in order to pursue a Marxist reinterpretation of the old populist correlation of conscious elite and spontaneous masses. By 1899 Lenin was fully aware of the need for such a new correlation between the Western Marxian theory and the Russian revolutionary prospect. In "Our Immediate Task," written that year to justify his new programing effort, he said:

> On the one hand, the Russian proletarian movement exists under conditions which are quite different from those in Western Europe. . . . On the other hand, Russian Social Democracy differs very much from the earlier revolutionary parties in Russia, so that the need to learn revolutionary technique and secret organization from the old Russian masters . . . does not in any way relieve

us from the duty of assessing them critically and of elaborating our own organization independently.[12]

Neither complete reliance on the Western Marxian program nor on the Russian revolutionary experience could be satisfactory. Thus began a distinctly new Leninist perspective on the prospect of a Marxist-oriented revolution in semi-Western Russia.

From 1899 to the outbreak of World War I in 1914

Before 1899 Lenin tended to exaggerate Russia's Western equivalence in order to accept the Marxist faith. Since 1899 he pointed to the difference between Russia and the West in order to work for a Russian revolution. The revolutionary potentiality of Russia had to be recognized for what it was, instead of being viewed entirely in the light of a Western Marxian model. The emphasis on Russia's difference from the Western model enabled Lenin to revise the Western-oriented Marxian strategy.

Already in *The Development of Capitalism in Russia*, a work completed in 1899, Lenin began to emphasize Russia's variation from the Western capitalist model: "In no capitalist country have institutions irreconcilable with capitalism survived in such abundance, institutions which retard the country's development and immeasurably worsen the position of the producers who 'suffer as much from capitalism as from the insufficient development of capitalism,' to quote the phrase of Marx." [13]

Before 1899, Lenin had emphasized the commercial capitalist development of Russian agriculture; now, after 1899, he emphasized the persistence of servile relations in her agriculture.[14] As he pointed out in "One Step Forward, Two Steps Back" (1904), "the Russian peculiarities of the general capitalist relations" should be emphasized.[15]

Marxian theory provided the general understanding of capitalism, but Russian history held the key to the specific development of capitalism in Russia. Lenin now repeatedly attacked Plekhanov for his excessive dependence on general Western theory, to the neglect of the specific Russian development.[16] In 1912 he attacked P. Miliukov and P. Axelrod on the same ground. They were, Lenin said, opportunists because "by uttering dreamy phrases about

'Europeanism,' they evade the difficult and urgent question of how a particular class, in non-European conditions, ought to act *for* a stubborn struggle to secure a *basis* for Europeanism [in Russia]." [17] Conversely, Lenin's attack against the populists and their Socialist Revolutionary descendants also shifted grounds. Before 1899, in conjunction with Plekhanov, he criticized the populists for their view concerning the exceptional character of Russia. But now, after 1899, with his own emphasis on Russian peculiarity within the general capitalist framework, Lenin did not attack the populists for emphasizing the uniqueness of Russia. For instance, in two articles written in 1902 specifically to criticize the position of the Socialist Revolutionaries, he did not even mention the old quarrel concerning the peculiarity of Russia.[18]

However, unlike the populists and the Socialist Revolutionaries, a Marxist could never consider Russian peculiarity as being unique. From the Western Marxist perspective, the world is divided into West and non-West (that is, East). Hence, if Russia were not entirely Western, she must be semi-Asiatic. "Asia" was an anti-Western model used by Lenin to characterize Russia's non-Western peculiarities.

In the first issue of *Zaria* (April, 1901), Lenin described the tsarist government as hiding behind a "Chinese wall." [19] In "A Valuable Admission" (*Iskra*, No. 6, July, 1901), he included Russia as a part of Asia, "where the masses of the people are so wretched and ignorant." [20] In "The Serf-Owners at Work" (*Iskra*, No. 8, September, 1901), Lenin said that Russia's "Asiatic government must seek support in Asiatic large landownership and a servile system of 'granted land.' " This led to the creation of "a class of Asiatic satraps." [21] In the pamphlet "What Is to Be Done?", he referred to the presence of "Asiatic reaction" in Russia.[22] In his January, 1905, notes, Lenin wrote that Russia had ties with both the West and the East (that is, Persia and China), thus implying that she was not entirely Western.[23] In "The Two Tactics of Social Democracy in a Democratic Revolution" (1905), he referred to the "Asiatic development of capitalism" in Russia as compared with European capitalism, and "the oppressive features of Asiatic bondage" in Russia.[24] In "The Platform of the Reformists and the Platform of the Revolutionary Social Democrats" (1912), he wrote: "What a lot of old China there is in Russian life . . . in our tsarism." [25] There are numerous other examples of Asiatic Russia, all along similar lines. Finally in "Left-Wing Populism and Marxism" (*Trudovaia Pravda*, No. 19, June, 1914), Lenin made pre-Emancipation Russia the equivalent of China! "But serfdom *can* keep, and for centuries has kept, millions of peasants in a down-trodden state (for example, in Russia from the ninth to the nineteenth century, in China for even more centuries)." [26]

In all such characterizations of Asiatic Russia, Lenin used "Asiatic" to mean non-Western, politically despotic, or economically stagnant. In this respect he conformed to the West European and Russian-Westerner image of the inferior East. Taking the Marxist viewpoint, he believed that pre-Emancipation Russia's agrarian economy was much closer to the Asiatic mode of production than to the European feudal mode. In "Notes on Plekhanov's Second Draft Program" (1902), Lenin criticized Plekhanov's use of the term "feudal handicraft" to describe the middle period of Russian history. "Here, an expression seems to have been chosen . . . which is least applicable to Russia, for it is questionable whether the term 'feudalism' is applicable to our Middle Ages." [27] In a report to the unity congress of the Russian Social Democratic Labor party, in 1906, Lenin characterized the economy of the Muscovite state land as Asiatic.[28] In "The Agrarian Program of Social Democracy in the First Russian Revolution, 1905–07" (1907), he characterized the old agrarian relations of Russia as being "partly feudal and partly Asiatic." [29] But in "The Essence of 'The Agrarian Problem in Russia'" (1912), Lenin explained: "The difference between 'Europe' and Russia stems from Russia's extreme backwardness. In the West, the bourgeois agrarian system is fully established, serfdom was swept away long ago. . . . But purely capitalist relations in our country are still overshadowed to a *tremendous* extent by servile relations. . . . In the West *this* kind of 'problem' . . . was solved long ago. In Russia, its solution has been delayed." [30]

Here Lenin seemed to equate pre-Emancipation Russia with the feudal West. Yet in "Left-Wing Populism and Marxism" (1914), he equated pre-Emancipation Russia with old China.[31] Lenin was never very clear what constituted Russia's pre-1861 economy. It is fair to say that he characterized pre-1861 Russia as semifeudal and semi-Asiatic.

The quest for the semi-Western, semi-Asiatic peculiarity of Russia within a general Western capitalist framework enabled Lenin to point to a mixed socioeconomic development in Russia— mixed, in the sense that it did not conform to Marx's Western-oriented model. This was a recognition of the historical particularism of Russia, from the universal Marxist perspective.

Universal Marxian theory provided for its own correlation of economic determinism and political voluntarism. According to it, a socialist proletarian revolution should emerge on the basis of mature capitalist development. The transplantation of Marxian theory to Russia required a change in the economic base for the expected political revolution. Without that Western base of capitalism, in order to maintain the expectation in the Marxian goal of socialism, an increase in political voluntarism was necessary. This increased sense of political voluntarism must depend upon the specific revolutionary prospect of Russia.

But political voluntarism was not purchased at the expense of universal theory. Lenin continued to be motivated by Marxian theoretical values. In this period from 1899 to 1914 he provided a reinterpretation of the universal demand of Marxian theory, in order to complement the demand of Russian particularism. This was already evident in his "Our Program" (1899):

> We do not regard Marx's theory as something complete and inviolable; on the contrary, we are convinced that it has only laid the foundation stone of the science which socialists *must* develop in all directions if they wish to keep pace with life. We think that an independent elaboration of Marx's theory is especially essential for Russian socialists; for this theory provides only general *guiding* principles, which in *particular*, are applied . . . [differently in different countries].[32]

Such a correlation between the demands of Marxist theory and of a socialist revolution in semi-Western, semi-Asiatic Russia was the key to the Leninist perspective during the 1899–1914 period. It was on this basis that Lenin provided his solution to the relations between the elite and the masses. This would be, theoretically, a revolutionary unity of Bolshevik elite and proletarian masses. The Bolshevik elite would be *conscious* of the necessity of a Marxist-oriented revolution, whereas the masses would possess *spontaneous* economic grievances. Practically, the emphasis was on the volun-tarist manipulation by the conscious elite.[33] From the same per-spective, Lenin pointed to the fundamental importance of the agrarian question in the bourgeois-democratic revolution of Russia. In conformity with Marxist theory, the prospective revolution in Russia would be bourgeois-democratic; but in accordance with Russian potentiality, the content of the revolution would be agrarian.[34] On the basis of the 1905 revolutionary experience, Lenin broadened his strategy into the revolutionary democratic dicta-torship of the proletariat and the peasantry. He stressed the ability of the Bolshevik elite to seize control of a bourgeois-democratic revolution in Russia, by exploiting the spontaneous grievances of both the urban and rural masses, and then to lead the bourgeois-*democratic* revolution to a post-bourgeois, that is, socialist, conclusion.[35] Finally, Lenin pointed to a Bolshevik ap-proach to the national question in a bourgeois-democratic revolu-tion. From the viewpoint of the situation in Russia, the demand for national self-determination was progressive; but from the viewpoint of the ultimate socialist goal, national self-determination was merely an intermediary stage. Therefore the Bolshevik ap-proach to the national question must be twofold.[36] All these are now familiar concepts of Leninist voluntarist strategy. But the perspective behind these manipulations was new in that it was based upon the Leninist correlation of Marxist theory and Russian revolutionary prospect. Lenin's Menshevik contemporaries cer-tainly did not agree with either his assessment of the Russian revolutionary prospect or his interpretation of the Marxist theory.

From 1914 to the Bolshevik victory in 1917

Between 1899 and 1914 Lenin had conceived of Russia as being semi-Western and semi-Asiatic, with her ultimate Western equiva-lence postponed until the triumph of socialism. The emphasis was on the difference between Russia and the West. Now between

1914 and 1917 he continued to see domestic Russia as semi-Western, semi-Asiatic; but at the international level he saw a changing relationship of Russia to the West.

For Lenin, the war of 1914 was an imperialist war. It was the signal for the final stage in bourgeois-capitalist history. In this stage, the struggle between the bourgeoisie and the proletariat would assume a world-wide scope.[37] This view became the basis for his pamphlet, "Imperialism, the Highest Stage of Capitalism" (1916). Lenin's theory of imperialism was not new; he borrowed a great deal from J. A. Hobson, Rudolf Hilferding, Rosa Luxemburg, and Otto Bauer.[38] With this theory Lenin provided a justification to counter the threat of Social Democratic revisionism in the West, and to prospect for revolutionary unrest in the colonial East.[39] It was an integrated world view.

But from the viewpoint of Russia's relation to the West, Lenin's theory of imperialism made Russia fully the equivalent of the West at the international level. In his theory of imperialism, the contradiction of capitalism assumed international significance: it was imperialist nations against colonial and semicolonial nations. The imperialist conflict at the international level overshadowed the domestic conflict between bourgeoisie and proletariat. In this international arena Russia was clearly an imperialist nation, along with the major Western powers.

Though internally semi-Western, internationally Russia became Western. The significance of the renewed integration of Russia and the West, made possible by Lenin's theory of imperialism, was announced by him in "The Defeat of Russia and the Revolutionary Crisis" (1915):

> The imperialist war has *connected* the revolutionary crisis in Russia, a crisis on the basis of a bourgeois-democratic revolution, with the growing crisis of the proletarian socialist revolution in the West. This connection is so direct that no separate solution of the revolutionary [tasks] is possible in any one country: the bourgeois-democratic revolution in Russia is now not only a prologue to, but an indivisible, integral part of the socialist revolution in the West.[40]

On the basis of the imperialist crisis, once more Russia's destiny would converge with the destiny of the West. If in the previous period of 1899–1914 Lenin, for the sake of Russian particularism, had to de-emphasize Russia's equivalence to the West, now in 1914–1917 he could, for the sake of the universal Marxist faith, restore that sense of Russia's Western equivalence.

From the Bolshevik victory in 1917 to 1924

The October victory entirely transformed the picture. This narrow victory depended on the voluntarist seizure of power by Lenin. The course of events in 1917 was not leading to an inexorable Bolshevik conclusion. In contrast to the Socialist Revolutionaries, the Mensheviks, and the Kadets, Lenin alone in 1917 commanded both the will and the organization to seize power. If it had not been for his preoccupation with power, the Bolsheviks would not have had their October victory. That was his contribution, which no one can deny. But the occasion for the seizure of power was not of his own making. The chaos of 1917 was due to the collapse of the old tsarist order, under the disrupting pressures of the war. Behind that was the prewar problem of the tension between autocratic order and a schismatic, westernizing society. The events of 1917 were precipitated by numerous contingent and personal factors. Who is to say that the course of events would have remained the same, if Nicholas II had not been such a nullity? But we can definitely say that neither the Marxian theory of capitalism nor the Leninist theory of imperialism provided a valid prognosis for the actual course of events leading to 1917. The October victory was a vindication of Lenin's political voluntarism. But the coming of 1917 was no testimony to Marxist theory.

However, Lenin never advocated the seizure of power for its own sake. He did everything in the name of Marxist theory. He tried to see Russian revolutionary prospect from a revised Marxist perspective. Therefore, from the viewpoint of the unity of theory and practice, the October victory was the realization of a Western-oriented revolution in backward Russia. At a time when Western Europe was still capitalist, Russia achieved the Western goal of socialism. Bolshevik Russia became the socialist leader of the world. At least from the Marxist perspective, the perennial problem of Russia's equivalence to the West was overcome. This enabled

Lenin to claim in 1918: "Things have turned out differently from what Marx and Engels expected; they have given us, the Russian toiling and exploited classes, the honored role of vanguard of the international socialist revolution; and we now see clearly how far the development of the revolution will go; the Russians commenced; the Germans, the French and the English will finish, and socialism will be victorious." [41] And on the fourth anniversary of the October Revolution Lenin said that the Bolshevik victory had "opened a new era in world history." [42]

If before October, 1917, the emphasis was on Russia's equivalence to the West, now after the Bolshevik victory it was on the value of the unique Bolshevik experience within the universal Marxist perspective. In " 'Left-Wing' Communism, An Infantile Disorder" (1920), Lenin insisted that "the Russian model reveals to *all* countries something that is very essential in their near and inevitable future." [43] Before 1917 the tension between the demands of Western theory and of Russia could hopefully be eliminated if Russia were to become the equivalent of the West. Now, after 1917, Western theory and Russian particularism would coalesce in insisting on the successful Bolshevik exemplar within the Marxist perspective. In enjoying the October victory both as a Russian revolutionary and as a dedicated Marxist, Lenin could have his cake and eat it too.

THE LENINIST IDEA OF CHINA

Lenin's idea of China was ancillary to his preoccupation with the correlation of Marxian theory and Russian revolutionary practice. Therefore the changing significance of his idea of China depended on his changing correlation of Western theory and Russian practice.

During the initial period of his intellectual development, from 1893 to 1899, Lenin was preoccupied with Russia's equivalence to the West. Universal value resided in the Western theory of Marxism, and Russia was already Western in the capitalist sense. Therefore he was not interested in the East. He rarely used the adjectives "Asiatic" and "Chinese" to describe unprogressive features of Russia; [44] and he never discussed China or Asia specifically.

But after 1899, when he began to de-emphasize Russia's Western equivalence, Lenin repeatedly used "Asiatic" and "Chinese" to describe what he considered to be the non-Western features of both pre-Emancipation and post-Emancipation Russia. Both adjectives meant non-Western, politically despotic, or economically stagnant.[45] Here he simply borrowed from the contemporary European and Russian Westerner's stereotype of the inferior East. In addition, in the early 1900's, he saw the East as a colonial market for Europe's capitalist production. Here he was entirely dependent on the Marxian idea of the East.[46] The only variation was that Lenin believed tsarist Russia could substitute the underdeveloped domestic market of Central Asia and Siberia for the necessary colonial market in the East.[47]

In 1900 Lenin wrote an article on the Boxer rebellion in China, for the first issue of *Iskra*. He condemned the role of the tsarist government in suppressing the Boxer rebellion. He believed this suppression to be the policy of Russian capitalists and war entrepreneurs, contrary to the interest and sympathy of the Russian people. In fact, he said: "The Chinese people suffer from the same evils as those from which the Russian people suffer— from an Asiatic government that squeezes taxes from the starving peasantry and that suppresses every aspiration towards liberty by military force, from the oppression of capital which has penetrated into the Middle Kingdom." [48] The article revealed Lenin's idea of the role of a colonial market for capitalist production, and his stereotyped understanding of "Asiatic" despotism. His sympathy was clearly with the Chinese rebels. But, aside from mentioning that both the Russian and the Chinese were suffering from despotic governments, Lenin gave no hint of any possible alliance between the Russian proletariat and the Chinese peasantry. He was primarily concerned with tsarist policy toward the Boxer rebellion.[49]

From 1899 to 1905, when Lenin was preoccupied with the correlation of the conscious elite and the spontaneous masses in Russia, he did not foresee any relation between Eastern colonial unrest and the Bolshevik struggle in Russia.[50] In the same period, whenever he talked of the national question, he meant the nationality problem of tsarist Russia. He gave no inkling of any national

question in the East.[51] During the Revolution of 1905, which
was provoked by a war with an Eastern power, Lenin mentioned
Asia in only one article, "The Defeat at Port Arthur" (*Vpered*,
No. 2, January, 1905). In it he rejoiced that "progressive, advancing
Asia has inflicted an irreparable blow upon backward and reactionary Europe." [52] However, in the rest of the article, he was
engrossed in speculating on the European impact of this defeat
in Asia. To him, it was an indication that the proletariat's victory
in Europe would soon come! Many years later, with the benefit
of hindsight, he claimed that the Revolution of 1905 had given rise
to revolutionary movements in Turkey, Persia, and China.[53] But
back in 1905 he had no such estimate of the revolutionary prospect
in the East.

Lenin was primarily interested in Western Marxian theory and
a Russian revolution. Up to the end of 1907 he viewed Asia
through the stereotyped model of West Europeans and Russian
Westerners, including Marx. At the 1907 International Socialist
Congress at Stuttgart, Lenin supported a resolution for the total
condemnation of colonialism, instead of the condemnation of
merely "capitalist colonialism." Interestingly, he supported total
condemnation on the ground of Marxian theoretical consistency,
rather than of any awareness of revolutionary prospects in Asia.[54]
At the end of the same year, in "The Agrarian Program of Social
Democracy in the First Russian Revolution, 1905–07," Lenin
was still debating with Plekhanov the Marxian concept of Asiatic
despotism. The controversy was undertaken entirely along Marxian
theoretical line, without any indication of awareness of changes
in Asia.[55]

But 1908 was a turning point in Lenin's attitude toward the
East. The years of domestic lull in Russia after 1905 had left
Lenin in a quandary. His Bolshevik program seemed less and less
relevant to the political and intellectual tendencies of post-1905
Russia. In spite of corruption and police intimidation, Duma
politics was a change from autocratic politics. Against his distaste
for parliamentary politics Lenin was gradually forced to participate
in it.[56] Intellectually, the 1900's was a period, in Russia, which
saw the growth of both liberal and conservative thought. The
intelligentsia's radical heritage itself came to be questioned by

conservative thinkers, as was evidenced by the publication of the pamphlet *Vekhi* in 1909.[57]

Against this background, Lenin began to look abroad for encouragement. But the Social Democrats in the West, in this period, were confronted with their own revisionist crisis. He therefore looked toward the East for revolutionary support. In the article "Inflammable Material in World Politics" (1908), Asia for the first time became politically alive for Lenin, instead of remaining a stagnant stereotype. In the article, he condemned tsarist policy in Persia, applauded the victory of the Young Turks, and pointed to British fear of unrest in India. Lenin continued:

> In China, the revolutionary movement against medievalism has also made itself felt with particular force during the last few months. In truth, nothing definite can as yet be said about this particular movement . . . but there cannot be any doubt about the rapid growth of a "new spirit" and of "European tendencies" in China, especially after the Russo-Japanese war; hence the transformation of the old Chinese riots into a conscious democratic movement is inevitable.[58]

And here for the first time he predicted an alliance between international socialism and the revolutionary democratic struggle in Asia:[59] an alliance of the proletariats of Europe and Asia against the capitalists!

In 1908 Lenin was exaggerating the capitalist development of Asia, just as, before 1899, he had been exaggerating Russia's capitalism. In both instances this exaggeration was undertaken to justify a revolutionary program strategically dependent on the proletariat. In fact, Lenin's position in 1908 was similar to that of Trotsky in the twenties. In his "Draft Resolution on the Present Situation and the Tasks of the Party" (December, 1908), Lenin said: "The general sharpening of the situation on the world market, due [among other factors] to the revolutionary movements in the East, which mark the creation of national capitalist states, results in keener competition, leads to more frequent international clashes, thereby intensifying the class antagonisms between bourgeoisie and proletariat."[60]

As a further indication of his lack of familiarity with Asia,

Lenin in the article "Inflammable Material in World Politics" used Russian analogies to explain the recent changes in Asia. He referred to Sultan Abdul Hamid as "the Turkish Nicholas II," and compared the poverty and starvation of India to those of Russia.[61] This tendency became even more pronounced in 1912–1913, when he wrote a series of articles analyzing the Chinese Revolution of 1911.

Events of change seemed to mount in such rapid succession for Lenin, that by early 1911 he could claim "1905 was the beginning of the end of 'Oriental' immobility." [62] This statement significantly abandoned the stereotyped concept of Asiatic stagnation. But in addition Lenin was consciously trying to relate recent changes in Asia with the Russian Revolution of 1905. By early 1912, under Lenin's leadership, the Sixth All-Russian Conference of the R.S.D.L.P. at Prague took cognizance of the Chinese Revolution of 1911. According to the conference's resolution, framed by Lenin, the Chinese Revolution not only testified to the coming liberation of Asia, but also to the end of the dominance of the European bourgeoisie.[63]

Among Lenin's articles on the Chinese Revolution written in 1912–1913, the most important ones were "Democracy and Populism in China" (1912), "Regenerated China" (1912), "Big Achievement of the Chinese Republic" (1913), "Backward Europe and Progressive Asia" (1913), "Cultured Europeans and Barbaric Asians" (1913), and "The Awakening of Asia" (1913). They revealed the enormous impression the Chinese Revolution had made on Lenin.

In these articles Lenin analyzed events in the China of 1911 in the light of the Russian model of 1905: Basically the Chinese Revolution was a bourgeois revolution, comparable to the French Revolution of 1789 and to the Russian Revolution of 1905.[64] With this revolution, China might even be considered a capitalist country! [65] But the bourgeois revolution in China was complicated by the presence of nonbourgeois democratic elements, just as the Russian Revolution was complicated by the combination of various antitsarist democratic forces. In fact, Lenin felt that the Chinese Revolution was an exact duplicate of the Russian Revolution. To him, Yuan Shih-k'ai was a representative of the liberal democratic interest,[66] whereas Sun Yat-sen was a representative of the populist, that is, agrarian democratic, interest.[67] Subjectively, the Chinese revolutionaries under Sun were socialist in orientation; but objectively the conditions of China were backward and semi-feudal. In China, "feudalism was based on the predominance of agriculture and natural economy; the source of feudal exploitation of the Chinese peasant was his *attachment* to the land." [68] Therefore, Lenin feared, the program of the Chinese populist revolutionaries would ultimately degenerate into a "program for the destruction of feudal exploitation *alone*." [69] Chinese freedom had been won by the alliance of peasant democracy with the liberal bourgeoisie, said Lenin. The near future would show whether the peasants, without the leadership of a proletarian party, would succeed in holding their democratic position against the liberals, who were only waiting for the opportune moment to desert to the Right.[70]

Lenin tended to be distrustful of both the "liberals" and the "populists." He believed the future of China must lie with an as-yet-unformed Chinese Social Democratic party. The role of that future party must be to criticize the petty-bourgeois tendency of Sun Yat-sen, and to accentuate his revolutionary democratic potentiality.[71]

By 1913 Lenin felt the democratic revolutionary movement in the East had been so consolidated that no matter what the future of the Chinese republic might be, no power on earth could hope to restore "the old serfdom in Asia." [72] He was confident that the Chinese republic would be able to weather the threat of an international capitalist consortium.[73] In the article curiously entitled "Backward Europe and Progressive Asia," Lenin claimed that "everywhere in Asia powerful democratic movements are growing, expanding and becoming strong." [74] This, said Lenin, was an indication that "the peoples of Asia have become democratically conscious." [75] He was witnessing not only the success of the Chinese revolutionaries, but also the democratic revolutionary uprisings of India and Java.[76] This awakening of Asia would be the signal to begin the struggle for power in Europe by the progressive proletariat! [77]

By early 1914, in his "On the Right of Nations to Self-

Determination," Lenin broadened his national question to include Asia. In the East, he said, the intrusion of capitalism had called forth national movements everywhere. The period of bourgeois-democratic revolution in both eastern Europe and Asia had not begun until 1905.[78]

> In this period . . . the task of [the Social Democratic] parties with regard to national policy must be twofold: recognition of the rights of all nations to self-determination, since burgeois-democratic reform is not yet completed . . . ; then, a close, unbreakable alliance in the class struggle of the proletarians of all nations in a given state, throughout all the changes of its history, irrespective of any reshaping of the frontiers of the individual states by the bourgeoisie.[79]

This was clearly based upon the analogy of the Bolshevik attitude toward the domestic national question within mixed bourgeois-democratic Russia.

From 1908 to 1914, after his disillusionment at home and in the West, Lenin was casting about for revolution in Asia. In the process he gradually abandoned his pre-1908 stereotype of the stagnant East. Instead, he viewed the East in the light of the Russian model of 1905. But the war of 1914 once more redirected Lenin's intellectual focus back to Russia and the West. And the revolutionary East faded into the background. Nevertheless, Eastern unrest could be related to his Western preoccupation through the theory of imperialism and the national question.

Lenin considered the war of 1914 as an imperialist struggle for colonies by the leading powers.[80] This struggle had led for instance to their exploitation of Turkey, Persia, and China.[81] In "Imperialism, the Highest Stage of Capitalism," he laid the theoretical foundation for the imperialist exploitation of the East:

> The epoch of modern capitalism shows us that certain relations are established between capitalist alliance, *based* on the economic division of the world; . . . and in connection with this certain relations are established . . . on the basis of the territorial division of the world. . . .
> The characteristic feature of this period is the final partition of the globe. . . . For the first time the world is completely divided up, so that in the future *only* redivision is possible.[82]

In this world of imperialist exploitation, Lenin called China a semicolonial country, on the way toward becoming a full-fledged colony.[83]

The incorporation of the problem of the East in the national question was accomplished by Lenin in early 1914, before the start of the war.[84] Now it was worked out in greater detail in "The Socialist Revolution and the Right of Nations to Self-Determination" (March, 1916). In this article Lenin divided the world into three major parts: The first was composed of the advanced capitalist nations in the West; in these countries the historically progressive role of the bourgeoisie belonged to the past. The second was eastern Europe, where the bourgeois–democratic movement had emerged only in the twentieth century; here the proletariat should champion the right of nations to self-determination. The third was composed of semicolonial countries such as China, Persia, and Turkey, as well as the colonial countries.

In these countries, says Lenin, the bourgeois–democratic movements have either hardly begun, or are not completed. Socialists must not only demand the unconditional and immediate liberation of the colonies without compensation, but must render determined support to the more revolutionary elements in the bourgeois–democratic movements for national liberation in these countries, and assist their rebellion—and if need be, their revolutionary war—*against* the imperialist powers that oppress them.[85] In accordance with this analysis, Lenin emphasized the progressive character of the twentieth-century bourgeoisie in Asia, and the need for the proletariat to support Eastern wars for national liberation.[86]

His theoretical formulation of the contradiction between the imperialist West and the colonial, semicolonial East, and his emphasis on the progressive tendency of Asian national-liberation movements finally led Lenin to posit a potential alliance between the Russian Bolsheviks and the Asian nationalist revolutionaries. This was different from his 1908 concept of an alliance between the Russian Bolsheviks and the Asian proletariat. In "A Few Theses" (October, 1915) he said that the Russian proletariat should be prepared to conduct a revolutionary war, in co-operation with the colonial East as well as with the European proletariat.

"There is no doubt that a victory of the Russian proletariat would create unusually favorable conditions for the development of revolution in both Asia and Europe." [87] But he failed to detail a strategic program.

During the crucial revolutionary year of 1917 Lenin was preoccupied with Russia. Any mentioning of the East by him was done in a cursory fashion: In "The Tasks of the R.S.D.L.P. in the Revolution" (April, 1917), he insisted that one of the conditions for peace should be "the liberation of *all* colonies and *all* oppressed nations." [88] In "What Declarations Were Made by Our Party on War before the Revolution" (May, 1917), he said that the Russian proletariat must systematically support the uprisings in colonial and dependent East, and that the victory of the Russian proletariat would create unusually favorable conditions for the development of revolutions in both Asia and Europe.[89] In "Foreign Policy of the Russian Revolution" (June, 1917), he mentioned the prospect of a revolutionary alliance with "the workers and peasants of colonial and semicolonial countries." [90] The only exception was his June 22 speech before the First All-Russian Congress of Soviets, where he emphasized the significance of the East. In that speech he asserted that the foreign policy of the Russian Revolution should appeal to oppressed classes and nationalities of the world: "If we actually carry out such a policy . . . all peoples of Asia would see that . . . the Russian workers and peasants really place themselves at the head of all the oppressed nationalities, and that their struggle against imperialism is to them of great revolutionary importance." [91]

From 1908 to 1914 Lenin abandoned his stereotype of the stagnant East and became interested in Asiatic revolutionary prospect; but from 1914 to October 1917 he once more became preoccupied with Russian revolutionary prospect and was not much concerned with Asia. This pattern seemed to persist after the October victory. His immediate concerns after October were the consolidation of victory at home and the expectation of socialist revolution in the West: In "Declaration of the Rights of the Toiling and Exploited People" (January, 1918), Lenin appealed for a complete break with "the enslavement of hundreds of millions of toiling people in Asia." [92] And in "Rough Draft of a

Program" (March, 1918), he appealed for "support of the democratic and revolutionary movement in all countries in general, and in the colonial and dependent countries in particular."[93] In the article "The Immediate Tasks of the Soviet Government," written in March and April 1918, Lenin pointed to the intensified rivalry between Japan and the United States in the Pacific area.[94] But this time he did not mention any revolutionary prospect in Asia. Nor did he mention it in the speech commemorating the first anniversary of the October Revolution.[95] And in his March, 1919, speech before the Eighth Congress of the Russian Communist party, he merely mentioned that the class antagonism in Asia should also be taken into account.[96]

The turning point this time seemed to have occurred during the summer and autumn of 1919. This was the low ebb of Bolshevik fortune. During that summer communist efforts in Bavaria, Austria, and Hungary were nearing collapse and the prospect of proletarian uprisings in Britain and Germany seemed to be fading. In fact, in August of that year Britain was able to sign an anticommunist alliance with Russia's neighbor, Persia; and within Russia the various White forces were at the peak of their activities.[97] Therefore, once more as in 1908, when confronted with difficulties at home and in the West, Lenin turned to Asia to prospect for revolutionary support.

In a pamphlet written during July, 1919, "The Tasks of the Third International," Lenin appealed for revolutionary struggle to liberate the colonial countries,[98] although just four months earlier, in his speech closing the First Congress of the Third International, he had not even mentioned any revolutionary prospect in Asia.[99] Between July and September the Bolshevik government appealed to the peoples of China, Mongolia, Persia, and Turkey, for an anti-imperialist alliance with the Russian people.[100] In the Karakhan declaration to the Chinese people, dated July 25, 1919, the Bolshevik government asserted: "If the Chinese people wish . . . to become free and to avoid the fate which the Allies prepared for them at Versailles . . . they must understand that their only allies and brothers in the struggle for freedom are the Russian workers and peasants and their Red Army."[101]

In his November 22, 1919, speech before the Second All-Russian

Congress of Communist Organizations of the Peoples of the East, Lenin for the first time detailed the Eastern strategy of the Bolsheviks. He appealed for the unity of the revolutionary movement of Eastern peoples with the revolutionary struggle of the Bolsheviks. This was to be an anti-imperialist alliance between the native bourgeois–nationalists and the Russian proletariat. Such an alliance had already been anticipated in Lenin's 1914 article, "On the Right of Nations to Self-Determination." But, in addition, Lenin made three revealing observations in this speech: There was no set proletarian strategy in the East, but rather communist strategy must be adapted to the peculiar conditions and problems of Asia; communist strategy in the East must seek the support of native bourgeois nationalists; in this period of difficulties, the alliance with the East was quite necessary for the Bolsheviks.[102]

Lenin's main strategy was to de-emphasize the potential conflict between the emergent native communists and the native nationalists, in order to obtain an international alliance between the nationalists in the East and the Bolsheviks in Russia. But this strategy would be a problem of commitment for the native communists in Asia. The difference was one between a Russian and an Asian Marxist perspective.

This difference emerged between Lenin and M. N. Roy at the Second Congress of the Third International, July, 1920. But already the problem was anticipated in the resolution of the Second Congress of the Communist Organizations of the Peoples of the East. Point three of the resolution emphasized the two stages of communist activities in the East: support for the bourgeois–nationalist movement and creation of an ultimate proletarian class program. The latter was fundamentally important, and therefore should never be sacrificed merely for the sake of the immediate support for the bourgeois–nationalist movement.[103] But the *finesse* between support for the bourgeois–nationalist movement and the ultimate proletarian goal would be the source of endless interpretations and controversies, up to the present.

In an interview with a Japanese correspondent in June, 1920, Lenin expressed his eastward orientation as follows: "Real communism can succeed only in the West; however, the West lives on account of the East; European imperialist powers support themselves mainly in Eastern colonies; but they, at the same time, are arming and training their colonies; thus, the West is digging its own grave in the East." [104] In actuality it was a Bolshevik necessity to seek Eastern support, in this period. But by wishful thinking Lenin insisted that it was Western dependence on the colonial East which provided for Bolshevik opportunity in the East.

The Leninist idea of China and the East received its most extensive treatment at the Second Congress of the Communist International, which met in Moscow during July and August, 1920. Here the strategy announced in the November 22, 1919, speech was worked out in greater detail; and the strategic problem of proletarian support for bourgeois nationalism in Asia came into the open. At this congress Lenin played the leading role in formulating the Eastern strategy of the Communist International.

The theses on the fundamental tasks of the Second Comintern Congress, drawn up by Lenin in early 1920, represented a significant shift from his Western orientation during the First Congress. Now he gave recognition to the importance of rural workers and asserted that there must be proper correlation between the proletariat and the toiling and exploited masses.[105] In his July 19 report on the international situation, Lenin spoke of the imperialist oppression of 70 percent of the world's population. This, he said, led to uprisings of the oppressed as well as conflicts among the imperialists. That gave him hope:

> The amalgamation of the revolutionary proletariat of advanced capitalist countries with the revolutionary masses of those countries where there is no proletariat or hardly any, with the oppressed masses of colonial, Eastern countries, is taking place at this congress. . . . The imperialist war has drawn the dependent peoples into world history. And one of the most important tasks that confronts us now is to ponder over how the foundation stone of the organization of soviet movement can be laid in the non-capitalist countries.[106]

Because of this shift toward the East, the agrarian question became important at the Second Congress. Lenin had anticipated it by preparing a set of draft theses on the agrarian question, in June. In the draft, he spoke of the need for the proletariat to act as the vanguard of the toiling and oppressed masses everywhere. He divided the rural population into three strata, of which only the poorest could be expected to support the proletariat. He urged the communists to organize as speedily as feasible rural soviets of wage earners and semiproletarians.[107]

However, the crucial issue at the Second Congress was the theses on the national and colonial question. In June Lenin had written a preliminary draft, which became the basis for deliberation by a commission of the congress. Eventually a revision of Lenin's draft emerged from the commission, plus a set of supplementary theses by M. N. Roy. Following is a brief summary of Lenin's twelve-point draft, with the commission's revision indicated in parenthesis:

(1) Bourgeois democracy would approach the question of national equality solely in an abstract, formal manner. (2) In contrast, the communists should approach it as a historically concrete problem. (3) The imperialist war of 1914 revealed the bourgeois democrats' hypocrisy about national equality, and intensified the revolutionary struggle of the proletariat and the toiling masses everywhere. (Among others, the following sentence was added: "The proletariat can attain genuine national freedom and unity only by means of revolutionary struggle after the downfall of the bourgeoisie.") (4) The communists should promote a joint revolutionary struggle of the proletariat and the toiling masses, for without the overthrow of capitalism the abolition of national oppression and inequality was impossible. (5) The anti-Bolshevik policy of the international bourgeoisie is rallying the communist movement of the advanced countries and the national liberation movement of the colonial, oppressed countries around Soviet Russia. (6) This close alliance must be determined by the stage of development reached by the communist or the bourgeois democratic liberation movement in each country. (The phrase "revolutionary liberation movement" was substituted for Lenin's "bourgeois democratic liberation movement.") (7) Federation is a transitional form toward the complete union of all nations. (8) The communists should strive for an ever closer federal association. (9) The communists must explain that the soviet system alone is capable of realizing true equality of nations.

(10) Proletarian internationalism demands the subordination of proletarian struggle in each country to the international struggle of the world proletariat and the sacrifice of bourgeois national interests for the sake of the overthrow of international capital. (11) In feudal-patriarchal countries, the communists must support the native bourgeois democratic liberation movement (changed into "revolutionary liberation movement," with the following sentence added: "The form which this support shall take should be discussed with the communist party of the country in question, if there is one."), must fight against clerical and other reactionary elements, must render special assistance to the antifeudal peasant movement (with the phrase "organizing the peasants and all the exploited wherever possible into soviets" added), should support but must not be merged with the bourgeois democratic national movement (changed into "revolutionary liberation movement"), and must explain to the toiling masses the deception of the imperialists (with the phrase "with the help of the privileged classes in the oppressed countries" added). (12) "The more backward a country is the stronger in it is small-scale agriculture, patriarchalism, and ignorance, which inevitably cause the deepest of petty bourgeois prejudices. . . ." Therefore the communists should treat these surviving national sentiments with caution.[108] (The quoted sentence was deleted from the final version.) [109]

In the draft theses Lenin was primarily concerned with the international strategy of the Bolsheviks against the Western imperialist nations. He was willing to support the Eastern bourgeois nationalist movement, in return for an anti-imperialist alliance. But Roy objected by saying the native bourgeoisie in the East would be unreliable and the Eastern revolutionary movement must depend on the native proletariat and peasantry.[110] Lenin finally conceded Roy's point by agreeing to substitute the phrase "national revolutionary" for the phrase "bourgeois democratic."

In a speech reporting on the work of the commission, July 26, Lenin defended the substitution: "[The communists] should support the bourgeois liberation movements in the colonies only if these are really revolutionary, when those who represent these movements would not oppose us in our efforts to educate and organize the peasantry and the masses of exploited people, in general, in the revolutionary spirit." [111] But in regard to the question whether the capitalist stage of development was inevitable for the backward countries, Lenin was very cautious: "If the revolutionary victorious proletariat undertakes among them a systematic propaganda, and if the Soviet governments render them all the assistance they possibly can, it will be wrong to assume that the capitalist stage of development is inevitable for the backward nationalities." [112]

He insisted that Eastern revolutionary progress depended on Bolshevik Russia, just as Marx and Engels in the late nineteenth century had insisted that Russian revolutionary progress depended on socialist Europe. Therefore he naturally refused Roy's insistence that the Comintern accept as a fundamental principle the complete dependence of the Western proletarian movement on the triumph of the revolution in the East! [113] The most he conceded, as he did in the article "The Second Congress of the Communist International" (August–September, 1920), was the necessity for the Western proletariat and Eastern toilers to unite. [114]

The difference between Lenin and Roy was the difference between a Russian Marxist concerned with safeguarding Bolshevik Russia and prospecting for international proletarian victory and an Asian Marxist committed to the prospect of communist victory in the East. The First (Baku) Congress of the Peoples of the East, September, 1920, in its resolution pointed out that the toilers' revolution in the East must go beyond the mere destruction of international imperialism. It must also destroy all forms of internal exploitation. And here it must depend on the sovietization of the peasantry. [115] In its de-emphasis of the role of bourgeois nationalists, the Baku resolution was closer to Roy's supplementary theses than to Lenin's draft theses. Again this was the case with the theses on the Eastern question, adopted in November, 1922, by the Fourth Comintern Congress. [116] But the actual implementation of communist strategy in the East, such as the Comintern policy regarding the Kuomintang-led nationalist movement in China, was closer to Lenin's position than to Roy's. [117]

After the Second Comintern Congress, Lenin did not further develop his idea of China. In the report delivered to the Eighth All-Russian Congress of Soviets, December 22, 1920, Lenin said that "the alliance and friendly relations between Russia and the oppressed nations of the East are becoming firmer." [118] But in "Once Again on the Trade Unions, the Present Situation and the Mistakes of Comrades Trotsky and Bukharin" (January, 1921), he admitted that he had little knowledge of China and was unfamiliar with the details of the situation there.[119] There were references to the revolutionary prospect of China in a number of speeches and articles in this period.[120] And in "Our Revolution" (January, 1923), Lenin emphasized the unique role of Russia between the East and the West. Russia was only semi-Western, and therefore could better introduce novel features into Eastern development.[121]

In his last article dealing with China and the East, "Better Fewer, But Better" (March, 1923), Lenin wrote that the imperialist war of 1914 had dislodged Eastern countries from their traditional immobility. "Their development has been completely shifted to the general European capitalist pattern." [122] Therefore, in the final analysis, the struggle against international imperialism must depend upon the alliance of Russia, India, and China. He advised preparation for the impending conflict "between the counter-revolutionary imperialist West and the revolutionary nationalist East." [123] This is reminiscent of his 1913 phrase, "backward Europe and progressive Asia."

AN EVALUATION

Throughout his career, Lenin had to correlate Western-oriented theory and Russian-preoccupied practice. These were the two fixed poles in his intellectual horizon. His changing correlation ultimately circumscribed the development of his idea of China. From 1893 to 1899, he insisted that Russian economy was capitalist. Universal value resided in the Western theory of Marxism, and Russia was already the equivalent of the West. Therefore during this period he was not even remotely interested in the East.

From 1899 to 1907, Lenin still was not specifically interested in the East. His Western orientation remained the same as before. But now he was describing Russia as semi-Western. This was necessitated by his commitment to prospect for revolutionary unrest in Russia. Since Russia was semi-Western, he used the stereotyped concept of the static, inferior East to characterize her non-Western features. Therefore he fell back upon the reservoir of the European-Russian, as well as Marxian, concepts of the stagnant East. He had no need to change this existing image of Asia. His use of the stereotyped concept of Asia to describe the valueless aspect of Russia was similar to that of other Russian Westerners such as Belinsky and Plekhanov, in spite of his differences with them.

From 1908 to 1914, Lenin finally became interested in China and the East. He was still committed to a Marxist solution for semi-Western Russia but his westward orientation was, in this period, getting him nowhere. Therefore he began to look about for revolutionary support in Asia. If his approach during 1899–1907 was to see the East as valueless and hence stagnant, now it was to see the East as potentially valuable. Suddenly, static and inferior Asia became revolutionary and democratic Asia. But Asia was a distant, unfamiliar concept and the Marxian crutch of Asiatic society certainly was unsuitable for a potentially changing East. Therefore Lenin relied upon his own Russian experience and began to regard Asia in the light of the Russian model of 1905. It was an image of Asia in accord neither with Marxian theory nor with the historical particularism of the East, but rather in accord with his own Russian revolutionary perspective.

From 1914 to 1919, revolutionary, democratic Asia receded into the background of Lenin's intellectual perspective. Once more the focus of his attention shifted back to Russia and the West. The war revived his sense of Russia's equivalence to the imperialist West. The revolution led him to be preoccupied with Russia. Victory created both the problem of domestic consolidation and the expectation of proletarian support from the West. Potentially the East was relevant to his Western-oriented outlook, through his theory of imperialism and his analysis of the national question; and after 1917 he could point out the value of the Bolshevik model for revolutionary, democratic Asia. He paid lip service to these potential correlatives but the East was not really significant within such a Western-oriented scheme of things.

From 1919 to 1923, Lenin repeated his search for revolution in China and the East. Once more he was confronted with difficulties at home and disappointed in the West. Hence the East regained its significance. With the Bolsheviks victorious in semi-Western Russia, he saw a Bolshevik course of development in the future of Eastern countries. But now he did not approach the national revolutionary prospect of Asia in terms of this Bolshevik model, nor in terms of the Marxist proletarian program. Rather, he approached it within the perspective of the strategic needs of Bolshevik Russia. A Bolshevik Russia as the custodian of proletarian leadership could demand much more than semi-Western Russia. He could appeal to both Marxist theory and the uniqueness of Soviet Russia for such an insistence. This was the basis for his quarrel with M. N. Roy.

Lenin began with the idea of a static, inferior China, but eventually shifted to the idea of a revolutionary, democratic China. The change was not motivated by any consideration for the universalist implication of Marxist theory. If he could realize his expectation in Russia and the West, he would not have been as much interested in the East. And when the change occurred, his idea of a revolutionary, democratic China accorded less with the historical particularism of twentieth-century westernizing China. It fitted more his model of the Russia of 1905. To the degree that he succeeded in getting away from the Western Marxian model for his mixed semi-Western Russia, to that degree he imposed his Russian model on the East. From a distance he saw in his Marxist mind the kind of China which his Bolshevik heart desired.

Within the Russian context, Lenin had succeeded in providing a Bolshevik solution of the tension between Western values and Russian particularism. With that success he had transformed the Russian intellectual situation. But the transformation did not depend upon any fundamental revision of his idea of China. Lenin's idea of China was ancillary to the central problem of Russia's equivalence to the West. The change in his idea of China was ultimately circumscribed by his changing approach to the crucial problem of Russia's equivalence to the West.

Chapter Four

The Chinese Situation

Maoism is another chapter in the history of Marxism. It is a theoretical as well as practical response to the westernization of twentieth-century China. In some respects, the westernization of China and its concomitant intellectual dilemma resemble the westernization of Russia and its intellectual dilemma. Both have the theme of the tension between the West and a westernizing society. But even typologically there are several important differences. For one thing, prewesternizing Confucian China had a universal tradition of thought which prewesternizing orthodox Russia lacked; and this universal tradition, through transformation, persisted into the twentieth century. For another, the gulf separating China and the West appeared to contemporary perspectives greater than that separating Russia and the West; Russia could somehow be considered semi-Western, but China always had to occupy the other extremity of a Western-oriented intellectual spectrum. Finally, China's westernization compressed into one hundred years what took westernizing Russia two- to three-hundred years to experience. We can assume that the former experience tended to be much more disruptive and undigestible. Besides the typological differences, the consciousness by westernized Chinese intellectuals of what had happened to westernizing Russia made that consciousness different from Russia's. And the West which confronted Russia in the nineteenth and early twentieth centuries was different from the West which confronted China in the late nineteenth and twentieth centuries. History is cumulative. Not even problems remain the same. But the Marxist linear perspective seeks to arrest the flux of history through the use of a comparative model. If Leninism developed, among other factors, in interaction with the Western model of Marx, then Maoism developed, among other factors, in interaction with the Bolshevik model of Lenin. Maoism represents a particular type of Chinese response to Western Marxism through the Bolshevik model.

Pre-Western traditional China had her own coherence. Politically, its government was based upon the interdependence between dynastic mandate and Confucian bureaucracy. Governmental authority was not delimited by law, but glossed over by the Confucian ideal of ethical exemplar and moral suasion. The vast empire was fundamentally held together by the basic commonality of Confucian views and goals among both the ruling and the ruled. Socially, it was not a caste society, but one based upon literary qualification, which anyone supposedly could acquire. In practice the possibility of social ascent through the examination system was maintained. Intellectually, the Confucian scholars saw China as a sociopolitical order in harmony with the universe. This was an immanent cosmos, in which order depended on itself rather than on any transcendent frame of reference. Ethical authority, social flexibility, and Confucian immanence tended to reinforce each other to maintain a coherent whole. At times, with the build-up of mass discontent or outside pressure, the coherence was disrupted. But, cyclically, it was always, more or less, restored at the beginning of a new dynasty. In the intellectual climate of traditional China, no other alternative to this immanent coherence was possible. Neither Taoism nor Buddhism could provide a this-worldly substitute for it.[1]

The Confucian intelligentsia of pre-Western China was intimately woven into the fabric of this immanent order. Confucian thought with its emphasis on inner harmony was the justification of the status quo. It was a way of thinking oriented toward the reinforcement, rather than the negation, of the existing order.[2] With Confucian education the key to pre-eminence in society, the pressure for social ascent could be sublimated into socially preservative intellectual activities. Moreover, this was not an elitist hoax, because in traditional China intellectual excellence did lead to social pre-eminence. But intellectual excellence was also the key to political ascendancy. The Confucian literati and the mandarin bureaucrats were rather one single social continuum; and the correlation of the refinement of thought with the wielding of power tended to blunt the contrast between the ideal of authority and the practice of power. The tension between thought and reality was at a minimum.

If in the West thought has usually functioned as a critique of reality, in traditional China it reinforced the status quo. What Hegel erroneously claimed as the identity of the real and the rational in the West was in China approximated through the equivalence between the real and the reasonable. Traditional China was certainly no utopia. But Confucian thought was able to conceal much of the tension of that society; and the Confucian intelligentsia functioned as the preservative of that coherent order.

The westernization of China during the past hundred years, from the Opium War to the Revolution of 1949, entirely disrupted the pre-Western correlation of ethical authority, social flexibility, and Confucian immanence. Just before this period, China had been undergoing the downward phase of a traditional dynastic cycle. But the added pressure of westernization broke the cycle. Endemic dynastic difficulties had already led to the impoverishment of the masses and the straining of governmental authority. The influx of Western commerce and the growth of urban compradore centers compounded the disparity between the wealthy and the poor, and throttled the traditional avenue to social ascent.[3] Without social cohesion, pre-eminence in society depended more upon monetary wealth. Governmental authority, already strained, was further weakened by the onslaught of Western military-diplomatic forces. Instead of central civilian bureaucracy, a pattern of regional militarism emerged. This was the source of power in westernizing China, behind the changing façades of claimed authority. It could be justified neither by Confucian ethics nor by Western legality. Without the community basis for authority, naked power had to maintain itself. None was powerful enough to maintain it for all of China.

Within the past hundred years, the intellectual history of China also underwent an enormous transformation. The classical literary education was gradually eroded by the introduction of Western rational, scientific education. This was dramatized by the abolition of the traditional examination system in 1905. Western-oriented education was supported in varying degrees by both the government and the foreign missionaries.[4] At first, a few students went abroad for advanced training. But the real impetus for overseas education came during the decade between the first Sino-Japanese war and the Russo-Japanese war, 1895 to 1905. Throughout the 1900's, more students from China went to nearby Japan than anywhere else abroad; by the 1920's the United States ranked second.[5] At home the translation of Western works increased accordingly. In the late nineteenth century, the influence of British translations predominated. But in the early twentieth century, translations of Japanese works and of Japanese translations of Western works prevailed.[6] Through all these, a succession of Western intellectual thoughts filtered into the consciousness of increasingly westernized Chinese intellectuals. From the late nineteenth to the early twentieth century, these were: Darwin's evolution, Kropotkin's mutualism, Schopenhauer's idealism, Dewey's pragmatism, Bergson's vitalism, Russell's logical analysis, and Marxism.[7]

Together with these changing intellectual influences, there was, in accordance with the westernization of Chinese society, a corresponding shift in the social origins of the Chinese intellectuals. During the second half of the nineteenth century, intellectuals tended to come from the landed gentry-mandarin background. They remained sensitive to the pre-Western tradition of Confucian China. In the twentieth century, intellectuals came increasingly from urban, nonmandarin backgrounds. They were more Western in orientation, and less sensitive to the agrarian, traditional elements of westernizing China.[8]

Various possible schemes for the periodization of modern Chinese intellectual history are available.[9] They all deal with the process of China's westernization. But there is a fundamental gap separating the westernization of Chinese society from contemporary intellectuals' consciousness of that westernizing process. The latter is more specifically the westernization of Chinese intellectual consciousness, centering on the problem of interaction between tradition-oriented and Western-oriented thought.[10] From this viewpoint, modern Chinese intellectual history can be divided into two major periods: that of the Confucian intellectuals of the second half of the nineteenth century; and that of the Western-oriented intellectuals of the first half of the present century. The intellectuals in each period viewed the westernization of China from qualitatively different vantage points.

The Confucian intellectuals of the second half
of nineteenth century

The universality of pre-Western Confucian thought was intimately
related to the cyclical stability of the Chinese empire. Tradition in
a stabilized, slow-changing society could maintain itself; and beyond
the empire there was no value. By the latter half of the nineteenth
century, Confucian thought had not only lost its old correlatives
of social flexibility and ethical authority; it also lost the pre-Western
context of China as a universal empire, *t'ien-hsia*. China became a
mere westernizing nation in a non-Chinese universe, *kuo-chia*. The
self-enclosed, stabilized context for universal tradition had collapsed. In a westernizing situation, native traditions were no longer
universal, but became the focus of particularism, whereas Western
rational values being linear and utilitarian in orientation could claim
universality. The intellectuals of this period, educated in the pre-
Western Confucian tradition, still maintained the universalist claim
of the Confucian perspective. They did not view China's westernization as a competition between native particularism and Western
universal value. Instead, through the universality of the Confucian
perspective, they sought to particularize the challenge of Western
rational values. There was a qualitative lag between China's westernization and the nineteenth-century Confucian consciousness
of it.

The Western-oriented intellectuals of the first half
of twentieth century

In the 1900's the intellectuals came increasingly from urban, non-
gentry background, and were Western-educated. They therefore
became more sensitive to the challenge of Western value than the
Confucian intellectuals of the latter half of the nineteenth century.
They recognized their world as a *kuo-chia* situation, that is, their
own China in a Western-defined universe. Within that Western-
oriented intellectual framework, each had to redefine his Chinese
identity. The intellectuals accepted the challenge of Western values
as universal and the claim of China as particular. Their conscious-

ness of the tension between Western universality and Chinese particularism approximated much more the ambivalent situation of a westernizing China; whereas the Confucian consciousness of the second half of the previous century distorted the situation as a tension between Chinese universality and Western particularism.

THE PROBLEM OF CHINA'S EQUIVALENCE TO THE WEST

Whether the tension was seen as between Chinese universality and Western particularism or between Western universality and Chinese particularism, it was in response to the underlying interaction between Western values and Chinese traditions. In this competition, rational values from the West had the advantage over native traditions, although neither rational value nor native tradition remained unchanged.[11] But the concern of Chinese intellectuals under Western pressure was with the changing problem of Chinese identity. It was not a general problem, but a specific modern Chinese one. The process of China's intellectual westernization shows

> a Chinese concern to establish the equivalence of China and the West. Many different intellectual choices have been made in modern China, but the choosers' considerations were not, nor could they have been, entirely intellectual; always, along with the search for right answers, or ideas acceptable to anyone, there continued a search for ideas that *Chinese* could accept. Commitment to the general, commitment to the special, and a sequence of intellectual expedients to make these commitments seem to coincide—these appear to me to characterize the thought of modern China.[12]

The Confucian intellectuals of the second half of nineteenth century

This was the period when the intellectuals used their universal Confucian perspective to understand the westernization of China. They gradually acknowledged the challenge of specific Western accomplishments. But they held tenaciously to their universalist Confucian perspective.

In the 1860's the Grand Secretary Wo-jen, a Manchu scholar close to the imperial throne, out-Confucianed the Chinese literati and completely rejected any compromise with westernization. In a memorial to the T'ung-chih emperor, he pointed out: "Now if these brilliant and talented scholars . . . have to change from their regular course of study to follow the barbarians, then the correct spirit will not be developed, and accordingly the evil spirit will become stronger. After several years it will end in nothing less than driving the multitudes of the Chinese people into allegiance to the barbarians." [13]

Wo-jen accepted the universal validity of Chinese ways. In his opposition to Western infiltration he was remarkably sensitive to the integrity of Chinese culture. But there was in his opposition already a note of desperation. How long could an obscurantist insist upon Chinese cultural integrity, when his situation was no longer an indigenous, but rather a westernizing, one?

On the other hand, Tseng Kuo-fan (1811–1872), the orthodox Confucian leader of the T'ung-chih restoration, was willing to study Western armament and technology: "We should carefully watch and learn their superior techniques and also observe their shortcomings. We should not boast of, nor neglect our ceremonies. If they esteem sincerity and cultivate harmony, we should by no means open any frontier hostility with them; if they abandon good relations and break their covenant, we should then have the weapons to oppose them." [14]

Tseng was a much more confident Confucian than Wo-jen. With that confidence he could accede to the practical demands of technological westernization. But where could one draw a line in the inundation of Western forces? In his confidence, Tseng rather than Wo-jen underrated the danger of westernization for China.

In the 1890's, Governor-General Chang Chih-tung (1837–1909), a reformer after Tseng's own heart, revived a traditional intellectual formula which would theoretically stabilize the relation between Confucian value and technical westernization: "In order to render China powerful, and at the same time preserve our own institutions, it is absolutely necessary that we should use Western knowledge. But unless Chinese learning is made the basis of education, and a Chinese direction given to thought, the strong will become anarchists, and the weak, slaves." [15]

Chinese learning was to be the "foundation" (*t'i*), whereas Western technology was for "use" (*yung*). As any good neo-Confucian knew *t'i* was more important than *yung*. The *t'i-yung* dichotomy superimposed a Confucian hierarchic order upon the unfamiliar westernization of China. To the universal Confucian perspective this made sense. But the actual competition between Chinese traditions and Western values was not undertaken between Confucian lines. And Western challenges recognized no Confucian rules.

The *chin-wen* reformers such as K'ang Yu-wei (1858-1927) and Liang Ch'i-ch'ao (1873-1929) argued in the 1890's for a greater degree of westernization than had previously been advocated. To support their reform program, K'ang and Liang insisted that such reform ideas were not just Western in origin, but represented the true Confucian tradition. They said that Confucius himself had been a progressive reformer, but unfortunately the *ku-wen* text had corrupted this true Confucian approach. Thus the true Confucian tradition and Western values were equivalent, and only post-Confucian corruption had brought about divergence between China and the West.[16] K'ang in his *Ta-t'ung shu* saw both China and the West as belonging to the same scheme of universal history. Both had a common origin in the Age of Chaos; and both were destined for the same Age of Great Peace.[17] Liang in the 1890's tried to argue that Western ideas and Chinese ideas were really the same.[18] In a land of stable tradition the insistence on orthodoxy was a heterodox innovation. By reinterpreting Confucian orthodoxy in a changing situation K'ang and Liang, in spite of their protest, contributed much toward the subversion of that tradition.

All four intellectual positions from Wo-jen to Tseng, to Chang, to K'ang and Liang retained the universal Confucian perspective. But with the gradual awareness of China's accelerating westernization, their approaches toward Western pressure became less intransigent. In the process they had to modify the Confucian tradition to accommodate Western pressure. The task became increasingly hopeless.

The Western-oriented intellectuals of the first half of twentieth century

With the continuing westernization of China's society, by the twentieth century her intellectuals no longer presupposed the universality of Confucian tradition, but were seeking Chinese identity in a Western-dominated universe. This changed orientation is best revealed in the position of twentieth-century traditionalists. If K'ang Yu-wei in the 1890's was a reformer on the basis of the equivalence of Confucian tradition and Western values, then by the 1910's K'ang the traditionalist insisted that Western politics based upon a Western foundation could not be transplanted on to Chinese foundation.[19] The scholar Yen Fu (1853–1921), who had earlier been most prominent as a reform advocate and a translator of Western thought into Chinese, now agreed with K'ang: "The foundation (*t'i*) and the use (*yung*) mean the same thing. . . . We cannot force the two cultures to be the same or similar. Therefore, Chinese knowledge has its foundation and function; Western knowledge has also its foundation and function. If the two are separated, each can be independent; if the two were combined, both would perish."[20] Their cohort, the reactionary Ku Hung-ming (1857–1928), insisted on the preservation of Chinese tradition for its own sake. All three, K'ang, Yen, and Ku, were westernizers before they became traditionalists. Theirs was a world of romantic particularism, in which China was unique. Being no longer confident in the equivalence between China and the West, their insistence on Chinese uniqueness provided them with a safeguard against Western universality. Regardless of right or wrong, they accepted Confucious because he was after all a Chinese.

Nationalists such as the Liang Ch'i-ch'ao of 1899–1919 and Sun Yat-sen (1866–1925) sought the redefinition of China through the Western ideal of the nation-state. Liang, in his "Renovation of the People as the Most Urgent Task of Present-Day China" (1902) wanted simultaneously the preservation of inherited Chinese characteristics and the borrowing of Western innovations.[21] Equally, Sun in the T'ung-meng hui manifesto of 1905 appealed for the rediscovery of China's pre-Manchu past, as well as the borrowing of Western republicanism and agrarian socialism.[22] They might disagree in regard to the evolutionary or revolutionary means. But both, the Liang of 1899–1919 and Sun, could agree on the disparity between China and the West, and hoped that nationalism would bring about China's Western equivalence. The plausibility of the nationalist position depended on both the nationalization of China's past as well as the projection of her nation-state future.

Radicalism as an intellectual position in twentieth-century China reached its height during the twenties, after the May Fourth movement. It was an attempt to seek identity through the universal demand of Western value, without recourse to Chinese particularism. Temporarily at least the radical could iconoclastically deny his Chinese past and insist that he was a universalist. For example, the philosopher Hu Shih (1891–1962) did not quarrel with the popular contrast between China and the West in the 1920's, but quarreled with the popular insistence that the spiritual East was superior to the materialist West. Instead, he believed it was Western spirituality over Eastern materiality, since the East had always been engulfed by the material needs of mere subsistence.[23] The other leading radicals of the early twenties, such as the novelist Lu Hsün (1881–1936) and the early Chinese Marxists, Ch'en Tu-hsiu (1879–1942) and Li Ta-chao (1888–1927), agreed, in varying ways, to the contrast between inferior China and superior West.[24] But Western-oriented radicalism in itself was an unstable position, psychologically difficult to maintain. A Chinese radical eventually had to render accounts to his Chinese roots. The way was thus open for Hu to tend toward intellectual renovation as the means for the reconciliation of China and the West. Ch'en and Li would see in communism the great equalizer between China and the West.

The Chinese communist position in the twenties accepted the disparity between semifeudal, semicolonial China and the capitalist West. China's past, now redefined in Western Marxist terms, occupied a different stage in the universal process of historical materialism. But the gulf was narrowed, and a Chinese communist revolution could hopefully transform China from a laggard to a progressive socialist in company with Bolshevik Russia. The Western-derived Marxist position could simultaneously claim rational universality and criticize the nonprogressive capitalist West on its own terms. The Chinese communist resolution of the problem of China's equivalence to the West ultimately depended on the practical achievement of that Marxist revolutionary promise for China.[25]

The four major intellectual positions in the twentieth century, from traditionalism to communism, presupposed the particularity of the Chinese claim and the universality of Western values.

Traditionalism in its insistence upon Chinese uniqueness was fighting against an assumed universalist West. On the other hand, radicalism depended entirely on Western-oriented values—psychologically an untenable position. Nationalism and communism sought the reconciliation of the demands of China and the West. Both hoped that through successful nationalization or communization China would become the equivalent of the West.

MODERN CHINESE IDEAS OF RUSSIA

But the gulf between China and the West was too wide to be easily bridged. Frequently, during the past hundred years, Chinese thinkers emphasized the contrast between China and the West. Initially, around the mid-nineteenth century, the contrast was seen as one between Chinese civilization and Western barbarism— thus seen, for example, by the opium-suppressing commissioner Lin Tse-hsü; by the scholar Wei Yuan, who had compiled the famous geography book *Hai-kuo t'u-chih;* by the Manchu diplomat Ch'i-ying; by the Manchu scholar Wo-jen; and even by the Taiping leaders. By the late nineteenth century the contrast between China and the West became one between Chinese ethical culture and Western mechanistic science. The contrast was thus seen by the T'ung-chih Confucian leader Tseng Kuo-fan; the *yang-wu* mandarin reformer Li Hung-chang; Governor-General Chang Chih-tung; Feng Kuei-fen, the initiator of the self-strengthening school; the journalist-reformer Wang T'ao; and the diplomat Hsüeh Fu-ch'eng. By the early twentieth century, the contrast appeared much more varied: Cheng Kuan-ying, the comprador-scholar, believed the contrast consisted in the difference between an agrarian China and the commercial West; Huang Jen-chi, the anti-Western critic, emphasized Chinese moral righteousness against Western might and profit-seeking; Yen Fu, the scholar-translator, pointed to the homogeneous stability of China and the heterogeneous progress of the West; for Ch'en Tu-hsiu the contrast was between aged, Confucian, reactionary, authoritarian China and the young, scientific, democratic, libertarian West; and for Li Ta-chao it was between Chinese quietism and Western activism. By the 1920's, once more these varied contrasts tended to be summarized into the simplicist contrast between spiritual

China and the material West. Such were the approaches of
Liang Sou-ming, Sun Yat-sen, and the Liang Ch'i-ch'ao of
1919–1929.[26]

For the Chinese thinkers who accepted the dichotomy between
China and the West this gulf created no new problem. But for
the westernizers who wanted to bring about China's eventual
equivalence to the West, that is, the *chin-wen* reformers, the
evolutionary nationalists, the revolutionary nationalists, and the
radical converts to communism, the gulf was an enormous problem.
For these westernizers, the West was the source of universal
values, and yet China was the center of their particularist preoccupation. How was it possible to reconcile the divergence
between Western rational values and Chinese historical particularism?

If another country, known to China and yet neither Chinese
nor originally Western, could be pointed to as a model of successful westernization, would not the solution to the problem
of China's Western equivalence be facilitated? The idea of another
country as a model-catalyst to induce one's own westernization
is not a logical necessity. But historically (which is not logically),
it could be decisive in influencing the specific course of westernization in one's own country. The Chinese choice of Western
values was not a random one, but rather circumscribed by the
successful experience of that westernizing model. The model could
facilitate the reconciliation between Western rationality and
Chinese historicity. Within the past century two countries were
used as models by Chinese westernizers: Japan and Russia.*

As early as the 1860's, Japan was mentioned as an example of

* We are concerned here with the role of the Russian model in modern
Chinese intellectual history, just as we were concerned, in chapter 2, with
the role of the Western model in nineteenth-century Russian intellectual
history. But it is equally possible to point to the role of the classical model
in Renaissance intellectual development, of the Chinese model in the
philosophy of the Enlightenment, and of the medieval model in nineteenth-
century romanticism. The classical model enhanced the Renaissance
acceptance of rationality as a field of value concentration, amidst the
collapse of the medieval synthesis. The function of the Chinese model in
the philosophy of the Enlightenment was to provide an exemplar of the
realization of natural law, in order to criticize the *ancien régime*. On the
other hand, the medieval model of nineteenth-century romanticism was
antirational, useful in fending off the pressure of universal rationalism on
romantic particularism.

a nation willing to be westernized.[27] With the emergence of Japan as the victor from the wars of 1894–1895 and 1904–1905, she became even more popular as the westernizing model for the Chinese advocating various types of westernization for China. There was general agreement that Japan, being close to China both in geography and experience, was the most suitable model. Such for instance were the arguments of Chang Chih-tung and K'ang Yu-wei.[28] But by the 1890's the Russian model began to compete with the Japanese model.

China had had some commercial and cultural dealings with Russia since the treaty of Nerchinsk (1689). Because of that background, some Chinese thinkers in the second half of the nineteenth century distinguished Russia from the other Western countries, and were well disposed toward her. Wei Yuan in his 1841 preface to *Hai-kuo t'u-chih* suggested that China under barbarian pressure might well find an ally in Russia.[29] This pro-Russian diplomatic orientation was carried on, in the late nineteenth century, by Li Hung-chang, Chang Chih-tung, and Governor-General Liu K'un-i. They too looked upon Russia as a potential ally against Western aggression.[30] In addition to these, Hung Jen-kan, a Taiping leader, already began to cite Russia as a model of reform. In his "New Chapters on Finance and Politics" (1859), Hung said that the political and religious welfare of Russia depended on the reforms of Peter the Great.[31] The imperial censor, Wei Mu-t'ing, in his memorial of 1861, also mentioned the reform model of Peter.[32] But there were others, during this initial period, who tended to be suspicious of Russia— for example, Feng Kuei-fen and Prince Kung in the 1860's.[33]

By the 1890's, the *chin-wen* reformers, such as K'ang Yu-wei and Liang Ch'i-ch'ao, seized upon the idea of westernizing Russia as a model for the reform program of China. They used both Petrine Russia and Meiji Japan as reform models. Among his memorials of 1898, K'ang wrote both "Account of the Political Reform of Peter the Great of Russia" and "Study of the Political Reform of Meiji Japan." [34] In a January, 1898, memorial, he wrote: "I beg Your Majesty to adopt the purpose of Peter the Great of Russia as our purpose and to take the Meiji reform of Japan as the model for our reform." [35]

Similarly, Liang in his "General Discussion on Reform" (1896) pointed to both Japan and Russia as reform models for China.[36] In his article "On Liberty" (1902), Liang selected the emancipation of 1861 and the constitutional promise of 1881, in Russia, as some of the leading events in the history of liberty.[37] The *chin-wen* model of Russia was limited by the simultaneous availability of the more familiar model of Japan. Both reform models were restricted by the Confucian universal perspective in regard to superior China. Nevertheless, within these limits, the *chin-wen* reformers used the reform model of Russia as an argument to facilitate the westernization of China.

The *chin-wen* reform model of Russia was passed on to the evolutionary nationalists. From 1899 to 1911, Liang Ch'i-ch'ao as the leader of the evolutionary nationalists grouped Russia and China together as nations in transition, and said that "if today there is to be a plan for China, we can well decide upon it by scrutinizing Russia." [38] But there was a rivalry between the Japanese model and the Russian model among *chin-wen* reformers and evolutionary nationalists. This was revealed in the 1905 Chinese newspaper editorials concerning the outcome of the Russo-Japanese war. Moderate newspapers in China agreed that Japan's triumph over Russia was a triumph of constitutional monarchy over autocracy.[39] It proved to them the intrinsic value of constitutional reform. They still preferred the model of Meiji Japan to that of Petrine Russia.

Before 1905, the revolutionary nationalists under Sun Yat-sen, concentrated mainly in Japan, were not favorably disposed toward Russia. They also preferred the successful model of Japan. To them Russia was too remote and her revolutionary movement too lacking in accomplishment. Besides, their idea of Russia was dependent mainly upon Japanese sources, which in this period just before the Russo-Japanese war certainly was not too friendly.[40] In April, 1903, nationalist-inspired Chinese students in Japan demonstrated against Russian demands in Manchuria.[41] The revolutionary nationalist, Ch'en T'ien-hua, was anti-Russian in his pre-1905 writings; he emphasized that Russia was the strongest and most aggressive of China's enemies.[42]

The Russian Revolution of 1905 transformed the Chinese

significance of the Russian model. Pre-1905 Russia was a model of monarchical reform which suited the preoccupation of both the *chin-wen* reformers and the evolutionary nationalists. But after 1905, constitutional reformers, including Liang Ch'i-ch'ao, became cool to the idea of a revolutionary Russia.[43] On the other hand, the post-1905 model of revolutionary Russia played a significant role in stimulating the revolutionary nationalism of the T'ung-meng hui; whereas before 1905 the revolutionary nationalists were not much interested in the Russian model of monarchical reform. *Min pao*, the post-1905 organ of the T'ung-meng hui, immediately took notice of the Russian Revolution of 1905.[44] Sun Yat-sen in 1906 compared the Russian Revolution with the French Revolution.[45] As a result of increased interest in the Russian revolutionary movement, *Min pao* began to publish articles on nihilism, anarchism, and the socialist revolutionaries.[46] Twice in *Min pao* it was suggested that the Chinese revolutionary nationalists imitate the agitation and assassination techniques of the Russian revolutionaries.[47] As the model of revolutionary Russia increased in popularity among the revolutionary nationalists, the model of a much less revolutionary Japan became less inspiring.*

The Revolution of 1905 was the great divide which separated the constitutional reformers from the revolutionaries in their attitudes toward the Russian model. Before 1905 the former were in favor of the Russian model of monarchical reform, after 1905 the latter became inspired by the Russian model of revolution. Correspondingly, the revolutions of 1917 further separated the attitudes of various Chinese intellectuals toward the Russian model. As the revolutionary events proceeded in 1917, Chinese moderate opinion became increasingly cautious. On the other hand, the revolutionary nationalists were encouraged by these Russian events. But even more significantly, the revolutions of 1917 converted some radicals, such as Ch'en Tu-hsiu and Li

---

* With the collapse of the Manchu dynasty in 1911, the Japanese model of constitutional monarchy became much less applicable to China. Besides, the deterioration of Chinese-Japanese relations after the Twenty-One Demands of 1915 put to an end the popular prospect of Japan as a progressive model for China. Thereafter, Japan became increasingly a symbol of conservatism and pan-Asiatic solidarity.

Ta-chao, to Marxism. The Russian model, now the Bolshevik model, induced the birth of Marxism in China.

The April, 1917, issues of both *Tung-fang tsa-chih: Eastern Miscellany*, representing moderate yet progressive Chinese opinion, and *Hsin ch'ing-nien: La Jeunesse*, representing iconoclastic radical opinion, took immediate notice of the February Revolution in Russia.[48] Their tone was generally sympathetic. However, their opinions about the revolution soon began to diverge. Already in the same issue of *Hsin ch'ing-nien*, Ch'en Tu-hsiu wrote "The Russian Revolution and the Awakening of the Chinese People." He sought a moral lesson in the revolution for the Chinese people. This, he said, was "not a revolution against the Russian tsar, but one against international monarchism and aggression."[49] His enthusiasm was echoed by many others. For instance, a Tsing-hua student, Sun Hao-hsüan, wrote elsewhere that the Russian Revolution resulted from a great popular enlightenment about tsarist autocracy.[50] On the other hand, the moderate *Tung-fang tsa-chih* became gradually more troubled by the trend of revolutionary events inside Russia.[51]

The February Revolution had already separated the moderate opinion from the radical opinion in China; and this trend was continued after the October Revolution. The January, 1918, issue of *Tung-fang tsa-chih* carried an article entitled "Further Account of the Internal Situation of Russia," in which the author expressed distress that the extremist Lenin was in control in Russia.[52] For the next two years, numerous articles in the magazine dealt with Russia, which testified to a sustained new interest in that country. However, almost all these articles were translated from Western-language magazines. Their attitudes toward Russia ranged from cautious reserve to outright hostility.[53] In fact, during this period the only article written by a Chinese appeared in the June, 1919, issue. That article certainly was not friendly toward the Bolsheviks.[54] In contrast to this moderate magazine, the radical *Hsin ch'ing-nien* became more enthusiastic about the Bolshevik victory. By the summer of 1918 distinctly pro-Bolshevik articles began to appear in that magazine. In May, 1919, *Hsin ch'ing-nien* published a special issue dealing entirely with Marxism.[55]

The revolutions of 1917 separated the moderates from the radicals in China. But within the radical ranks, the attitude of the revolutionary nationalists toward the Bolshevik model was different from the attitude of the radicals toward the same model. The revolutionary nationalists were already favorable toward the 1905 model of revolutionary Russia. Now they extended the same favor to the 1917 model of revolutionary Russia. In early 1918, Sun Yat-sen sent a telegram to congratulate Lenin, expressing his fraternal solidarity.[56] It was Sun's belief that the Chinese revolutionary nationalists and the Bolsheviks were identical in their opposition to the old regime and in their aspiration for a new order. In 1923, Sun argued on this basis of comparability for the adoption of the Bolshevik party model: "Why have they succeeded in Russia, and why have we not in China? It is because the Russian Revolution owed its success to the struggle of the Party members. . . . Therefore, if we wish our revolution to succeed, we must learn the methods, organization, and training of the Russians; then there can be hope of success." [57]

Sun de-emphasized the distinction between the Russian Bolsheviks and the Chinese revolutionary nationalists. For that matter, he also failed to differentiate the revolutions of 1917 from the Revolution of 1905.

Sun's view as a revolutionary nationalist was already formed. It sought to transform China in terms of the Western value of the nation-state. With his goal set, the Bolshevik model was merely a revolutionary inspiration for him. So long as he remained committed to the cosmopolitan value of the nation-state, Sun was basically insensitive to the Marxist value implied in the Bolshevik model. His cosmopolitan perspective, which saw the world as being composed of a multitude of unique, yet equal nation-states, predisposed him to reject the linear perspective of historical materialism. Thus the Bolshevik model was merely an auxiliary to Sun's nationalist program.

On the other hand, some radicals were influenced by the Bolshevik model in an entirely different way. Theirs was an intellectual position oriented toward the universal demand of Western rational values, without any concession being made to Chinese particularism. It was a Western-oriented critique of China. In its total opposition to China they were unable to produce an effective program for the westernization of China. But the psychological roots of the radicals still lay in China. And the Bolshevik model could best be the midwife for the conversion of some Chinese radicals to communism.

Marxism has always been a radical Western value. But before 1917 it seemed irrelevant to China. Therefore, the few Marxist writings available in Chinese translation before 1917 never acquired popularity.[58] After the Bolshevik triumph in semi-Western Russia, Marxism seemed increasingly possible for even more backward China. Thus the Chinese popularity of Marxism. Chinese radicals, by becoming communists after 1917, could maintain the Western radicality of their view, and in addition could acquire a new program for the westernization of old China. Such seems to have been the case for Ch'en Tu-hsiu and Li Ta-chao.

Both Ch'en and Li, before 1917, were typically radical in emphasizing the contrast between an inferior China and a superior West.[59] However, even before the May Fourth movement, the Bolshevik model had gradually detached Ch'en and Li from radicalism to communism. Already in April, 1917, Ch'en looked upon the Russian Revolution as a model for China.[60] In July, 1918, Li compared the Russian Revolution with the French Revolution. He saw the former as socialist, international, and pacific, the latter as political, nationalist, and military.[61] He certainly favored the former. In the October, 1918, issue of *Hsin ch'ing-nien*, Li wrote his well-known "The Victory of Bolshevism." He said: "The victory of Bolshevism, therefore, is the victory of the spirit of common awakening in the heart of each individual among mankind in the twentieth century." [62]

In February, 1919, Li wrote "Youth and Village," in which he asked Chinese youths to model themselves after the Russian populist youths.[63] From 1917 to 1919, Ch'en and Li were predisposed toward Bolshevism. But their writings revealed that they were not yet theoretically consistent Marxists. After the May Fourth movement, they completed their journey to historical materialism.[64] As finally explained by Li Ta-chao, in his "The October Revolution and the Chinese People" (November, 1922): "Our toiling masses, already under tremendous oppressions, suddenly heard the October Revolution's outcry for 'the overthrow of international capitalism' and 'the overthrow of international imperialism.' Such a voice was especially poignant, sober and significant for us." [65]

If we discard rhetoric and dogma and substitute the term "radical intellectuals" for the term "toiling masses," Li's observation acquires much historical validity. The Bolshevik model enhanced the Chinese significance of Marxism and revealed a Bolshevik course for China's progress to the universal Marxist goal.

The Russian model had played a significant role in the intellectual efforts of those Chinese westernizers who sought to bridge the gulf between Western rationality and Chinese historicity. This was true for the *chin-wen* reformers and the evolutionary nationalists. It was even truer for the revolutionary nationalists. And it became crucial for the conversion of some radicals to communism. As the Russian model itself became more radical, it tended to influence the more radically predisposed segments of Chinese westernizers.

PRE-MAOIST CHINESE COMMUNIST IDEAS OF CHINA

Much has been written about the communist movement in China during the 1920's. In terms of the problem of China's equivalence to the West, the movement represented a continuation of the need to reconcile Western values and Chinese particularism. This would have to be accomplished both in theory and in practice.

However, such a reconciliation was complicated in the twenties by the presence of other factors. For one, the current international communist movement had its strategic base in Bolshevik Russia; and any good communist had to take into consideration the strategic needs of the one and only socialist state. For another, the Chinese background of the efficacy of the Russian model induced Chinese Marxists to be swayed by the analogy of Soviet experience. Both factors detracted from a proper reconciliation of Western Marxist theory and Chinese revolutionary practice.

From this point of view, several major lines developed, during the twenties, in the pre-Maoist Chinese communist ideas of China.

One was the official Comintern-Chinese Communist party (C.C.P.) line from 1923 to 1927, dictated from Moscow. The other was the revised official line of 1928–1930, also dictated from Moscow. A third was the private line of Ch'en Tu-hsiu and his cohort P'eng Shu-chih. The fourth was the Li Ta-chao line.

The basis of the official Comintern-C.C.P. line on China, in the mid-twenties, was the Leninist theses on the national and colonial question, adopted by the Second Comintern Congress in 1920. Lenin approached the national and colonial question from the perspective of the international strategic concern of Bolshevik Russia. From that vantage point, he emphasized the temporary alliance with the bourgeois–nationalist movement in the semi-colonial, semifeudal countries. In opposition to that, M. N. Roy saw the national and colonial question in terms of the native communist prospect within the semifeudal, semicolonial country. Therefore, he de-emphasized the alliance with the native bourgeois nationalists, and instead promoted the autonomous role of the native communist party and the prospect of the sovietization of the agrarian masses. This is not a difference between revolution from the top and revolution from the bottom, because any communist worth his name would be an elitist manipulating from the top. It is fundamentally a difference between a Russian- and an Asian-preoccupied perspective.

The first manifesto of the C.C.P. "on the current situation," June, 1922, pointed out that China was feudal and semicolonial, under the control of militarists and imperialists. In such a situation, "the proletariat's present urgent task is to act jointly with the democratic party [i.e., the Kuomintang] to establish a united front of democratic revolution to struggle for the overthrow of the military and for the organization of a real democratic government." [66]

The manifesto of the Second National Congress of the C.C.P., in July, 1922, justified this united-front tactic against leftist doctrinaire criticism: "At present the Chinese Communist Party must, in the interest of the workers and poor peasants, lead the workers to support the democratic revolution and forge a democratic united front of workers, poor peasants, and petty bourgeoisie." [67]

Both the manifesto of the Third National Congress in June, 1923,[68] and the fourth manifesto of the C.C.P. "on the current situation" in January, 1925,[69] continued the same approach. As late as May, 1927, after Chiang Kai-shek had taken the initiative in breaking with the communists, the Fifth National Congress of the C.C.P. still refused to emphasize agrarian unrest in China. At this last congress, the emphasis on the importance of the agrarian question was increased. But fundamentally the party was still committed to the alliance with the Kuomintang.[70] The August 7, 1927, Emergency Conference of the C.C.P. reconfirmed it: "Under present conditions, unless we achieve hegemony within the Kuomintang, we shall not be able to achieve hegemony of the Chinese proletariat. We must reorganize the Kuomintang and make it a genuine mass organization of the urban and agrarian toiling masses." [71] Stalin had not yet given the signal to abandon the coalition ship; therefore the course remained the same.[72]

The idea of China as revealed in this official Comintern-C.C.P. line was that of a semicolonial, semifeudal China, where the Kuomintang played the leading role in the anti-imperialist democratic revolution, and the C.C.P. played a mere supporting role. As long as the C.C.P. desired to maintain the coalition with the Kuomintang, it could not afford to antagonize the moderate element within the Kuomintang by prospecting for agrarian discontent. Such was the restraint throughout the mid-twenties, in spite of constant lip service being paid to the importance of the agrarian question in backward countries. This was Lenin's post-1919 idea of China, that is, a semicolonial China seen by a Russian-preoccupied Marxist. From this perspective, the revolutionary prospect of China was subordinated to the international strategic concern of Bolshevik Russia.

By late 1927, the official Comintern-C.C.P. policy of alliance with the Kuomintang was abandoned. Armed insurrections were advocated instead. In this brief period armed insurrection was attempted at Nanchang (August), in Hunan (September), and at Canton (December). The November, 1927, enlarged plenum of the Central Committee of the C.C.P. confirmed this shift by claiming a "rising revolutionary wave." It pointed out, "the co-ordination of worker uprisings and peasant uprisings is the most important problem facing the party." [73] But the policy of seeking victory through armed uprising, necessitated by Stalin's domestic struggle against Trotsky, led to a series of disastrous defeats in China. Finally, the ninth plenum of the Executive Committee of the Comintern (E.C.C.I.), held in Moscow in February, 1928, announced a new line on China:

> The present period of the Chinese revolution is the period of the bourgeois-democratic revolution, which neither from the economic aspect . . . , nor from the aspect of the national struggle against imperialism . . . , nor from the aspect of the class nature of the government . . . , has yet reached its conclusion. The characterization of the present stage of the Chinese revolution as one which is already a socialist revolution is false. . . . At the present moment we are not confronted with a new and powerful advance of the revolutionary mass movement throughout the country. [74]

The new line was reconfirmed by the Sixth National Congress of the C.C.P., held in Moscow during the late summer of 1928. According to the political resolution of that congress, the two immediate tasks were the overthrow of imperialism and the promotion of an agrarian revolution, under the dictatorship of the workers and the peasants. [75] However, this revised Comintern-C.C.P. line, as carried out by Li Li-san during 1929–1930, was basically an attempt to use the rural based military force to gain an urban base for the communist revolution in China. [76] He was under order to instigate armed insurrection and to recapture the urban proletarian base of the revolution. [77]

The revised Comintern-C.C.P. line abandoned the old dictate of a national democratic alliance. But it was still a Moscow-ordered program for revolution, distrustful of, yet reluctantly drawn to, the peasantry, and still exaggerating the ideological commitment to the urban proletariat. From a Russian-preoccupied viewpoint, the lesson learned from the failure of 1927 in China was negative. The revised line was indicative of the intellectual disorientation of the communist leaders, following the disaster of 1927. It revealed little evidence of acquaintance with the particularity of Chinese conditions. Instead, it fell back upon ideologically conditioned response.

Opposed to the official Comintern-C.C.P. lines was a private

Ch'en Tu-hsiu-P'eng Shu-chih line.[78] Ch'en in 1920, as a recent convert to communism, had this to say about the prospect of socialism in China: "Fortunately, we, in China, are beginning our tasks of industrialization and education while capitalism is still undeveloped. We can thus use methods of socialism to develop our education and industrialization, thus avoiding the errors of Europe, America and Japan." [79]

And again, about the same time, he said: "In the Soviet Union the republic overthrew the feudal system only to be replaced by socialism a half year later. This is clear proof that there need not be any long interim between feudalism and socialism." [80]

From 1922 to 1927, Ch'en as the head of the C.C.P. had to support the official Comintern-dictated policy of alliance with the Kuomintang. Yet even in 1924, his follower P'eng wrote that the Chinese bourgeoisie had become counter-revolutionary and that the Chinese peasantry could not be expected to have the Marxist revolutionary spirit. Therefore, P'eng continued, the only class really capable of revolutionary initiative was the Chinese proletariat. He complained that the alliance with the Kuomintang had throttled the proletariat's initiative.[81] Ch'en, in "A Statement of Our Views" (December, 1929), emphasized that the "wrong" diagnosis of the bourgeois revolution and of the Kuomintang had led to the failure of 1927. Instead, he advocated a soviet movement of the proletariat, the petty bourgeoisie, and the impoverished masses in the cities and the countryside.[82]

The idea of China implied in the private Ch'en-P'eng line was overshadowed by its excessive commitment to the theoretical validity of Marxism and to the efficacy of the soviet model for China. If the official Comintern-C.C.P. lines sacrificed the native prospect of the Chinese communists for the sake of the international strategic concern of Bolshevik Russia, then the private Ch'en-P'eng line unduly exaggerated the prospect of an independent proletarian leadership and of a soviet movement in China. It revealed a lack of sophistication concerning the particularity of revolutionary potentiality in China. In this regard, similar to the attitude of the early Russian converts to Marxism, the private Ch'en-P'eng line tended to exaggerate the immediate prospect of post-capitalist development in democratic revolutionary China.

The only exception to the party lines mentioned above was the
line adopted by Li Ta-chao. In February, 1919, Li had written an
article "Youth and the Village," in which he had urged the Chinese
youths to emulate the Russian populists by going back to the
villages and by attending to the problems of the rural masses. He
said: "China is an agrarian country, where most of her working
people are peasants. And if the peasants are not liberated, the
Chinese people cannot be liberated." [83] This was a remarkable
statement for a Western-oriented radical, given the urban bias of
most westernized intellectuals in modern China. In his 1925
article on "Land and the Peasants," Li concluded: "If the broad
peasant masses of China can be organized for participation in the
national revolution, then the success of the Chinese revolution
cannot be far off." [84] In the following year Li was placing his
revolutionary hope upon the armed peasant secret societies! [85] As
Maurice Meisner pointed out in his dissertation, Li as a Chinese
Marxist placed the revolutionary spirit in the Chinese nation as a
whole. This was the justification for his support of the official line
of co-operating with the Kuomintang in the national revolution.
But when that began to fail, during the last few years of his life,
1925–1927, he transferred the revolutionary spirit from the nation
to the peasantry as a whole.[86] Li lacked a sense of the possibility
for the C.C.P. to manipulate the peasantry, a sense of the necessity
for a Bolshevized elitist consciousness. In addition, from 1920 to
1925, Li himself had abandoned his populist-peasant line in favor
of a nationalist revolution.[87]

Within the Chinese communist correlation of theory and practice, the idea of China must be pragmatic enough in order to
recognize the specific revolutionary prospect in China. Yet such
pragmatic idea must be fitted into the universal Marxist framework, for otherwise it will have no universal, that is, Marxist
universal, value.

However, a cursory review of the major pre-Maoist Chinese
communist ideas of China shows that such reconciliation was not
achieved in the 1920's. Both official Comintern-C.C.P. lines revealed
a Bolshevik-Russian-preoccupied perspective, whereas the private
Ch'en-P'eng line revealed excessive commitment to the validity of
Marxist theory as well as to the Soviet model. Therefore, except

for Li Ta-chao's populist line, the other lines were remote from the particularity of agrarian China in discontent. This, however, is no argument for mere pragmatic revolution. For the Chinese communists, such a revolution must be undertaken in the name of Marxism. Li's peasant line, without sufficient theoretical orthodoxy and without organized communist party control, might easily become merely a peasant revolution.

From the point of view of a Chinese Marxist revolutionary, a new reconciliation between Western Marxist theory and Chinese revolutionary practice must be sought by de-emphasizing the applicability of the Bolshevik model. Such a correlation cannot be accomplished from the Soviet-Russian preoccupied viewpoint. This is the background for an understanding of the Maoist idea of China.[88]

Chapter Five

Mao

THE UNITY OF THEORY AND PRACTICE IN MAOIST THOUGHT

Mao Tse-tung is neither a simple Chinese chauvinist nor an orthodox Marxist theoretician. As a Chinese Marxist revolutionary, he has worked for the revolutionary transformation of China. But that transformation has always been justified in the name of Marxism. Correspondingly, universal Marxist theory will have to be revised in order to incorporate specific Chinese reality. Only in this way can the problem of China's equivalence to the West be solved, so that the specific demand of revolutionary China be reconciled with the universalist demand of Marxist value. Within this reconciliation, Mao has always emphasized revolutionary practice and the support of practice-oriented knowledge. This is his version of the Marxist unity of theory and practice. His idea of China is an integral part of his version of that unity.[1]

Such an approach to the relation between theory and practice was already evident during Mao's pre-Marxist period, before 1920. In the article "A Study of Physical Education" (*Hsin ch'ing-nien*, April, 1917), Mao pointed to the central importance of physical education as the basis for individual will and initiative.[2] Two years later, he had advanced from individual will to mass movement. In "The Great Union of the Popular Masses" (*Hsiang-chiang p'ing-lun*, July–August, 1919), he pointed to the union with the popular masses as the method for the transformation of China.[3] Both individual will and popular masses are concepts which indicate a mind fundamentally committed to activism. Yet Mao was no mere activist. He had intellectual pretensions, and aspired to provide a theoretical justification for his activist program. In the 1917 article, he said: "If one becomes conscious of the problem, a program of physical education will come easily, and we will attain our goals and make our influence felt as a matter of course."[4] And in the

1919 article, he said: "It is not that basically we have no strength; the sources of our impotence lies in our lack of practice."[5]

There was a traditional Chinese background for the concern with the duality of knowledge and action.[6] It was admitted that thought and action were related. But the proverbial question has always been: Is it more difficult to know or to act? Against that background, Mao had opted for the latter by subordinating knowledge to action.

Actually, it was not until 1920 that Mao became converted to communism.[7] The transition from the traditional duality of knowledge and action to the Marxist duality of theory and practice constituted no fundamental break in Mao's mental make-up. Within the traditional duality, he had subordinated knowledge to action. And now within the Marxist duality of theory and practice he emphasized the importance of practice over theory. Mao maintained his preference for activism.

Nevertheless, within this preference, he still had to reconcile revolutionary practice with practice-oriented theory. In different periods, not only did Mao's revolutionary practice change, but theoretical justification also varied. In terms of this shifting correlation between theory and practice, Mao's Marxist development can be divided into five major periods: The initial Marxist period, from his conversion to Marxism in 1920 to approximately 1926; the formative Maoist period, beginning with his emphasis on a peasant-based revolution in 1927 to the consolidation of his control within the party by 1935;[8] the mature Maoist period, from 1935 to the completion of his concept of new democracy by early 1940; the civil-war period, from 1940 to 1949; and the post-1949 period, following the revolutionary victory.*

The initial Marxist period, from 1920 to 1926

In this period Mao showed himself to be not really versed in Marxist theory. In a November, 1920, letter to Ts'ai Ho-shen, he pro-

---

* All periodizations are arbitrary; none can fit the past exactly. Mao's public career as well as the Chinese communist movement, with which he has been so closely identified, can be periodized in other ways. The present scheme intends to emphasize the major phases of Mao's intellectual development.

posed several reasons why education could not bring about the transition from capitalism to communism. From the Marxist viewpoint the position he took was sound. But not so his reasons to justify this position. His first reason was psychological, that is "how then can one hope that [the capitalist] will repent and turn to the good?" The second reason was that the rulers must be "overthrown by the people." The third reason was that "the proletarians are discontented, and a demand for communism has arisen and had already become a fact." [9] Such "reasons" were mere declaration of Mao's revolutionary enthusiasm. They did not provide the immanent socioeconomic explanations, which usually form the core of Marxist thinking.

At the level of revolutionary practice, Mao in this period was a faithful follower of the official Comintern-C.C.P. line of co-operating with the "bourgeois democratic" party, the Kuomintang. In "The Peking *Coup d'Etat* and the Merchants" (*Hsiang-tao*, July 11, 1923), he wrote: "The work for which the merchants should be responsible in the national revolution is both more urgent and more important than the work that the rest of the people should take upon themselves." [10] This was a straight party line, completely submerging his own penchant for a mass line. And, as subsequent events in China proved, it led to disaster.

Mao was therefore neither a good Marxist theoretician nor a practical revolutionary. His theory was distorted by populist revolutionary enthusiasm. And his practice was in conformity with the official Comintern-C.C.P. line. No wonder all official editions of Mao's selected works ignored his pre-1927 writings. The only exception was the article "Analysis of the Classes in Chinese Society" (1926) in the 1951 edition. But that article was entirely rewritten by the editorial committee.[11]

Among other things, in the original version of the article Mao had insisted on the equivalence between China and the West: "The attitudes of the various classes in China toward the national revolution are almost identical with the attitudes of the various classes in Western capitalist countries toward the socialist revolution. . . . This is because all contemporary revolutions are basically one, and their goals and means are identical. The goal is an anti-imperialist one; and the means depends upon the coalition war of oppressed nations and oppressed classes." [12] By insisting on the similarity between Chinese and Western class attitudes, Mao was able to transpose Western Marxist strategy to Chinese society. But this rigid transposition prevented him from devising a strategy appropriate to the specific revolutionary potentiality in China, as well as from understanding the theoretical difference between the Eastern democratic revolution and the Western socialist revolution. He abandoned this insistence after his initial Marxist period.

The formative Maoist period, 1927–1935

This was the most trying period for the Chinese communist movement. It began with the strategic bankruptcy of the official party line of co-operating with the Kuomintang. The urban base of the infant movement was destroyed by Chiang Kai-shek. The problem of the Chinese revolution became a football in the factional struggle within Russia between Stalin and Trotsky. There was a successive change of party leadership in China, a fluctuating expectation between the rising and declining revolutionary wave, between an urban-based and a rural-based insurrection, and between an anti-imperialist and an antifeudal revolution. It ended with the Long March from Kiangsi to Yenan, lasting from the autumn of 1934 till the autumn of 1935.

During this disorienting period, Mao gradually staked out a claim for himself. In November, 1927, he set up a soviet regime in Hunan. In August, 1929, he set up the Kiangsi soviet, and became its provisional chairman in November, 1931. The following autumn he succeeded in moving the urban-based central committeemen to his Kiangsi region. Throughout the early 1930's, Mao fought off five anticommunist campaigns led by Chiang Kai-shek. In 1935 he led the successful Long March out of Kiangsi, and was finally confirmed with the chairmanship of the Central Committee and the Politburo of the C.C.P. at the Tsun-i conference in January of that year.

Throughout the period, Mao was preoccupied with the strategic maneuver of his peasant-based revolutionary movement. Probably because of this preoccupation, and possibly because he realized his own lack of theoretical sophistication, he avoided all theoretical implications in his speeches and writings, and employed a minimum of Marxist category of thought.[13]

"On the Rectification of Incorrect Ideas in the Party" was a resolution written by Mao for the Ninth Party Conference of the Organization of the Fourth Red Army, in December, 1929. It seems to be his most "theoretical" statement during this period. In it, he emphasized the need to train party members in the Marxist method of political and class analysis; to investigate social and economic questions and to base tactics upon such investigation; and to criticize the spirit of idealism in the party.[14] He was primarily concerned with the practical problems of organization and discipline in the party; not with Marxist theory.

In none of his writings and speeches of the period did Mao discuss further what he meant by the Marxist method of political and class analysis. As for the investigation of social and economic conditions, he wrote, in addition to his well-known "Report on an Investigation of the Peasant Movement in Hunan" (February, 1927), a series of reports on rural investigation in 1933–1934.[15] All these reports discussed the actual conditions in the countryside, employing very little Marxist terminology.

The only other indication of theoretical interest was revealed in his January 5, 1930, letter to Lin Piao, in which Mao tried to differentiate the subjective and objective forces in China.[16] He said: "Although the subjective forces of the Chinese revolution are weak, the *objective* forces are also weak, therefore the revolution in China will certainly approach a rising wave much faster than in Western Europe" [17] (Italics added). By subjective forces Mao meant the revolutionary forces, and by objective forces the counter-revolutionary forces. In fact, the 1951 edition of *Hsüan-chi* substituted the word "counter-revolutionary" for "objective." [18] Mao, in his pre-Marxist period, was concerned with the dichotomy between knowledge and action. Now he was concerned with the dichotomy between revolutionary ideology and counter-revolutionary objective conditions. Though not sound as Marxist theory, this new dichotomy does reveal two elements in Mao's thinking of the period: It was pragmatically sound, because most of the actual forces in China were not revolutionary in the Marxist sense, and Marxism represented the ideology of a very small minority; and it revealed an understanding of the subjective revolutionary forces closely approximating Lenin's emphasis on the elitist role of revolutionary consciousness.

Since the level of his theoretical concern in this period was so low, it is at the level of practice that we can discover his preoccupation. Mao was immersed in the practice of his peasant-based communist movement. This approach to practice was best exemplified in a letter written by Mao during the period: "To summarize, the method of strategy and work should be decided on the basis of the actual conditions. You should realistically assess the situation, and decide the actual strategic approach in terms of the tendency and demands of the mass struggle. Only then can you obtain great and substantive results." [19] Such an emphasis upon specific practice based on actual mass conditions has been an ingredient of Mao's thinking ever since 1927.

However, revolutionary momentum cannot rely solely on practice, no matter how realistic. There must also be an utopian stimulus. Since Mao showed neither interest nor sophistication in Marxist theory, that stimulus could not come from the universalist claim of Marxist value. It came, in this period, from his belief that the Soviet model was applicable to China. Mao tried to correlate the specifics of the communist-manipulated agrarian discontent with the ideal of the Soviet model. This was the basis for the establishment of the soviet form of government, first in Hunan then in Kiangsi. And during 1934 Mao spoke and wrote often on the importance of the Soviet model for China.[20]

For Mao, in this period, the unity of theory and practice did not involve a correlation of specific practice with Marxist values. It was rather a correlation of specific practice with the ideal of the Soviet model, without much concern for Marxist values. His concern for specific practice represented an advance over the official Comintern-C.C.P. lines of the 1920's as well as the private Ch'en-P'eng line. But his acceptance of the Soviet model was still an ideological lag.

The mature Maoist period, from 1935 to 1940

The period from the confirmation of his control of the party and the end of the Long March ordeal in 1935 to the completion of his concept of a new democracy in early 1940 was intellectually Mao's most fruitful time. In 1935, after the Long March, he had to start a communist movement all over again at Yenan. The domestic situation, with the ascendancy of the Kuomintang, was certainly not favorable to Mao. The only favorable development was the beginning of a discrepancy between Chiang Kai-shek's anticommunist drive and the growing anti-Japanese sentiment among that segment of urban, literate, vocal Chinese which constituted public opinion. The international scene, to which Mao had not paid much attention during his Kiangsi period, did not appear favorable either. The threat of Japanese aggression in North China was imminent. Elsewhere in Europe, there was the rising threat of Nazi Germany and Fascist Italy, which by August 1935 had prompted the Seventh Comintern Congress to announce the strategy of an antifascist popular front. Confronted with a new and difficult situation, Mao could only rely on his peasant-based, armed insurrectionary experience. Yet the added burden of the chairmanship of the Central Committee of the party forced him to look at the situation much more broadly than before. He thus abandoned his correlation of specific practice and the Soviet model, and sought instead a new framework for his revolutionary practice. Intellectually, he had to make a greater effort in this period, than during any other period in his career.

Such a shift in Mao's intellectual orientation became evident in his pamphlet "Strategic Problems of China's Revolutionary War" (December, 1936).[21] Unlike his writings and speeches of the previous period, this pamphlet tried to provide a theoretical veneer for his concern with revolutionary practice. He divided the laws of war in general from the laws of revolutionary war in particular and from specifically the laws of China's revolutionary war.[22] Each set of laws, he said, had its own characteristics. Military laws, like the laws governing all other concerns, are a reflection in our mind of objective reality; everything is objective reality except our mind.[23]

The ultimate justification for the study, according to Mao, is to resolve "the contradiction between the subjective and the objective."[24] After discussing in the first chapter how to study war, he then moved on, in the third chapter, to the topic of the characteristics of China's revolutionary war. He insisted: "It can thus be

seen that failure to understand the characteristics of China's revolutionary war means inability to direct it or to lead it to victory." [25] Mao's attempt at theory in this pamphlet included the appeal to practice-oriented knowledge, and especially emphasized the
subject–object contradiction and China's characteristics.

This theoretical concern again emerged in Mao's May, 1937, report to the national conference of the party at Yenan. He said:
"The contradiction between China and Japan has become a primary contradiction, while China's internal contradiction has become a secondary and subordinate contradiction. This has ushered
in a new stage of development in the current revolutionary situation." [26] He concluded his report with the following remark: "We
advocate the theory of the continuously developing revolution,
but not the Trotskyite theory of 'uninterrupted revolution,' *nor
the semi-Trotskyite theory of Li-sanism*. We stand for the attain-
ment of socialism through all the necessary stages of the democratic republic. We are opposed to tailism, but also to adventurism
and extreme impatience" [27] (Italics added).

Given such indications, we can say that by 1937 Mao had become interested in Marxist theory. Theory meant to him practice-
oriented knowledge and subject–object contradiction. However,
we have only the 1951 versions of the two theoretical articles, "On
Practice" and "On Contradiction." Both articles have probably
been revised. I would say that the content of the present version of
"On Practice" can be dated to Mao's theoretical concern of the
late 1930's, whereas the content of the present version of "On
Contradiction" appears more typical of the Mao of the early
1950's.[28] Substantively, "On Practice" emphasized that man's
social practice alone is the criterion for the truthfulness of his
knowledge. Knowledge begins with practice, reaches the theoretical level through practice, and then has to return to practice. Situations change; and practice-oriented knowledge has to change in
accordance with the changing situations.[29]

In his October, 1938, report to the Central Committee of the
C.C.P., entitled "On the New Stage," Mao continued to emphasize
practice-oriented knowledge. "We should not study the words of
Marxist-Leninist theory, but study their standpoint and approach

in viewing problems and solving them." [30] But now, practice-oriented Marxist theory meant for Mao the assumption by Marxism of a national form: "Communists are Marxist-internationalists, but Marxism must be given a national form, before it can be put into practice. There is no abstract Marxism, only specific Marxism. So-called specific Marxism is Marxism given a national form; it is Marxism applied to the specific struggle in the specific circumstances of China." [31]

For Mao, Marxism in a national form involved not merely the emphasis on the characteristics of that country, but also the history of that country, viewed through Marxist eyes, as the foundation for her current characteristics: "Our nation has a history of several thousand years, a history which has its specific pattern of development, its national characteristics and is full of treasures. . . . The China of today has developed from the China in history; as we are believers in the Marxist approach to history, we must not cut off our whole historical past." [32] In effect, Mao was implying that China's historical particularism, viewed through Marxist eyes, not merely provided the foundation for her characteristics, but also the link between China and the Marxist process.[33]

Finally, in "On New Democracy" (January, 1940), Mao said: "There is but one truth, and the criterion for determining it is not subjective boastfulness but objective practice." [34] What he meant by this remark was made clear in his "Dialectical Materialism" (March, 1940). There he insisted that there are only two philosophical schools, idealism and materialism: "When men think, they cannot avoid using concepts. This then can easily cause our knowledge to split into two aspects: one aspect is the individual and particular nature of things; the other aspect is the general nature of concepts. . . . Objective truth is demonstrated in the unity of generality and particularity." [35]

Mao has refined his understanding of the subject–object contradiction by defining it as a contradiction between reality and the conceptualization of it. Reality is specific, conceptualization is general. Idealism is excessive dependence on the generality of conceptualization, whereas mechanistic materialism is excessive dependence on the particularity of the outside material world. Ob-

jective truth depends on the active interaction between particularist reality and general conceptualization. This, concluded Mao in
1940, is the validity of dialectical materialism, with its emphasis on
the unity of general theory and specific practice.

In this period Mao was not only concerned with practice-
oriented knowledge, but also wished to discard the Soviet model
for China. In several places he pointed out that Bolshevik experience
was not automatically applicable to China. Strategic practice in
China should adapt Marxist value to the specific conditions of
China. In "Strategic Problems of China's Revolutionary War"
(December, 1936), he said: "They do not know that we should
cherish Soviet experience, and cherish it more than the experiences
of other countries throughout history. . . . But we should cherish
even more China's experience in revolutionary war, because there
are many conditions peculiar to the Chinese revolution and the
Chinese red army." [36] And in his October, 1938, report, "On the
New Stage," Mao pointed out: "In Britain, the United States,
France, Germany, Japan, and other countries, it is not possible to
maintain a protracted peasant war from the countryside against the
cities. . . . But a large semicolonial country such as the China of
today can undertake this type of war." [37]

He certainly implied that Russian experience belonged to the
former group, and therefore was inappropriate for China. While
de-emphasizing the function of the Soviet model, he began to hint
that the Chinese model was more appropriate for other semicolonial and colonial countries.[38]

The civil-war period, from 1940 to 1949

Much happened during this period. At the beginning, relations between the C.C.P. and the Kuomintang deteriorated. In 1942 the
C.C.P. undertook the *cheng-feng* ("rectification") movement.
During the later stage of the Second World War, both the C.C.P.
and the Kuomintang were preoccupied with their civil-war maneu-
vers. When V-J Day arrived, the race was on for both parties to
reoccupy territories held by the Japanese during the war. From
1945 to 1947, the United States sponsored a precarious truce between the parties, and tried to induce them to negotiate a political

settlement. But in 1947 civil war broke out, culminating in the Chinese communist victory of 1949.

For Mao this period was intellectually barren. He was preoccupied with revolutionary practice, and was no longer seeking new correlations. In his writings and speeches he merely mouthed the intellectual position at which he had arrived in the previous period. He continued to emphasize theory as practice-oriented knowledge. In the second preface to "Village Investigation" (March, 1941), he insisted: "The only method to understand conditions is to investigate society, to investigate the living conditions of the various classes in society . . . to use the basic viewpoint of Marxism—the method of class analysis." [39]

Mao's only excursion into theory was in connection with the *cheng-feng* movement of 1942.[40] There, typically, he summarized the correlation between Marxist theory and Chinese practice: "The 'target' is the Chinese revolution, the 'arrow' is Marxism-Leninism. We Chinese communists seek this 'arrow' *for no other purpose than to* hit the 'target' of the Chinese revolution and the revolution of the East" [41] (Italics added).

If there was any new emphasis here, it was Mao's concern with two types of subjectivist deviation: One, dogmatism, excessive reliance upon abstract theory; the other, empiricism, excessive dependence on experience. As far as he was concerned, dogmatism represented a greater threat than empiricism; [42] party sectarianism and party "eight-legged" formalism were manifestations of subjectivism.[43]

In his speeches and writings of this period, Mao tried to maintain his concept of practice-oriented knowledge and to avoid deviations to the right and left. In "On Coalition Government" (April, 1945), he said: "Dogmatism departs from concrete practice, whereas empiricism mistakes partial experience for universal truth; both kinds of opportunistic thought go against Marxism." [44]

The same concern emerged during the last two years of the civil war just before the victory of 1949, when Mao had to caution against excessive optimism and dogmatism.[45] Finally, in September, 1949, he saw the communist victory as the triumph of the historical materialist view of history over the bourgeois idealist view of history.[46] This was a return to his concept of the rivalry between the idealism of the oppressor class and the materialism of the oppressed class, as explained in "Dialectical Materialism" (1940).

The post-1949 period, following the revolutionary victory

The wars of the 1940's did not alter the political tendency in China. They merely accelerated its development. Since the late twenties, the Kuomintang under Chiang had depended increasingly on the support of the moderate and preservative elements in China. Chiang's approach to politics had been a combination of traditionalist nationalism and Confucian ethics, as the superstructure for his military basis of power. On the other hand, since the late twenties, the Chinese communist movement under Mao increasingly justified its military power in terms of the reconciliation of Marxist values with Chinese revolutionary practice. Mao throughout his career has solicited the support of the impoverished, discontented masses in China. Military power was necessary in schismatic China, where the cohesion of traditional society had collapsed. But the chance for practice-oriented Marxism to reintegrate westernizing, schismatic China was greater than for tradition-oriented nationalism.[47] As the war exposed the chaotic situation of China, the manipulative relevancy of Maoist ideology increased at the expense of the conservative Kuomintang ideology.

Fortune is not made by man. But individuals can exploit fortune when it emerges. Mao's victory in 1949 testified to his ability to seize the opportunity for power which China's chaotic situation granted him. Yet this victory was a much less unexpected event than the Bolshevik victory of 1917. The latter opened an entirely new era in Marxist revolutionary politics, the former was another confirmation of it. However, since Mao had always insisted on the unity of Marxist theory and Chinese practice, the victory of 1949 was a confirmation of his correlation of theory and practice.

Optimism is the keynote to Mao's intellectual orientation in the post-1949 period. In September, 1949, he said: "We believe that revolution can change everything, and that before long there will arise a new China with a big population and a great wealth of products, where life will be abundant and culture will flourish. All pessimistic views are utterly groundless."[48]

In this period Mao confidently revised theory to relate it to the new practice of socialist construction. Such theoretical revision is already evident in the 1951 version of "On Contradiction." In the 1930's, when Mao had talked about contradiction, he meant the contradiction between subjective thought and objective reality. In "Dialectical Materialism" of 1940, he saw idealism and materialism as two possible correlations between subjective thought and objective reality. In the 1940's he introduced no new elements into his understanding of the subject–object contradiction. Now, in the 1951 version of "On Contradiction," he saw contradiction as a universal principle underlying all processes of development, yet with each contradiction possessed of its own particularity.[49] He implied that even in a socialist society contradictions exist, though of a different, nonantagonistic type.[50] In "On the Historical Experience of the Dictatorship of the Proletariat" (April, 1956), he said: "To deny the existence of contradictions is to deny dialectics. The contradictions in various societies differ in character, so do the forms of their solution, but society at all times develops through continual contradictions. Socialist society also develops through contradictions between the productive forces and the conditions of production." [51] And in "On the Correct Handling of Contradictions among the People" (February, 1957), he said: "Contradictions in a socialist society are fundamentally different from contradictions in old societies, such as capitalist society. Contradictions in capitalist society find expression in acute antagonisms and conflicts, in sharp class struggle, which cannot be resolved by the capitalist system itself. . . . Contradictions in socialist society are, on the contrary, not antagonistic and can be resolved one after the other by the socialist system itself." [52]

However, theoretical justification could not resolve the problem of the practice of socialist construction. Soviet experience as well as the needs of a one-party dictatorship in a developing society indicated the direction of political centralization and economic modernization, after the revolution. The crucial problem was not the direction of socialist construction, but its *pace*. On this issue Mao did not rely on the Soviet experience. In *The Question of Agricultural Co-operation* (July, 1955), he said: "The Soviet Union's great historical experience in building socialism inspires our people and gives them full confidence. . . . However, there are different ways of looking at this question of international experience." Mao criticized those who believed that, because Stalin had failed in his agricultural collectivization in the early 1930's, China should not try to accelerate her agricultural collectivization.[53]

In such a situation, said Mao, the pace of socialist construction should depend on the interaction between a conscious party and mobilized mass support. In September, 1949, he had claimed: "Of all things in the world, people are the most precious. Under the leadership of the C.C.P., as long as there are people, every kind of miracle can be performed." [54] He repeated this in July, 1955: "We must believe in the masses; we must believe in our party; these are the two cardinal principles. If we doubt these principles, we can do nothing." [55]

Mao's emphasis on the unity of party and masses in the post-1949 era is no idle phrase-mongering. The victory of 1949 confirmed the pragmatic validity of his brand of practice-oriented Marxist consciousness. That victory also confirmed the pragmatic validity of his type of mass mobilization. Both party consciousness and mass mobilization had been necessary for that victory. Therefore, after 1949 he depended on their correlation as the key for the pace of socialist construction.

Moreover, the victory of 1949 forced Mao to generalize the validity of the Chinese communist revolutionary experience. Since 1927, for the sake of practice-oriented knowledge, he had emphasized China's specific characteristics; and since 1935 he had pointed out that the Soviet model was not applicable for her. In the late 1930's, he began to hint that the new democratic model of China might be more appropriate for other semicolonial and colonial countries than the Soviet model.[56] Now, after 1949, a significant competition started between the new democratic model and the Soviet model. This was especially true for 1949–1951 and since 1957.[57] As explained in a footnote to the 1951 edition of *Hsüan-chi:* "Just as the Chinese people have done, all or at least some of the colonial peoples in the East can hold for an extended period big or small base areas and revolutionary regimes, carry on a protracted revolutionary war to encircle the cities from the countryside, and proceed gradually to take over the cities and win nation-wide victory in their respective countries." [58]

In the optimistic atmosphere after 1949, Mao revised theory to justify postrevolutionary practice, paced the domestic socialist construction of China in accordance with the ability of the party to mobilize the masses, and sought abroad the general validity of China's new democratic model against the Soviet model.

THE MAOIST IDEA OF CHINA

Mao's idea of China has been an integral part of his practice-oriented knowledge. It did not motivate his revolutionary practice, rather the idea depended upon the exigency of his revolutionary practice. But the idea as the justification for his practice cannot depend entirely upon the requirements of practice. To the extent that he wants to remain a Marxist revolutionary in China, Mao must also fit his specific idea of China into the general process of Marxism. Thus the Maoist idea of China is neither sound scholarly knowledge, nor good Marxist theory. It has rather been the result of his reconciliation of the conflicting demands of Chinese revolutionary practice and universal Marxist values. This reconciliation varied from one period to another.

The initial Marxist period, from 1920 to 1926

"Analysis of the Classes in Chinese Society" was the most extensive article written by Mao from this initial period. Here he described China as "economically backward and semicolonial." [59] But he insisted on the similarity between Chinese class attitudes and Western class attitudes. He claimed: "In any country, anywhere, there are three categories of people: upper, middle, and lower. If analyzed in more detail, there are five categories: the big-property class, the middle-property class, the small-property class, the semi-propertyless class [sic], and the propertyless class." [60]

The terms *tzu-ch'an chieh-chi* and *wu-ch'an chieh-chi* have become the Chinese translations for "bourgeoisie" and "proletariat." However, literally, they mean propertied class and class without property. Mao, in this article, did not know enough

Marxist theory, and mistook these terms in their literal Chinese meanings. Therefore he applied the five-class spectrum to both the rural and urban segments of Chinese society.

Mao's concept of class was un-Marxist. In Marxist terminology, class is not based specifically upon wealth or property, but rather upon social relations to the economic mode of production. In different economic modes, there are different types of wealth or property. But for Mao, failing to distinguish different modes of production and urban-rural class relations, social structure was a pyramid based simply upon wealth.

In addition, in his analysis of class relations, Mao placed more weight upon the population figure, than upon the Marxist analysis of the economic and political structure of power. The reliance upon quantity is revealed in the chart on the next page, taken from Mao's article.[61]

On the basis of this chart, Mao concluded that the "big-property class" represented the enemies of the revolution, whereas the small-property, the "semi-propertyless," and the propertyless classes were all friends. The "middle-property class" he considered to be vacillating. "How numerous are our real friends? 395 million. How numerous are our enemies? One million." [62] Even if the "middle-property class" were to side with the "big-property class," Mao claimed, it would still be 395 million against 5 million!

These figures were all imaginary, and the ratio of 395:5 was fantastic. In this analysis, Mao considered the industrial proletariat the main revolutionary force, and the urban coolies the main supporting force. Next in importance were the "agrarian property-less class," the peddlers, and the poor peasants. Then came the shop assistants, the handicraftsmen, and the "semi-wealthy" peasants. Mao adroitly combined acceptance of the urban orientation of the official Comintern-C.C.P. line with recognition of the rural numerical superiority.

The idea of China as contained in this article typified Mao's intellectual development during his initial Marxist period. It revealed poor understanding of Marxist theory and was the result of rigidly fitting Chinese society into a set of pseudo-Marxist categories of thought. Mao relied too much on projected quantitative figures and had too much revolutionary enthusiasm.[63]

Class	Quantity	Attitude to the Revolution
THE BIG-PROPERTY CLASS	1,000,000	extremely antirevolutionary
THE MIDDLE-PROPERTY CLASS	4,000,000	right-wing antirevolutionary, left-wing hostile yet may join revolution, entire class as a whole antirevolutionary
THE SMALL-PROPERTY CLASS (TOTAL):	150,000,000	
the wealthy right wing	15,000,000	in peace antirevolutionary, in war may become revolutionary
the satisfied middle wing	75,000,000	in peace neutral, in war will join revolution
the dissatisfied left wing	60,000,000	will welcome the revolution
THE SMALL-PROPERTY CLASS (TOTAL):	200,000,000	
the semi-landholders	50,000,000	will join the revolution
the semi-wealthy peasants	60,000,000	will decidedly join the revolution
the poor peasants	60,000,000	will bravely struggle for the revolution
the handicraftsmen	24,000,000	same as the semi-wealthy peasants
the shop assistants	5,000,000	same as the semi-wealthy peasants
the peddlers	1,000,000	same as the poor peasants
THE PROPERTYLESS CLASS (TOTAL):	45,000,000	
the industrial proletariat	2,000,000	the main force of the revolution
the urban coolies	3,000,000	main support for industrial proletariat
the agrarian propertyless	20,000,000	will bravely struggle for the revolution
the roving propertyless	20,000,000	can be converted to revolutionary asset

Nevertheless, in spite of these ideological fetters, this specific idea of China showed Mao's desire to come to grips with what he considered to be the reality of revolutionary and counter-revolutionary forces in China. In his desire to reach that reality, he relied on mass support and indigenous discontent, rather than on Marxist theoretical dictate and external anti-imperialist agitation. Typically, in this article, the counter-revolutionary classes were allied with the external imperialists, whereas the revolutionary classes were indigenous. The article is not significant for its poor theory, but for its desire to understand Chinese reality.

The formative Maoist period, from 1927 to 1935

The shift to a reliance upon the internal forces of China, without the rigidity of an externally superimposed strategic dictate, became apparent in Mao's "Report on an Investigation of the Peasant Movement in Hunan" (February, 1927). Mao claimed: "The further development of the peasant movement is a tremendous problem. Within a short time, hundreds of millions of peasants will rise in Central, South and North China, with the fury of a hurricane; no power, however strong, can restrain them. . . . All revolutionary parties and comrades will be judged by them. Are we to get in front of them and lead them or criticize them behind their backs or fight them from the opposite camp?" [64]

Falling back upon his quantitative approach, Mao considered the peasantry to constitute 70 percent of those supporting the democratic revolution, with the urban forces accounting for the remaining 30 percent.[65] Within the peasantry, his estimate of the ratio between the rich, moderately wealthy, and poor peasants has shifted to become 10 percent rich peasants, 20 percent moderately wealthy peasants, and 70 percent poor peasants.[66]

Therefore, Mao concluded in the report, "it is the rising up of the democratic forces in the countryside to overthrow the feudal forces in the villages, which is the true goal of the revolution." [67] In the rural democratic revolution, "this leadership by the poor peasants is very essential. Without them, there will be no revolution." [68]

The need to recognize the internal forces of China lead Mao, in this period, to seek the characteristics of contemporary China. He abandoned his previous emphasis on the equivalence between Western and Chinese classes. He did this with a minimum dependence on Marxist category of thought.

In his 1928 draft resolution for the Second Party Conference of the Hunan-Kiangsi Border Area, Mao justified the prospect of his communist insurrection movement upon a unique combination of factors: warfare within the white political power, the legacy of the national revolution of 1925–1927, the continuation of a revolutionary situation, and the presence of a Red army and a well-organized communist party.[69] In his November, 1928 report to the Central Committee from the Chingkang mountains, he again emphasized the peculiar combination of factors in China. This time he singled out the following: a sound mass basis, a sound party, a red army of adequate strength, a terrain favorable for military operation, and a self-sufficing economy.[70]

In his January 5, 1930, letter to Lin Piao, he analyzed China in a long series of contradictions—contradictions within imperialism, between imperialism and colonies, between imperialism and the proletariat, within the Chinese ruling classes, between the ruling classes and the broad masses, between imperialism and Chinese capital, between the Chinese bourgeoisie and the Chinese proletariat, within the landlord class, between the landlord class and the peasantry, and so on.[71] What emerged from this analysis was the image of an essentially structureless society filled with tension and strife. Finally, in Proclamation No. 1 of the Central Executive Committee of the Chinese Soviet Republic, December 1, 1931, Mao saw the contradiction in Chinese society as between "the warlords, bureaucrats, landlords, and capitalists" on the one hand, and "the workers, peasants, soldiers, and toilers" on the other.[72]

Mao's idea of China in this period primarily sought to justify his strategy of a peasant-based, armed insurrection movement. In this justification Mao emphasized the characteristics of contemporary China. These were the rural basis of Chinese society and mass discontent, and a series of factors which favored the development of an armed insurrection movement. The emphasis on China's characteristics was necessary for the pragmatic success of revolutionary strategy. It was made possible by Mao's inclination to rely upon the indigenous forces within a society and to solicit mass support. It was not related to the universalist demand of Marxist theoretical value.

The goal of this armed insurrection movement, based on the characteristics of contemporary China, was a reorganization of Chinese society along the Soviet model. In 1934, Mao said: "Rural soviet (and city soviet) is the basic organization of the soviet system. It is that level of soviet most in touch with the masses. And it is that organ directly leading the masses to carry out the various revolutionary tasks of the soviet system." [73]

In his report to the Second All-China Soviet Congress, he insisted that "only the soviet and the red army can save China." [74] The tension and strife in economically backward, semicolonial China brought closer the goal of a soviet form of government. Mao's idea of China in this period was an adaptation of China to the Soviet model. Theoretical Marxism was practically ignored.

The mature Maoist period, from 1935 to 1940

In "Strategic Problems of China's Revolutionary War" (December, 1936), Mao continued to emphasize the characteristics of contemporary China. He summarized them as follows:

> A vast semicolonial country that is unevenly developed politically and economically and that has gone through a great revolution; a powerful enemy; a weak and small red army; and the agrarian revolution—these are the four principal characteristics of China's revolutionary war. From these characteristics are determined the guiding line for China's revolutionary war and its strategic and tactical principles. From the first and fourth characteristics emerged the possibility of the Chinese red army growing and defeating the enemy. From the second and third characteristics emerged the impossibility of the red army growing quickly or defeating the enemy quickly, but rather the possibility of the strategy of protracted war, and if things go wrong the possibility of defeat.[75]

However, within such characteristics, Mao in the previous period emphasized the "antifeudal" revolution. Now he shifted to the "anti-imperialist" revolution.[76] The shift camouflaged the relative weakness of the Chinese communist movement immediately after the Long March, by using the more popular slogan of anti-Japanese nationalism. It included the national bourgeoisie into the revolutionary bloc of the proletariat, the peasantry, and the petty bourgeoisie.[77] As late as May, 1937, Mao still insisted that "the tasks of China's anti-imperialist, antifeudal bourgeois democratic revolution, as proven in history, cannot be accomplished through the leadership of the bourgeoisie. They can be accomplished only through the leadership of the proletariat." [78]

But with the start of the Sino-Japanese War, Mao immediately changed this position. In September of the same year, he conceded: "It is impossible to put the program into practice without the agreement of the Kuomintang, because the Kuomintang remains at present China's biggest ruling party. Without its agreement, it is not possible to carry out the program throughout the country." [79]

For Mao, this was the strategy of the revolution in China. It was both anti-imperialist and antifeudal. But the shift of emphasis from one to the other depended on his estimate of the external and internal factors. After each shift a realignment of the revolutionary forces became necessary. In an anti-imperialist revolution, it was the four-bloc coalition of the proletariat, peasantry, petty bourgeoisie, and national bourgeoisie; in an antifeudal revolution the coalition contracted to the first three groups.[80] Mao is a voluntarist with a distinct sense of the reality of mass discontent. He predicated his revolutionary enthusiasm on his estimate of the characteristics of China. He has no commitment to the fundamental importance of social structure. For him, social structure can easily be manipulated for the sake of revolutionary prospect.

Actually the characteristics of China became the justification for Mao's revolutionary strategy. But as strategy began to shift in this period, he felt the need to seek a broader foundation for these characteristics. He did this along two lines, in the years 1936–1938: One, an emphasis on the inapplicability of the Soviet model for China,[81] and on the differences between big semicolonial China and other small colonial, semicolonial countries; [82] the other, an emphasis on China's recent history, with each stage of history different from, as well as preparing for, the next stage, and all stages being one linear process of development.[83] Both emphases sought to justify further the shifting strategy of Mao in this period.

This tendency to emphasize China's uniqueness and her historical particularism culminated in Mao's November, 1938, report to the Sixth Enlarged Plenum of the party's Central Committee, entitled "On the New Stage." Here he insisted that the anti-Japanese war was unprecedented in China's past. In fact, he continued, present-day China was unlike the capitalist countries, unlike the small semicolonial countries, even unlike the China of a few decades ago.[84] "On the basis of China's historical development, present-day China's anti-Japanese national united front, which is unlike any foreign united front such as the Front populaire, and also unlike the united front in China's past such as the first Kuomintang-C.C.P. co-operation, has present-day China's characteristics." [85]

The emphasis on China's uniqueness and her historical particularism indicated Mao's sensitivity to the particularist demands of China. This sensitivity is necessary for any successful revolutionary. However, Mao wishes to transform China in the name of a Western value system. Since 1937 he has become increasingly conscious of the universal demand of Marxist theory. Practice must be justified by universal theory, rather than by a simple appeal to characteristics. From this point of view, the report "On the New Stage" represented a turning point. In it, Mao claimed that "Marxism must be given a national form" and that national form involved the history of China. "Our nation has a history of several thousand years, a history which has its pattern of development, its national characteristics and is full of treasures. . . . The China of today has developed from the China in history; as we are believers in the marxist approach to history, we must not cut off our whole historical past." [86]

China's history was the link between the demand of China and the demand of Marxist values. Such a history had to take into account the characteristics of her past, thus justifying her uniqueness in the present. But it also had to be formulated in Marxist terms and be more or less integrated into the universal process of Marxist history. It was neither sound history nor good theory, but rather a reconciliation of the conflicting demands of the two. This is the purpose of history for Mao.

The concern with China's history became evident in Mao's article "The May Fourth Movement" (May, 1939):

> The process of China's bourgeois-democratic revolution . . . has passed through several stages of development: the Opium War, the Taiping movement, the Sino-Japanese war, the political changes of 1898, the Boxer movement, the Revolution of 1911, the May Fourth movement, the northern expedition, the warfare of the red army, etc. The anti-Japanese war of today is another new stage in its development. . . . Beginning with the Opium War, each stage in the development of the revolution has *its own distinct character and distinct appearance*, its characteristics. However, taken as a whole, they all bear the character of the bourgeois–democratic revolution. *This character is a fundamental one, commonly shared by the quantitatively different stages.* . . . [The democratic society] *came from the feudal society and will pass into the socialist society, by completing its struggle in accordance with definite historical periodization"* [87] (Italics added).

History not only justified the characteristics of contemporary China, but also provided a generalized framework of gradational development, leading from one stage to another.

The idea of China as contained in "The Chinese Revolution and the C.C.P." (December, 1939) [88] and in "On New Democracy" (January, 1940) represented Mao's tendency to emphasize Chinese history. In these pamphlets Chinese history from Mao's Marxist viewpoint became the link between the characteristics of China and historical materialism.

Chapter 1 of "The Chinese Revolution and the C.C.P." sought to fit China's premodern past into the universal framework of the historical materialist process: "Developing along the same lines as the other *great* nations of the world, the Chinese nation (chiefly the Han) first went through some tens of thousands of years of life in *egalitarian*, classless primitive *communist society*. Up to now approximately *5000* years have passed since the collapse of the primitive *communist society* and the transition to class society, first slave society and then feudal society" [89] (Italics added).

The characteristic of feudal China was a self-sufficing natural economy; a feudal ruling class of landlords, nobility, and the emperor owning most of the land; an exploited peasantry, supporting the feudal class, the bureaucracy, and the army of the feudal state; and the feudal state of the landlord class. The main contradiction in this feudal society, according to Mao, was between the peasantry and the landlord class.

Since he viewed traditional, dynastic China rigidly as a feudal period in Marxist historiography, Mao had to explain why China "remained stationary for a long time." [90] He stated that "the gigantic scale of peasant riots and wars in Chinese history is absent in the history of the world." [91] However, without new productive forces and new classes, and new leadership, peasant riots and wars invariably failed. "Thus, after each peasant revolutionary struggle, although some progress was made, the feudal economic relations and the feudal political order basically remained unchanged." [92] Mao seemed to imply that no internal dynamics existed in feudal China, and ultimately changes would have to depend upon the introduction of external forces: "By the mid-nineteenth century, only with the invasion of foreign capital did a fundamental transformation within this society occur." [93]

With the advent of Western capitalism, within the past hundred years, China entered the semicolonial, semifeudal stage, said Mao. The characteristics of this stage are: The end of the natural self-sufficient economy, and the beginning of a partnership of feudal landlord exploitation with the exploitation of compradore and usurer capital; the weakness of national capitalism, because of its tie with foreign capitalism and domestic feudal remnants; the replacement of the autocracy of emperor and nobility by either the rule of warlords and bureaucrats, or the joint dictatorship of landlords and big bourgeoisie; the imperialist control of China's political and military power, as well as her financial and economic lifeline; the unevenness of China's development, because of imperialist partition and domestic disunity; the extreme impoverishment of the broad Chinese masses, especially the peasantry because of imperialist-feudal oppression.[94]

Against this background, Mao then in chapter 2 of "The Chinese Revolution and the C.C.P." answered questions regarding the revolution in China. He described it as a new democratic national revolution, involving a protracted military struggle against both foreign imperialism and domestic feudal remnants. The two-fold task of the revolution was first democracy and then socialism.

Besides the imperialists, the chief enemies at home were the big landlords and the compradore-capitalists. Mao optimistically estimated that "during a revolution against imperialism and big landlords [the middle and small landlords] would either remain neutral or temporarily join the struggle." [95]

The national bourgeoisie, in contrast to the compradore-capitalists has a dual character, and therefore is vacillating.[96] The petty bourgeoisie, consisting of the intelligentsia, the urban poor, the functionaries, the handicraftsmen, the professionals, and the small merchants, is a reliable ally in the revolution.[97] Of the peasantry, the middle and poor peasants are necessary allies; but sometimes even the rich peasants should be included.[98] The proletariat must realize that, although it is most conscious and best organized, it can not win the revolution by itself.[99] Concluded Mao: "Among all the classes in Chinese society, the peasantry is the firm ally of the working class, the urban petty bourgeoisie is a reliable ally, and the national bourgeoisie is an ally during certain periods and to a certain extent; this is one of the fundamental laws proven by the history of contemporary Chinese revolution." [100]

In "On New Democracy," Mao expanded what he had said in "The Chinese Revolution and the C.C.P." He emphasized the division between the democratic and the socialist stages of the Chinese revolution.[101] Before the First World War and the October Revolution, he said, the Chinese revolution was part of the old bourgeois democratic revolutions. But since then the Chinese revolution has become related to the international proletarian revolution. It is therefore a new bourgeois democratic revolution: "Since the May Fourth Movement, the leadership of the Chinese bourgeois democratic revolution no longer belongs *primarily* to the Chinese bourgeoisie *alone*, but *is participated jointly by* the Chinese proletariat" [102] (Italics added).

Mao distinguished this new democratic revolution from both the bourgeois democratic revolution of the West and the socialist revolution of Russia.[103] He insisted that this type of revolution was appropriate for other colonial and semicolonial countries.[104]

So far as the politics of new democracy was concerned, Mao projected a joint dictatorship of all revolutionary classes, and was permissive toward the bourgeoisie: "Today, whoever can lead the people to drive out Japanese imperialism and carry out democratic politics will be the savior of the people. *If the Chinese bourgeoisie is able to fulfill this responsibility, it will be greatly respected. If not, then this responsibility must fall upon the shoulders of the proletariat.*" [105] (Italics added).

As for the new democratic economy, Mao envisaged the nationalization of the big banks, the big industries, and the big commercial enterprises. "But, at the same time, it does not take over other capitalist private properties." [106] In the villages he envisaged the confiscation of "the land of the big landlords." [107]

New democratic culture, continued Mao, as the reflection of new democratic politics and economy, must be anti-imperialist and antifeudal. He said: "So far as national culture is concerned, it is at present not yet a socialist culture. It is wrong to assume that the national culture as a whole at present is or should be a socialist national culture. . . . We have not yet this kind of politics and economy, therefore cannot yet have this kind of national culture." [108]

The idea of China as contained in "The Chinese Revolution and the C.C.P." and "On New Democracy" represented the culmination of Mao's effort to clothe specific China in a universal Marxist garb. Primitive, ancient, and feudal China was viewed rigidly in the universal perspective of Marxist historiography. "Feudal" China, in spite of its peasant rebellions, lacked internal dynamics. The historicity of China's dynastic-bureaucratic past was sacrificed for the sake of the concept of feudalism. Yet, lacking immanent dynamics, the concept of feudal China was not good historical materialism. On the other hand, Mao saw China of the period after the Opium War increasingly in terms of specific, recognizable indigenous forces. His concept of semicolonial, semifeudal China was based on a combination of Chinese history with Marxist theory. For China after May Fourth, Mao's concept of the new democratic revolution emphasized the specificity of contemporary China, in contradistinction to both the Western and the Russian revolutionary models. [109]

The Maoist idea of China, from December, 1939 to January, 1940, sought to reconcile the conflicting demands of theory and practice. Therefore, premodern China was seen more in terms of the demand of Marxist theory, modern China in terms of the demands of practice. Mao approached contemporary China with even greater commitment to voluntarist practice than to Marxist theory.

The civil-war period, from 1940 to 1949

Throughout this period, Mao maintained his idea of a new democratic China, as the basic ideological justification for his revolutionary practice. There was no change in his idea, only a variation in accordance with practical shifts in tactics. In his November, 1941, speech to the Shensi-Kansu-Ninghsia Border Assembly, Mao said that "Chinese society is one with two small heads and a large body; the proletariat and the big landlords and capitalists are the minorities; the broadest group are the intermediate classes." [110] There was increasing competition between the two small heads, the C.C.P. and the Kuomintang, the latter representing the big landlord and capitalist interests. But actually, Mao's shifting tactics during the anti-Japanese united front depended upon realistic prospecting to enlarge the role of the C.C.P. at the expense of the Kuomintang, rather than upon any ideological commitment to the class analysis as contained in his idea of a new democratic China. In practice, Mao was much more opposed to the Kuomintang, although in theory he still equivocated. For example, in his concluding speech before the Yenan Forum on Art and Literature, in May, 1942, he said: "We should also co-operate with those elements within the landlord and capitalist classes who are still resisting the Japanese, but we must not forget that they oppose a broadly based democracy for the Chinese people." [111]

Practice is fundamental, theory justifies practice. In April, 1945, Mao almost admitted as much, when he said that the Chinese communist demand for democratic representation was a means of propelling the C.C.P. into a coalition. But once the C.C.P. was in power, the situation would be entirely different.[112]

Mao's sense of competition between the C.C.P. and the Kuomintang increased in "On Coalition Government," his April, 1945 report to the Seventh National Congress of the party. In the report, he saw two prospects for China—either "a dictatorial fascist rule" under the Kuomintang,[113] or "a state of the united front of democratic alliance based on the overwhelming majority of the people." [114] His concept of a new democratic China was the ideological justification for the Chinese communist challenge against the Kuomintang.

Up until then, Mao has been primarily concerned with the indigenous forces and characteristics of China, as the justification for his practice. But since the mid-1940's, he sees an increasingly more favorable international situation, which enhances his optimism concerning the domestic development in China. The favorable international climate has been an addition, rather than a diversion, to his concern with China's characteristics. This trend became discernible in "On Coalition Government," where he prefaced his analysis of domestic China with the following assessment of the international scene:

> Contrary to the forecast of all reactionaries in China and abroad, the three great democracies of Britain, the United States, and the Soviet Union have consistently been united. Among them, there had been and will be certain controversies; but ultimately unity will prevail. . . . This condition is the product of the 1940's, during that most crucial turning point in world history. . . . Since the appearance of this condition, the world situation has been transformed. The entire fascist power and its followings will inevitably be eliminated.[115]

This optimism about the international situation by Mao continued into the immediate postwar period.[116] However, by the autumn of 1946, when he was interviewed by Anna Louise Strong, Mao saw the international situation much more as an open contention between American imperialism and the socialist democratic bloc:

> On the one hand, the U.S. imperialism is indeed preparing a war against the Soviet Union. . . . On the other hand, this propaganda is a smoke-screen put up by the U.S. reactionaries to cover many actual contradictions confronting U.S. imperialism. . . . The United States and the Soviet Union are separated by a vast zone which includes many capitalist, colonial and semi-colonial countries

in Europe, Asia, and Africa. Before the U.S. reactionaries have subjugated these countries, an attack on the Soviet Union is out of the question.[117]

This was the international framework in which Mao was to wage his struggle against the Kuomintang at home. Ideologically it was still an anti-imperialist, antifeudal revolution. Mao did not change his concept of a new democratic China. In this concept he could easily justify the transition from an anti-Japanese war to a civil war, as he did in early 1947: "The circumstances in which this situation has arisen are that U.S. imperialism and its running dog Chiang Kai-shek have replaced Japanese imperialism and its running dog Wang Ching-wei, and adopted the policies of turning China into a U.S. colony, launching a civil war and strengthening the fascist dictatorship." [118]

In this situation, Mao continued his strategy of a broadly based anti-imperialist, antifeudal united front. He insisted: "This is a very broad united front of the whole nation. In comparison with the united front in the period of the anti-Japanese resistance war, it is not only as broad in scope but has even deeper foundations." [119]

In late 1947, Mao saw the Chinese revolution reaching a turning point: "The strength of the world anti-imperialist camp has surpassed that of the imperialist camp. It is we, not the enemy, who are in the superior position. . . . We certainly should grasp our own destiny in our own hands. . . . This is the historic period in which world capitalism and imperialism are going down in their doom and world socialism and people's democracy are marching to victory." [120]

As the civil war turned in favor of the C.C.P., Mao with increasing frequency asserted that "the leadership in this revolution can and must be assumed by . . . the proletariat and the C.C.P." [121] Yet, at the same time, he continued to maintain a broad united-front strategy.[122]

In this entire period of shifting tactics from 1940 to 1949, Mao's idea of a new democratic revolutionary China did not fundamentally change. He evidently felt that this idea, a result of his correlation of the conflicting demands of theory and practice in late 1939 and early 1940, was sufficient to justify his practice and needed no further development.

The post-1949 period, after the revolutionary victory

The basic concern of the Maoist idea of China since 1949 has been with socialist construction. In "On the People's Democratic Dictatorship" (June, 1949), Mao provided a general guideline for the postrevolutionary development of new democratic China: "Our present task is to strengthen the people's state apparatus. . . . Given this condition, China can develop steadily, under the leadership of the working class and the communist party, from an agricultural into an industrial country, and from a new democratic into a socialist and communist society." [123] This, said Mao, would require the elimination of the landlord class and the bureaucrat–bourgeoisie, the remolding of the national bourgeoisie, the education of the peasantry, and the co-ordination between socializing agriculture and developing industry.[124]

For the first three years, from 1949 to 1952, efforts were directed toward political consolidation and economic restoration. Since 1953, the socialist economic plan was introduced.[125] But the problem of socialist construction led Mao to be concerned with the co-ordination between industrial and agricultural growth, and with the relation between economic growth and the sociopolitical development.

By the mid-1950's Mao began to emphasize the problem of co-ordination between industrial and agricultural growth:

In agriculture, under the conditions prevailing in our country, co-operation must precede the use of big machinery. We can see, then, that industry and agriculture, socialist industrialization and socialist transformation of agriculture, cannot on any account be separated, cannot be dealt with in isolation from each other. . . . What is more, there are two other things which some of our comrades do not think of linking up: The large funds which are needed to complete both national industrialization and the technical reconstruction of agriculture, and the fact that a considerable part of these funds is derived from agriculture.[126]

Within this co-ordination, Mao emphasized the growth of heavy industry. However, there are so many inherent financial and technical difficulties in economic growth, that Mao saw its solution and the prospect of accelerated economic growth as coming from the noneconomic sector. "The economic conditions of our country being what they are, technical reform will take longer than social reform." [127] Here is the key to the relationship between economic growth and sociopolitical development: development can accelerate growth. Mao's approach to the socialist construction of China is highly voluntarist.

The urge to accelerate the pace of socialist construction at home depended on Mao's general tone of voluntarist optimism since 1949. Herein lies the significance of his post-1949 correlation of theory and practice. In theory, the revised concept of nonantagonistic socialist contradiction enabled him to justify his manipulation of difficulties in postrevolutionary China.[128] In practice, the concept of the unity of conscious party and mobilized masses provided him with an indication of the possible pace of acceleration.[129]

However, in addition, Mao sought other ideological justifications. Domestically, by the second half of 1955, he felt conditions were favorable for acceleration: "In China, 1955 was the year of decision in the struggle between socialism and capitalism. . . . The first half of 1955 was murky and obscured by dark clouds. But in the second half, the atmosphere changed completely. . . . It is as if a raging tidal wave has swept away all the demons and ghosts." [130] Internationally, by November, 1957, after the orbiting of the first sputnik by the Soviet Union, Mao claimed: "The international situation has now reached a new turning point. There are two winds in the world today: the east wind and the west wind. . . . I think the specific characteristic of the situation today is the east wind prevailing over the west wind. That is to say, the socialist forces are overwhelmingly superior to the imperialist forces." [131]

All these factors were behind Mao's decision for the Great Leap Forward and the promotion of people's communes, in 1958. As Peter Schran pointed out in "On the Rationality of the Great Leap Forward and Rural People's Commune," one of the basic factors influencing the decision for acceleration was the belief in greater voluntarist emphasis within the sociopolitical sphere.[132] It is within this framework that we should evaluate the article by Mao, in April, 1958; he said:

Throughout the country, the communist spirit is surging forward. The political consciousness of the masses is rising rapidly. . . . The decisive factor, apart from leadership by the party, is our six hundred million people. . . . Apart from other characteristics, China's six hundred million people are, first of all, poor, and, secondly, "blank." That may seem like a bad thing, but it is really a good thing. Poor people want change, want to do things, want revolution. A clean sheet of paper has no blotches and so the newest and most beautiful words can be written on it, the newest and most beautiful picture can be painted on it.[133]

It is not the poor and blank people alone, but rather the people mobilized under the leadership of the party, which will promote the acceleration of socialist construction in China. The party possesses Maoist ideological consciousness and experience, and the people have proved in the past their revolutionary spontaneity. Together, they will be more important than the economic structure. What emerges is a highly voluntarist idea of China, whose direction and pace of growth will depend much more upon socio-political mobilization, than upon economic reality.*

AN EVALUATION

Ever since his pre-Marxist days, in the late 1910's, Mao has been a voluntarist in his approach to knowledge. Since 1920, and especially since the thirties, this has become practice-oriented approach to Marxist theory. His idea of China has been an integral part of both his theory and practice. It changes, in different periods, in accordance with his changing correlation of theory and practice.

From 1920 to 1926, during his initial Marxist period, Mao was not familiar with Marxist theory. He followed the Comintern-C.C.P. dictate of supporting the Kuomintang in an urban-oriented national revolution. By emphasizing the basic similarity between

* Since 1958, pronouncements by Mao have been infrequent. The policies and attitudes of Communist China are definitely based upon the post-1949 Maoist idea of China. However, since this is specifically a study of the Marxian-Leninist-Maoist ideas of China, and not a general study of Marxist ideas of China, I shall end the chapter here, and not delve into the post-1958 Chinese communist idea of China.

Western and Chinese social classes and their attitudes, he saw Chinese society in a rigid Western-oriented perspective. Yet, he wanted to reach the reality of social discontent in China.

In his formative period, from 1927 to 1935, Mao seemed even less interested in Marxist theory than before. He was primarily concerned with the adaptation of revolutionary practice to the reality of peasant discontent in China. To justify this adaptation he abandoned the insistence on the Western equivalence of the Chinese social structure, and began to emphasize the characteristics of contemporary China. The revolution in economically backward, semicolonial China would be a protracted armed struggle, with the goal of promoting the Soviet model.

During his mature period, from 1935 to 1940, Mao continued to emphasize the characteristics of China. But he now pointed out the inappropriateness of the Bolshevik experience for semicolonial, semifeudal China. Instead, he sought a theoretical framework for his specific China. In the process, China's history became for him the link between the conflicting demands of theory and practice. He saw the new democratic China more in terms of the specific demands of practice, and premodern China more in terms of the universality of the Marxist historical process.

From 1940 to 1949 Mao was preoccupied with revolutionary practice and not much interested in theory. He maintained his correlation of theory and practice and his idea of China, as developed in the previous period. There was no new development.

Since 1949 Mao has been preoccupied with the practice of socialist construction. He introduced the concept of nonantagonistic contradiction in socialist society, to justify his peculiarly manipulative practice. He continues to insist that Bolshevik experience is not appropriate for China, but now emphasizes the general validity of China's new democratic model for other colonial and semicolonial countries. Within this framework, his idea of China emphasizes the voluntarist role of conscious party and mobilized masses, at the expense of the economic and social factors in society. The superstructure has assumed substructural importance.

Mao began by seeing Chinese society in a rigid Western perspective. But increasingly he pointed out the characteristics of

China, as the basis for justifying his revolutionary practice. However, he contained specific China within the universal framework of historical materialism. He ends up with a China under the impact of his own postrevolutionary correlation of revised theory and voluntarist practice.

Notes

Introduction (pp. xi–xiv)

1. Cf. the distinction in William Dray, *Laws and Explanation in History* (London, 1957), pp. 156 ff.

2. Concerning perspective, cf. Karl Mannheim, *Ideology and Utopia: An Introduction to the Sociology of Knowledge* (New York, n.d.), pp. 103–108. Concerning presupposition, cf. R. G. Collingwood, *An Essay on Metaphysics* (Oxford, 1940), pp. 21–33.

3. "The mechanical and static comparison of institutions . . . fails to do justice to their dynamic functional relationships. . . . It is the task of the comparative historian to detect and interpret the variety of functions and relationships which an institution, a style of thought or art, an administrative or economic structure, or a political system may have had in the context of the periods and cultures studied." M. Raeff, "Russia's Perception of Her Relationship with the West," *Slavic Review*, XXIII (1964), 18–19.

4. As will be evident from what follows, my approach to the study of the Marxist ideas of China is historical, with emphasis on intrinsic differentiation due to contextual changes. On the other hand, K. Wittfogel approaches his study of the Marxist ideas of China in terms of theoretical and typological concerns. Cf. his *Oriental Despotism: A Comparative Study of Total Power* (New Haven, 1957) and "The Marxist View of China," *China Quarterly*, No. 11 (July–September, 1962), 1–20; No. 12 (October–December, 1962), 154–169. Inevitably, with different perspectives the results will vary. Since I approach thoughts in correlation with their changing contexts, I have not discussed the question of how original is Maoism. For that controversy, cf. K. Wittfogel and B. Schwartz, "The Legend of 'Maoism,'" *China Quarterly*, No. 1 (January–March, 1960), 72–86; No. 2 (April–June, 1960), 16–42.

Notes to Chapter I (pp. 1–29)

1. G. W. Leibniz, *The Preface to Novissima Sinica* (Honolulu, 1957), pp. 69–70.

2. Chapter I, "Essay on the Customs and the Spirit of Nations," in *Voltaire: The Age of Louis XIV and Other Selected Writings,* ed. J. H. Brumfitt (New York, 1963), pp. 274–285.

3. F. Quesnay, *Oeuvres économiques et philosophiques,* ed. A. Oncken (Frankfurt, 1888), p. 577.

4. *Ibid.,* p. 605.

5. Montesquieu, *Oeuvres complètes* (Paris, 1950), I, i, 171.

6. J. G. von Herder, *Outlines of a Philosophy of the History of Man* (London, 1800), pp. 291, 295, 297.

7. G. Hegel, *Lectures on the Philosophy of History* (London, 1894), pp. 121–145.

8. E. Rose, "China as a Symbol of Reaction in Germany, 1830–1880," *Comparative Literature*, III (1951–1952), 60–64.

9. A. Reichwein, *China and Europe: Intellectual and Artistic Contacts in the Eighteenth Century* (London, 1925), p. 150.

10. A. H. Rowbotham, *Missionary and Mandarin: The Jesuits at the Court of China* (Berkeley, 1942), pp. 256–257.

11. Mary G. Mason, *Western Concepts of China and the Chinese, 1840–1876* (New York, 1939), p. 11.

12. E. Cassirer, *The Philosophy of the Enlightenment* (Boston, 1955), pp. 209–220.

13. R. G. Collingwood, *The Idea of History* (Oxford, 1946), p. 78.

14. Cf. *ibid.*, pp. 59 ff.

15. Cf. R. G. Collingwood, *The Idea of Nature* (Oxford, 1945), pp. 127–129.

16. Hegel, *op. cit.*, pp. 9–10.

17. *Ibid.*, p. 66.

18. *Ibid.*, pp. 18–19.

19. G. Lichtheim, *Marxism: An Historical and Critical Study* (New York, 1961), p. 142.

20. In recent decades, scholars in the West have tended to emphasize the Hegelian heritage of the young Marx, in contradistinction to the analysis of the capitalist dynamics by the mature Marx. Specifically, this new emphasis involves the young Marx's concern with the Hegelian concept of alienation. Cf. R. C. Tucker, *Philosophy and Myth in Karl Marx* (Cambridge, 1961), pp. 11–27, 167–168. But in this work I wish to single out the other aspect of the Hegelian heritage in the young Marx, namely his concern with an immanent process of universal history. Along this line, cf. H. Popitz, *Der entfremdete Mensch: Zeitkritik und Geschichtsphilosophie des jungen Marx* (Basel, 1953) and B. F. Hoselitz, "Karl Marx on Secular and Social Development," *Comparative Studies in Society and History*, VI (1963–64), 142–163.

21. Karl Marx, *Early Writings* (London, 1963), pp. 120 ff.

22. K. Marx and F. Engels, *Historisch-kritische Gesamtausgabe: Werke, Schriften, Briefe* (Moscow, 1927 ff.), I, v, 11.

23. *Ibid.*, p. 12.

24. *Ibid.*, p. 14.

25. *Ibid.*, pp. 39 ff.

26. K. Marx and F. Engels, *Manifesto of the Communist Party* (New York, 1932), p. 9.

27. K. Marx, *A Contribution to the Critique of Political Economy* (Chicago, 1904), p. 13.

28. K. Marx, *Grundrisse der Kritik der politischen Ökonomie (Rohentwurf), 1857–1858* (Berlin, 1953), pp. 375 ff.

29. *Ibid.*, p. 386.

30. K. Marx, *Capital*, Vol. I: *The Process of Capitalist Production* (Chicago, 1906), p. 536.

31. K. Marx and F. Engels, *The Russian Menace to Europe* (Glencoe, Ill., 1952), p. 217.

32. *The Origin of the Family*, p. 19.

33. *Ibid.*, pp. 150–151.

34. *Ibid.*, pp. 158–159.

35. *Ibid.*, p. 23.

36. K. A. Wittfogel, "The Ruling Bureaucracy of Oriental Despotism: A Phenomenon that Paralyzed Marx," *The Review of Politics*, XV (1953), 350.

37. A. Smith, *An Enquiry into the Nature and Causes of the Wealth of Nations*, ed. E. Cannan, 5th ed. (New York, 1937), pp. 348, 360, 362, 645, 688, 789–790.

38. R. Jones, *An Essay on the Distribution of Wealth and on the Sources of Taxation* (London, 1831), pp. 109, 112–113, 139.

39. J. S. Mill, *Principle of Political Economy, with Some of Their Applications to Social Philosophy* (Boston, 1848), I, 16–18, 209, 503–504.

40. Marx and Engels, *Gesamtausgabe*, III, i, 476, 481.

41. F. Bernier, *Voyages de François Bernier, Contenant la Description des Etats du Grand Mogol, de l'Indoustan, du Royaume de Cashemire, etc.* (Paris, 1830), pp. 280, 316, 317.

42. Marx and Engels, *Gesamtausgabe*, III, i, 477, 480.

43. *Ibid.*, p. 480.

44. *Ibid.*, p. 486.

45. *Ibid.*, p. 487.

46. K. Marx, *Articles on India*, 2d ed. (Bombay, 1951), p. 24.

47. *Ibid.*, p. 26.

48. *Ibid.*, pp. 28–29.

49. Volume I of *Capital* was published in 1867; subsequent volumes were published after Marx's death, in 1885 (ed. F. Engels), in 1894 (ed. F. Engels), and in 1904 (ed. K. Kautsky).

50. Marx, *Capital*, I, 89.

51. *Ibid.*, pp. 366–367.

52. *Ibid.*, p. 100.

53. K. Marx, *Capital*, Vol. III: *The Process of Capitalist Production as a Whole* (Chicago, 1909), p. 913.

54. *Ibid.*, I, 393–394.

55. *Ibid.*, III, 924–925.

56. *Ibid.*, I, 655–656.

57. *Ibid.*, p. 91.

58. *Ibid.*, p. 654.

59. Marx and Engels, *Gesamtausgabe*, I, viii, 319–320.

60. *Ibid.*, p. 165.

61. *Ibid.*, p. 185.

62. *Ibid.*, pp. 182–183.

63. *Ibid.*, I, iv, 279.

64. *Ibid.*, I, v, 35.

65. *Ibid.*, I, vi, 508.

66. *Ibid.*, p. 638.
67. Marx and Engels, *Manifesto of the Communist Party*, p. 10.
68. Cf. Marx and Engels, *Gesamtausgabe*, I, v, 44.
69. *Ibid.*, III, i, 303.
70. K. Marx and F. Engels, *Letters to Americans, 1848–1895: A Selection* (New York, 1953), p. 49.
71. Marx and Engels, *Gesamtausgabe*, III, i, 384.
72. K. Marx, *Marx on China, 1853–1860: Articles from The New York Daily Tribune* (London, 1951), p. 4.
73. *Ibid.*, p. 7.
74. *Ibid.*, p. 52.
75. *Ibid.*, p. 59.
76. *Ibid.*, p. 64.
77. Marx and Engels, *Gesamtausgabe*, III, ii, 340.
78. *Ibid.*, p. 342.
79. Marx, *Marx on China*, p. 66.
80. K. Marx and F. Engels, *The Civil War in the United States* (London, n.d.), pp. 17–18.
81. Mark and Engels, *Gesamtausgabe*, III, iii, 56.
82. *Ibid.*, p. 59.
83. *Ibid.*, III, iv, 256.
84. Marx, *Capital*, III, 480.
85. *Ibid.*, I, 31, preface by Engels.
86. F. Engels, *Condition of the Working Class in England in 1844*, tr. Wischnewetsky (London, 1892), p. vi.
87. K. Marx and F. Engels, *Selected Correspondence, 1846–1895* (New York, 1942), p. 500.
88. K. Marx, F. Engels and F. Lassalle, *Aus dem literarischen Nachlass von Karl Marx, Friedrich Engels und Ferdinand Lassalle* (Stuttgart, 1902), III, 444–445.
89. Marx, *Marx on China*, p. 2.
90. *Ibid.*
91. *Ibid.*, p. 4.
92. *Ibid.*, p. 45.
93. *Ibid.*, p. 55.
94. *Ibid.*, p. 56.
95. K. Marx and F. Engels, *Sochineniia* (Moscow, 1928 ff.), XII, ii, 360.
96. Marx, *Marx on China*, pp. 64, 87; Marx and Engels, *Gesamtausgabe*, III, ii, 342.
97. Marx, *Capital*, III, 121.
98. Marx, *Marx on China*, p. 90.
99. *Ibid.*, p. 3.
100. Marx, *A Contribution to the Critique of Political Economy*, pp. 153–154.
101. Marx, Engels, and Lassalle, *Aus dem literarischen Nachlass*, III, 444–445.
102. *Ibid.*, p. 445.
103. Marx, *Marx on China*, pp. 1–2.
104. *Ibid.*, p. 11.

105. *Ibid.*, p. 35.
106. *Ibid.*, p. 39.
107. *Ibid.*, p. 51.
108. *Ibid.*, p. 56.
109. *Ibid.*, p. 65.
110. Marx and Engels, *Sochineniia*, XII, ii, 360.
111. *Ibid.*, p. 362.
112. Marx and Engels, *Manifesto of the Communist Party*, p. 13.
113. Marx and Engels, *Gesamtausgabe*, III, ii, 342.
114. K. Marx, *Capital*, Vol. II: *The Process of Circulation of Capital* (Chicago, 1909), p. 44.
115. *Ibid.*, III, 393.
116. *Ibid.*, I, 493.
117. K. Marx and F. Engels, *Briefe an A. Bebel, W. Liebknecht, K. Kautsky und andere* (Moscow, 1933 ff.), I, 270.
118. Marx and Engels, *Selected Correspondence*, pp. 500–501.
119. F. Engels, *Aus der Frühzeit des Marxismus: Engels' Briefwechsel mit Kautsky* (Prague, 1935), p. 374.
120. "The Turkish Question" (April, 1953) in K. Marx, *The Eastern Question* (London, 1897), p. 21.
121. *Op. cit.* (n. 100), p. 29 n.
122. "Russia and the Social Revolution," in Marx and Engels, *The Russian Menace to Europe*, p. 203.
123. In "Russia and the Social Revolution" (1873), Engels wrote: "A person who says that this revolution can be carried out easier in a country which has no proletariat or bourgeoisie, proves by this statement that he has still to learn the ABC of socialism" (*ibid.*, p. 205). Any exception "can happen only if in western Europe a victorious proletarian revolution is achieved before the complete disintegration of communal property. This would provide the Russian peasant with the preconditions to such a transformation of society" (p. 213). In his 1877 reply to the article by N. K. Mikhailovskii, Marx indicated that "in recent years [Russia] has made great efforts in [the capitalist] direction" (p. 217). In the second draft of his letter to Vera Zasulich, 1881, Marx wrote that, if Russia were isolated, she must undergo the entire course of economic development. But the situation was fundamentally different. "It is contemporaneous with a superior civilization, it is tied to a world market in which capitalist production predominates. By appropriating the positive results of this mode of production, [Russia] is in a position to develop and transform the yet archaic form of its village community, instead of destroying it" (pp. 222–223). In his preface to the second Russian edition of the *Communist Manifesto*, 1882, Engels wrote: "If the Russian revolution sounds the signal for a proletarian revolution in the West (the decomposition of the communal ownership of land in Russia can be evaded), so that each complements the other, the prevailing form of communal ownership of land in Russia may form a starting-point for a communist course of development" (p. 228), [parenthesized clause stricken out from the original manuscript]. By 1890, in "The Foreign Policy of Russian Tsarism," Engels wrote: "The internal development of Russia since 1856 . . . has had its effect; the social

revolution has taken gigantic steps forward; Russia is becoming daily more westernized" (p. 51). Finally, in "Russia and the Social Revolution Reconsidered" (1894), Engels pointed out that each economy must resolve its own problems. Nevertheless, he grudgingly admitted that the communal background of Russia "may serve as the starting point of a communist development," provided that it comes "in harmony with a revolution in western Europe" (pp. 240–241).

124. The Chinese Marxists, basing themselves upon Mao's successful correlation of Western theory and Chinese practice, are attempting to substitute their new democratic model for the Western Marxist model, in analyzing other developing societies. On the other hand, some social scientists in the West are debating the applicability of the *Gemeinschaft-Gesellschaft* dual model for the study of the developing societies. Obviously, neither seem to feel it is possible to study a society without presupposition. This is an inevitable problem in perspective. As Gunnar Myrdal said: "The value-loaded terms have a meaning and represent a theoretical approach, because the theoretical approach itself is determined by the valuations in the governing *ethos* of a society" ("A Methodological Note on Facts and Valuations in Social Science," *An American Dilemma* [New York, 1944], p. 1063, quoted in L. Bramson, *The Political Context of Sociology* [Princeton, 1961], p. 147).

Notes to Chapter II (pp. 30–53)

1. There are numerous approaches in interpreting the phenomenon of the Russian intelligentsia. One school, beginning with Tkachev, tends to emphasize the intelligentsia's isolation and alienation from the rest of Russian society. Cf. P. N. Tkachev, *Izbrannye Sochineniia na sotsialno-politicheskie Temy*, ed. B. P. Kozmin (Moscow, 1922–1923), I, 282; P. Struve in *Viekhi: Sbornik Statei o russkoi Intelligentsii* (Moscow, 1909); P. Miliukov in K. Arsenev et al., *Intelligentsiia v Rossii: Sbornik Statei* (St. Petersburg, 1910), p. 188; N. Cherevanin in *Obshchestvennoe Dvizhenie v Rossii v Nachale XX-go Veka* (St. Petersburg, 1909), I, 259; D. N. Ovsianiko-Kulikovskii, *Sobranie Sochinenii* (Moscow, 1923–1924), VII, 9; T. G. Masaryk, *The Spirit of Russia*, 2d ed. (London, 1955), I, 124; and N. A. Berdiaev, *The Russian Idea* (New York, 1947), p. 30. Another school tends to emphasize the iconoclastic radicalism of the Russian intelligentsia. Cf. R. V. Ivanov-Razumnik, *Istoriia russkoi Obshchestvennoi Mysli* (St. Petersburg, 1911–1914), I, 24; G. B. Sliozberg, *Dorevolutsionnii Stroi Rossii* (Paris, 1933), p. 16; F. I. Dan, *Proiskhozdenie Bolshevizma* (New York, 1946), p. 32; H. E. Bowman, "Intelligentsia in Nineteenth-Century Russia," *Slavonic and East European Journal*, XV (1957), 20; F. Stepun, "The Russian Intelligentsia and Bolshevism," *Russian Review*, XVII (1958), 263; and S. Tompkins, *The Russian Intelligentsia* (Norman, Okla., 1957), p. 271. A more conservative school tends to emphasize the persistence of religious-philosophical preoccupations within the Russian intelligentsia. Cf. Berdiaev, *The Russian Idea*, p. 253; G. P. Fedotov, *The Russian Religious Mind*, Torchbook ed. (New York, 1960), p. 50; N. O. Losskii, *History of Russian Philosophy* (London, 1952), pp. 402–409; and V. V. Zenkovskii, *A History*

of Russian Philosophy (New York, 1953), I, 156. More recently new light has been thrown on this complex phenomenon. Cf. L. H. Haimson, *The Russian Marxists and Origins of Bolshevism* (Cambridge, Mass., 1955), p. 8 on the tension between consciousness and spontaneity; F. Venturi, *Roots of Revolution: A History of the Populist and Socialist Movements in Nineteenth-Century Russia* (New York, 1960), p. 285 on the tension between elite and masses; G. Fischer, "The Intelligentsia and Russia," *The Transformation of Russian Society*, ed. C. E. Black (Cambridge, Mass., 1960), pp. 253–273 on the conflict of generations; R. Pipes, "The Historical Evolution of the Russian Intelligentsia," *Daedalus*, LXXXIX (1960): *The Russian Intelligentsia*, pp. 487–488 on the relation between intelligentsia and westernization, and the distinction between cultural and philosophical westernization; and Alan P. Pollard, "The Russian Intelligentsia: The Mind of Russia," *California Slavic Studies*, III (Berkeley, 1964), 1–32 on the origins of the term itself in the 1860's and 1870's. For the bibliography of the Russian intelligentsia, see N. M. Somov, *Bibliografiia russkoi Obshchestvennosti: K. Voprosu ob Intelligentsii* (Moscow, 1927–1931), mentioned in M. Malia, *Alexander Herzen and the Birth of Russian Socialism, 1812–1855* (Cambridge, Mass., 1961), p. 429.

2. A. Koyré, *La Philosophie et le Problème national en Russie au Début du XIXe Siècle* (Paris, 1929), pp. 9–10.

3. Cf. below, pp. 45–46.

4. P. N. Miliukov in *Ocherki po Istorii russkoi Kultury* (Paris, 1930 ff), II, 301–302 pointed out that, from the standpoint of the development of secular Russian literature, two cultural strata appeared in the eighteenth century, with the educated drawing further apart from the merely literate. This is the eighteenth-century background for the distinction made by R. Pipes between cultural and philosophical westernization in nineteenth-century Russia, in "The Historical Evolution of the Russian Intelligentsia," *Daedalus*, LXXXIX (1960), 487–488.

5. Cf. H. Rogger, *National Consciousness in Eighteenth-Century Russia* (Cambridge, Mass., 1960), pp. 266–267; and A. Radishchev, *A Journey from St. Petersburg to Moscow*, ed. R. P. Thaler (Cambridge, Mass., 1958), Introduction by R. P. Thaler, p. 22.

6. Cf. the eighteenth-century Russian historians in A. Mazour, *Modern Russian Historiography*, 2d ed. (Princeton, 1958), pp. 9–13, 30–45.

7. E.g. the letters of D. Fonvizin (1745–1792) mentioned in N. V. Riasanovsky, *Russia and the West in the Teaching of the Slavophiles* (Cambridge, Mass., 1952), pp. 1–2.

8. *Satiricheskie Zhurnaly N. I. Novikova*, ed. P. N. Berkov (Moscow and Leningrad, 1951), p. 488, quoted in Rogger, *op. cit.* (n. 5), pp. 74–75.

9. Cf. R. Pipes, "The Background and Growth of Karamzin's Political Ideas down to 1810," in *Karamzin's Memoir on Ancient and Modern Russia*, ed. R. Pipes (Cambridge, Mass., 1959), pp. 20–21.

10. M. Raeff, *Michael Speransky, Statesman of Imperial Russia, 1772–1839* (The Hague, 1957), p. 366.

11. A. Mazour, *The First Russian Revolution* (Berkeley, 1937), pp. 271, 264.

12. N. V. Riasanovsky, "Fourierism in Russia," *American Slavic and*

East European Review, XII (1953), 289–302; F. I. Kaplan, "Russian Fourierism of the 1840's," *ibid.*, XVII (1958), 161–172.

13. A Koyré, *Etudes sur l'Histoire de la Pensée philosophique en Russie* (Paris, 1950), p. 104; M. E. Malia, "Schiller and the Early Russian Left," *Russian Thought and Politics*, ed. H. McLean et al. (Cambridge, Mass., 1957), pp. 170, 180.

14. A. Herzen, *Selected Philosophical Works* (Moscow, 1956), p. 537.

15. Cf. A. von Schelting, *Russland und Europa im russischen Geschichtsdenken* (Bern, 1948), pp. 261 ff.

16. H. Kohn ed., *The Mind of Modern Russia* (New York, 1962), pp. 38–40.

17. *Sobranie Sochinenii*, VII, 6.

18. V. G. Belinsky, *Selected Philosophical Works* (Moscow, 1956), p. 102.

19. Quoted in N. V. Riasanovsky, *Russia and the West in the Teaching of the Slavophiles*, p. 76.

20. *Ibid.*, p. 83.

21. Herzen, *op. cit.* (n. 14), p. 15.

22. Quoted in Malia, *Alexander Herzen and the Birth of Russian Socialism*, p. 192.

23. *Ibid.*, p. 306.

24. Kohn ed., *The Mind of Modern Russia*, p. 169.

25. Venturi, *op. cit.* (n. 1), p. 35.

26. Pollard, "The Russian Intelligentsia," *California Slavic Studies*, III (1964), 26–27.

27. Cf. D. M. Wallace, *Russia on the Eve of War and Revolution*, ed. C. E. Black (New York, 1961), pp. 191, 383.

28. Pollard, *op. cit.*, p. 29; Venturi, *op. cit.*, p. 595 n. According to the calculation of N. A. Hans, by the end of this period, in 1880, approximately 47 per cent of the university students were of *dvoriane* and bureaucratic origins, the others being *raznochintsy*. Cf. *History of Russian Educational Policy (1701–1917)* (London, 1931), p. 239.

29. Pollard, *op. cit.*, p. 7.

30. A. Kornilov, *Obshchestvennoe Dvizhenie pri Aleksandr II (1855–1881)* (Moscow, 1909), p. 121.

31. Venturi, *op. cit.*, p. 276.

32. D. Pisarev, *Selected Philosophical, Social and Political Essays* (Moscow, 1958), p. 116.

33. *Ibid.*, p. 288.

34. N. A. Dobroliubov, *Selected Philosophical Essays* (Moscow, 1956), p. 417.

35. *Ibid.*, pp. 485–486, 542.

36. "The Importance of Authority in Education" (1857), *ibid.*, p. 22.

37. *Ibid.*, p. 439.

38. N. G. Chernyshevsky, *What Is to Be Done?* (New York, 1961), p. 56.

39. A. Gerschenkron, "The Rate of Industrial Growth in Russia since 1885," *Journal of Economic History*, Supplement VII (1947), 156, quoted in H. Schwartz, *Russia's Soviet Economy*, 2d ed. (Englewood Cliffs, N. J., 1954), p. 63.

40. R. Pipes, "Russian Marxism and Its Populist Background," *Russian Review*, XIX (1960), 335.

41. S. H. Baron, *Plekhanov, the Father of Russian Marxism* (Stanford, 1963), p. 60.

42. G. V. Plekhanov, *Sochineniia*, 2d ed. (Moscow, 1923 ff.), II, 37.

43. *Ibid.*, p. 321.

44. "Socialism and the Political Struggle," *ibid.*, p. 47.

45. "Our Differences," *ibid.*, p. 225.

46. *Ibid.*, p. 337.

47. *Ibid.*, III, 78–79.

48. *Ibid.*, II, 402.

49. "Socialism and the Political Struggle," *ibid.*, p. 84.

50. "Our Differences," *ibid.*, p. 301.

51. Baron, *op. cit.*, p. 88.

52. R. Pipes, *Social Democracy and the St. Petersburg Labor Movement, 1885–1897* (Cambridge, Mass., 1963), pp. 121, 125.

53. A. Kremer, *Ob Agitatsii* (Geneva, 1896), p. 16, quoted in Pipes, *Social Democracy*, p. 63.

54. Baron, *op. cit.*, pp. 192–196.

55. M. Weber, *The Theory of Social and Economic Organization* (New York, 1947), pp. 329–358.

56. Kohn ed., *op. cit.* (n. 16), p. 42.

57. *Ibid.*, p. 55.

58. *Ibid.*, p. 56.

59. Belinsky, *op. cit.* (n. 18), p. 22.

60. *Ibid.*, p. 115.

61. *Ibid.*, p. 125.

62. *Ibid.*, p. 128.

63. *Ibid.*, p. 130.

64. *Ibid.*, p. 132.

65. Herzen, *op. cit.*, pp. 145–146.

66. Cf. E. Sarkisyanz, "Russian Attitudes Toward Asia," *Russian Review*, XIII (1954), 247.

67. A. Herzen, *From the Other Shore; and The Russian People and Socialism* (London, 1956), p. 132.

68. *Ibid.*, p. 179.

69. A. S. Khomiakov, *Polnoe Sobranie Sochinenii* (Moscow, 1904), VI, 93.

70. F. M. Dostoevskii, *The Diary of A Writer* (London and New York, 1949), II 1044.

71. K. Leontiev, *Sobranie Sochinenii* (Moscow, 1912–1913), V, 383–388.

72. Cf. D. Bodde, *Tolstoy and China* (Princeton, 1950), pp. 62–63; A. Malozemoff, *Russian Far Eastern Policy, 1881–1904* (Berkeley, 1958), pp. 42 ff.

73. N. G. Chernyshevsky, *Selected Philosophical Essays* (Moscow, 1953), p. 218.

74. Chernyshevsky, *What Is to Be Done?* (New York, 1961), p. 176.

75. Cf. Plekhanov, *Sochineniia*, VII, 15–28, 165.

76. *Ibid.*, II, 236.

77. E.g. *ibid.*, II, 272, 285, 305, 306; XV, 32–33.
78. *Ibid.*, III, 74.
79. *Ibid.*, II, 236.
80. *Ibid.*, III, 78.
81. *Ibid.*, XXIV, 320.

Notes to Chapter III (pp. 54–81)

1. V. I. Lenin, *Sochineniia*, 4th ed. (Moscow, 1941 ff.), I, 53. The research for this chapter was completed before the appearance of *Polnoe Sobranie Sochinenii*, 5th ed. (Moscow, 1958 ff.). Therefore, the citations will be from the fourth edition, unless specified otherwise. I have compared, in detail, the relevant texts in the fourth edition with those in *Sochineniia*, 2d ed. (Moscow, 1926 ff.), and in *Leninskii Sbornik* (Moscow, 1924 ff.), as well as with English translations. Several articles in the fourth edition, not in the second edition, were transferred from the *Sbornik*. In addition, a few words and phrases were changed. These changes I noted in the footnotes. None of the alterations has affected the content of this chapter.

2. Cf., "On the So-Called Market Question" (1893), *Sochineniia*, I, 93, 107; "What the 'Friends of the People' Are and How They Fight the Social Democrats" (1894), *Sochineniia*, I, 173–174, 200–201, 227; "The Development of Capitalism in Russia" (1899), *Sochineniia*, III, 266–273, 475–484.

3. *Sochineniia*, I, 178.
4. *Ibid.*, II, 481.
5. For the former see *ibid.*, I, 227; for the latter, which occurred more frequently, see *ibid.*, I, 249, 272, 280, 446, 463; III, 157.
6. *Ibid.*, p. 331.
7. *Ibid.*, p. 480–481.
8. "What the 'Friends of the People' Are," *Sochineniia*, I, 272.
9. *Ibid.*, II, 312.
10. Cf. below, pp. 58–59.
11. Cf. "Draft and Explanation of a Program for the Social Democratic Party" (1895–1896), *Sochineniia*, II, 79, 80; "The Tasks of the Russian Social Democrats" (1897), *ibid.*, II, 308.
12. *Ibid.*, IV, 197.
13. *Ibid.*, II, 527, quoted in A. G. Meyer, *Leninism* (Cambridge, Mass., 1957), pp. 267–268.
14. E.g. "A Draft Program of Our Party" (1899), *Sochineniia*, IV, 221; "The Workers' Party and the Peasantry" (1901), *ibid.*, IV, 395; "Petty Bourgeois and Proletarian Socialism" (1905), *ibid.*, IX, 413; "The Agrarian Program of Social Democracy in the First Russian Revolution, 1905–07" (1907), *ibid.*, XIII, 215.
15. *Ibid.*, VII, 216.
16. "Opinion on Plekhanov's Second Draft" (1902), *ibid.*, VI, 41; "How Comrade Plekhanov Argues about Social Democratic Tactics" (1906), *ibid.*, X, 435.

17. "How P. B. Axelrod Exposes the Liquidators," *ibid.*, XVIII, 162–163.

18. "Why the Social Democrats Must Declare A Determined and Relentless War on the Socialist Revolutionaries," *ibid.*, VI, 151–154; "The Basic Thesis against the Socialist Revolutionaries," *ibid.*, VI, 243–246.

19. *Ibid.*, IV, 368.

20. *Ibid.*, V, 67.

21. *Ibid.*, p. 82.

22. *Ibid.*, p. 345.

23. *Leninskii Sbornik*, XVI, 43.

24. *Sochineniia*, IX, 32, 40.

25. *Ibid.*, XVIII, 357.

26. *Ibid.*, XX, 348.

27. *Ibid.*, VI, 28.

28. *Ibid.*, X, 303.

29. *Ibid.*, XIII, 251.

30. *Ibid.*, XVIII, 57.

31. *Ibid.*, XX, 348.

32. *Ibid.*, IV, 191–192.

33. Cf. "What Is to Be Done?" (1902), *Sochineniia*, V, 345 ff.; E. H. Carr, *The Bolshevik Revolution, 1917–1923* (New York, 1951–1953), I, 15 ff.; Haimson, *The Russian Marxists and the Origins of Bolshevism*, pp. vi, 8.

34. Cf. "The Workers' Party and the Peasantry" (1901), *Sochineniia*, IV, 397; "To the Rural Poor" (1903), *ibid.*, VI, 383; "The Attitude of Social Democracy toward the Peasant Movement" (1905), *ibid.*, IX, 212; "The Agrarian Program of Social Democracy in the First Russian Revolution, 1905–07" (1907), *ibid.*, XIII, 386.

35. Cf. "Revolutionary Democratic Dictatorship of the Proletariat and the Peasantry" (1905), *ibid.*, VIII, 264–274; "The Two Tactics of Social Democracy in the Democratic Revolution" (1905), *ibid.*, IX, 94.

36. Cf. "Critical Remarks on the National Question" (1913), *ibid.*, XX, 3 ff.; "The Right of Nations to Self-Determination" (1914), *ibid.*, XX, 367 ff.

37. Cf. "Under a Stolen Flag" (1915), *ibid.*, XXI, 126; "Resolutions of Conference of the Sections of R.S.D.L.P. Abroad" (1915), *ibid.*, XXI, 137–138.

38. Cf. B. J. Hovde, "Socialist Theories of Imperialism prior to the Great War," *Journal of Political Economy*, XXXVI (1928), 571–572; E. M. Winslow, *The Pattern of Imperialism* (New York, 1948), p. 183; J. Freymond, *Lenine et l'Impérialisme* (Lausanne, 1951), p. 8; D. G. Smith, "Lenin's 'Imperialism': A Study in the Unity of Theory and Practice," *Journal of Politics*, XVII (1952), 562; D. H. Kruger, "Hobson, Lenin, and Schumpeter on Imperialism," *Journal of the History of Ideas*, XVI (1955), 252–259.

39. As early as 1907, while commenting on the Stuttgart International Socialist Congress, Lenin had mentioned that it was the profit from exploiting colonial people which had infected the proletariat of the exploiting country with chauvinism. *Sochineniia*, XIII, 61. But, at that

time, he showed no awareness of any revolutionary prospect in the East. That prospect occurred to Lenin only after 1907, during the period of 1908–1914, when he was seeking revolutionary support wherever it was available. Below, pp. 66–70. Thus, the post-1914 *theoretical* formulation of the link between European revolution and Asian revolution occurred after his concern with the *practical* prospecting for revolutionary support in the East.

40. *Sochineniia*, XXI, 345–346.

41. "Report to the Third All-Russian Congress of Soviets," *ibid.*, XXVI, 429.

42. *Ibid.*, XXXIII, 33.

43. *Ibid.*, XXXI, 5–6.

44. E.g. *ibid.*, I, 218; II, 312.

45. Cf. above, pp. 58–59.

46. Cf. "The Development of Capitalism in Russia," *Sochineniia*, III, 522; review of Kautsky's *Bernstein und das Sozialdemokratische Programm* (1899), *ibid.*, IV, 182; "The Lessons of the Crisis" (1901), *ibid.*, V, 74–75.

47. Cf. "The Development of Capitalism in Russia," *ibid.*, III, 493; "Again on the Theory of Realization" (1899), *ibid.*, IV, 76.

48. "The Chinese War," *ibid.*, IV, 351.

49. Cf. also "Review of Internal Affairs" (1901), *ibid.*, V, 231; "Regarding the State Budget" (1902), *ibid.*, V, 308; "To the Rural Poor," *ibid.*, VI, 363.

50. Cf. "Our Program" (1899), *ibid.*, IV, 190–194; "Our Immediate Task" (1899), *ibid.*, IV, 195–200; "A Draft Program of Our Party" (1899), *ibid.*, IV, 209–233; "Declaration of the Editorial Board of *Iskra*" (1900), *ibid.*, IV, 326–331; "The Urgent Tasks of Our Movement" (1900), *ibid.*, IV, 341–346; "Where To Begin?" (1901), *ibid.*, V, 5–12; "What Is to Be Done?" *ibid.*, V, 321–485; "The Two Tactics of Social Democracy in the Democratic Revolution," *ibid.*, IX, 3–94.

51. E.g. "The National Question in Our Program" (1903), *ibid.*, VI, 412–420.

52. *Ibid.*, VIII, 32.

53. Cf. "Leo Tolstoy and His Epoch" (1911), *ibid.*, XVII, 31; "Lecture on the Revolution of 1905" (1917), *ibid.*, XXIII, 244.

54. *Ibid.*, XIII, 71.

55. *Ibid.*, XIII, 300–302.

56. L. Schapiro, *The Communist Party of the Soviet Union* (New York, 1960), p. 100.

57. Cf. P. B. Struve's criticism in *Viekhi: Sbornik Statei o russkoi Intelligentsii*, pp. 131–140.

58. *Sochineniia*, XV, 162.

59. *Ibid.*, p. 164–165.

60. *Ibid.*, p. 295.

61. *Ibid.*, p. 160, 161.

62. "Leo Tolstoy and His Epoch," *ibid.*, XVII, 31.

63. *Ibid.*, p. 434–435.

64. Cf. "Political Parties During the Five Years of the Third Duma" (1912), *ibid.*, p. 449: "The Sorry Defence of Liberal Labor Policy" (1912),

ibid., p. 499–500; "Democracy and Populism in China," *ibid.*, XVIII, 143.

65. "The May First Celebration of the Revolutionary Proletariat" (1913), *ibid.*, XIX, 195.

66. "Organ of the Liberal Labor Party" (1912), *ibid.*, XVII, 438.

67. "Democracy and Populism in China," *ibid.*, XVIII, 143–146. However, in "Discourse on 'Kadetism'" (1912), *ibid.*, XVIII, 271, 272, Lenin compared Sun to the bourgeois, Miliukov!

68. *Ibid.*, XVIII, 146.

69. *Ibid.*

70. "Regenerated China," *ibid.*, XVIII, 372.

71. "Democracy and Populism in China," *ibid.*, XVIII, 149.

72. "The Historical Destiny of the Doctrine of Karl Marx" (1913), *ibid.*, XVIII, 546.

73. "Big Achievement of the Chinese Republic," *ibid.*, XIX, 9–10.

74. *Ibid.*, XIX, 77–78.

75. "Cultured Europeans and Barbaric Asians," *ibid.*, XIX, 38.

76. *Ibid.*, XIX, 37–38; also "The Awakening of Asia," *ibid.*, XIX, 65–66.

77. *Ibid.*, XIX, 66.

78. *Ibid.*, XX, 371–372, 378.

79. *Ibid.*, XX, 404–405.

80. Cf. "Conference of the Foreign Sections of the R.S.D.L.P." (March, 1915), *ibid.*, XXI, 138; "Socialism and War" (August, 1915), *ibid.*, XXI, 277–278; "A Caricature of Marxism and 'Imperialist Economism'" (October, 1916), *ibid.*, XXIII, 22; "Draft of Revised Program of the R.S.D.L.P." (May, 1917), *ibid.*, XXIV, 431.

81. Cf. "Collapse of the Second International" (Summer, 1915), *ibid.*, XXI, 204–205; letter to A. M. Kollantai (Summer, 1915), *ibid.*, XXXV, 155; "The United States of Europe Slogan" (August, 1915), *ibid.*, XXI, 309; "Appeal on War" (August, 1915), *ibid.*, XXI, 335; correction to the pamphlet "To Whom Is the War Necessary?" by A. M. Kollantai (Autumn, 1915), *Leninskii Sbornik*, XVII, 327; "Speech at the International Meeting in Berne" (February, 1916), *Sochineniia*, XXII, 111; "Imperialism and the Split in the Socialist Movement" (Autumn, 1916), *ibid.*, XXIII, 104; "Draft Resolution on the War," Petrograd Conference of the R.S.D.L.P. (April, 1917), *ibid.*, XXIV, 133; "In the Footsteps of *Russkaia Volia*" (April, 1917), *ibid.*, XXIV, 91; "The Note of the Provisional Government" (May, 1917), *ibid.*, XXIV, 161; "Political Parties in Russia and the Tasks of the Proletariat" (May, 1917), *ibid.*, XXIV, 77.

82. *Ibid.*, XXII, 241–242.

83. *Ibid.*, p. 245.

84. D. Boersner, *The Bolesheviks and the National and Colonial Questions (1917–1928)* (Geneva and Paris, 1957), p. 58.

85. *Sochineniia*, XXII, 140; cf. also draft resolution on "The World War and the Tasks of the Social Democrats" (August, 1915), *Leninskii Sbornik*, XIV, 166; "Revolutionary Proletariat and the Right of Nations to Self-Determination" (November, 1915), *Sochineniia*, XXI, 371; "The Pamphlet by Junius" (August, 1916), *ibid.*, XXII, 296; "A Caricature of Marxism and 'Imperialist Economism'," *ibid.*, XXIII, 27–28.

86. Cf. "Socialism and War," *ibid.*, XXI, 272; "Opportunism and the

Collapse of the Second International" (end of 1915), *ibid.*, XXI, 402; "The Military Program of the Proletarian Revolution" (Autumn, 1916), *ibid.*, XXIII, 66–67; "Discussion on Self-Determination Summed Up" (October, 1916), *ibid.*, XXII, 322.

87. *Ibid.*, XXI, 368.
88. *Ibid.*, XXIII, 351.
89. *Ibid.*, XXIV, 358.
90. *Ibid.*, XXV, 68.
91. *Ibid.*, p. 27.
92. *Ibid.*, XXVI, 386.
93. *Ibid.*, XXVII, 132.
94. *Ibid.*, p. 209–210; cf. also "The Theses on the Contemporary Political Situation" (May, 1918), *ibid.*, XXVII, 326.
95. *Ibid.*, XXVIII, 126–131.
96. *Ibid.*, XXIX, 167.
97. Carr, *The Bolshevik Revolution, 1917–1923*, III, 131.
98. *Sochineniia*, XXIX, 467.
99. *Ibid.*, XXVIII, 453.
100. Cf. J. Degras ed., *Soviet Documents on Foreign Policy* (London, 1951 ff.), I, 158–167; X. J. Eudin and R. C. North, *Soviet Russia and the East, 1920–1927: A Documentary Survey* (Stanford, 1957), pp. 175–177, 184–186, 199–200.
101. Degras ed., *op. cit.*, I, 160.
102. *Sochineniia*, XXX, 130–141.
103. Eudin and North, *op. cit.*, p. 164.
104. V. I. Lenin, *Lenin i Vostok; Sbornik Statei* (Moscow, 1925), p. 63.
105. *Sochineniia*, XXXI, 160–164.
106. *Ibid.*, p. 207–208. Cf. *ibid.*, 2d ed., Vol. XXV for a slightly different version of the speech.
107. *Sochineniia*, XXXI, 140.
108. Cf. *ibid.*, p. 122–128 for Lenin's draft theses.
109. Cf. J. Degras, *The Communist International, 1919–1943: Documents* (London and New York, 1955–1960), I, 139–144 for the final version of the theses.
110. Cf. Roy's supplementary theses in Eudin and North, *op. cit.*, pp. 65–67.
111. *Sochineniia*, XXXI, 217. Cf. *ibid.*, 2d ed., Vol. XXV for a slightly different version of the speech.
112. *Ibid.*, XXXI, 219.
113. *Vestnik*, No. 1 (July 20, 1920), mentioned in A. S. Whiting, *Soviet Policies in China, 1917–1924* (New York, 1953), pp. 54–55.
114. *Sochineniia*, XXXI, 246.
115. Eudin and North, *op. cit.*, pp. 169–170.
116. Cf. Degras, *The Communist International*, I, 383–391.
117. E.g. the Sun-Joffe declaration of January 1923 in C. Brandt et al., *A Documentary History of Chinese Communism* (Cambridge, Mass., 1952), pp. 70–71.
118. *Sochineniia*, XXXI, 460.
119. *Ibid.*, XXXII, 73.

120. "Speech to the Meeting of the Activists of the Moscow Organization of the R.C.P.(B.)" (December, 1920), *ibid.*, XXXI, 423; "Plan for the Pamphlet 'On the Food Tax' II" (March–April, 1921), *ibid.*, XXXII, 302; "Speech to the Third Congress of Communist International" (July, 1921), *ibid.*, XXXII, 458; "The Tenth Anniversary of *Pravda*" (March, 1922), *ibid.*, XXXIII, 313; "On the Significance of Militant Materialism" (March, 1922), *ibid.*, p. 207.

121. *Ibid.*, p. 437.
122. *Ibid.*, p. 457.
123. *Ibid.*, p. 458.

Notes to Chapter IV (pp. 82–106)

1. Cf. M. Weber, *From Max Weber: Essays in Sociology* (New York, 1946), pp. 416–444; F. Michael, "State and Society in Nineteenth-Century China," *World Politics*, VII (1954–55), 419–433; Chung-li Chang, *The Chinese Gentry; Studies on Their Role in Nineteenth-Century Chinese Society* (Seattle, 1955), pp. 137–141; Ho Ping-ti, "Aspect of Social Mobility in China, 1368–1911," *Comparative Studies in Society and History*, I (1958–59), 358–359; R. M. Marsh, *The Mandarins; the Circulation of Elites in China, 1600–1900* (New York, 1961), pp. 82, 190; J. R. Levenson(*Confucian China and Its Modern Fate*, Vol. II: *The Problem of Monarchical Decay* (Berkeley and Los Angeles, 1964), pp. 25 ff.

2. Cf. Mannheim, *Ideology and Utopia*, pp. 192 ff., for the distinction between thinking which tends to preserve the status quo and thinking which seeks to overcome the status quo.

3. Y. C. Wang, "Western Impact and Social Mobility in China," *American Sociological Review*, XXV (1960), 854.

4. C. H. Peake, *Nationalism and Education in Modern China* (New York, 1932), p. 70; Kiang Wen-han, *The Ideological Background of the Chinese Student Movement* (New York, 1948), pp. 9–20.

5. Shu Hsin-ch'eng, *Chin-tai Chung-kuo liu-hsüeh shih* (Shanghai, 1927), p. 224.

6. Tsien Tsuen-hsuin, "Western Impact on China through Translation," *Far Eastern Quarterly*, XIII (1953–54), 323–324.

7. Kuo Chan-po, *Chin wu-shih-nien Chung-kuo ssu-hsiang shih* (Peking, 1935), pp. 357–384; also Chow Tse-tsung, *The May Fourth Movement; Intellectual Revolution in Modern China* (Cambridge, Mass., 1960), p. 294.

8. Y. C. Wang, "The Intelligentsia in Changing China," *Foreign Affairs*, XXXVI (1957–58), 322; cf. also R. C. North's analysis of the social origins of some twentieth-century Chinese leaders in *Kuomintang and Chinese Communist Elites* (Stanford, 1952), pp. 46–47.

9. See Kuo, *op. cit.*, pp. 195–196; Fei Min, *Chung-kuo chin-tai ssu-hsiang fa-chan chien-shih* (Shanghai, 1949); S. Y. Teng and J. K. Fairbank, *China's Response to the West: A Documentary Survey, 1839–1923* (Cambridge, Mass., 1954), pp. iii–vi; Shih Chün ed., *Chung-kuo chin-tai ssu-hsiang shih ts'an-k'ao tzu-liao chien-pien* (Peking, 1957); Y. C. Wang, "Intellectuals and Society in China, 1860–1949," *Comparative Studies in Society and History*, III (1960–61), 421; Chow, *op. cit.* (n. 7), p. 327.

10. In making the distinction between a changing situation and the relative degree of intellectual awareness of that changing situation I am indebted to two articles by J. R. Levenson: *"T'ien-hsia* and *Kuo* and the 'Transvaluation of Values'," *Far Eastern Quarterly*, XI (1951–52), 447–451; " 'History' and 'Value': The Tensions of Intellectual Choice in Modern China," *Studies in Chinese Thought*, ed. A. F. Wright (Chicago, 1953), pp. 146–194.

11. For the distinction between native tradition and western value in a westernizing situation, cf. above, p. 45.

12. J. R. Levenson, *Confucian China and Its Modern Fate; the Problem of Intellectual Continuity* (Berkeley, 1958), p. xvi.

13. Teng and Fairbank, *op. cit.*, p. 76.

14. *Ibid.*, p. 63.

15. Chang Chih-tung, *China's Only Hope* (New York, 1900), p. 63, quoted in Levenson, " 'History' and 'Value,' " p. 190 n.

16. Ch'ien Mu, *Chung-kuo chin san-pai-nien hsüeh-shu shih* (Shanghai, 1937), pp. 705, 709.

17. *Ta T'ung Shu; the One-World Philosophy of K'ang Yu-wei* (London, 1958), p. 72. Although the book was not written before 1902, its content was present in K'ang earlier writings dating back to the eighties. Cf. R. C. Howard, "K'ang Yu-wei (1858–1927): His Intellectual Background and Early Thought," *Confucian Personalities*, ed. A. F. Wright and D. Twitchett (Stanford, 1962), pp. 295–296.

18. J. R. Levenson, *Liang Ch'i-ch'ao and the Mind of Modern China* (Cambridge, Mass., 1959), p. 2.

19. Cf. Ch'ien, *op. cit.*, p. 681.

20. Teng and Fairbank, *op. cit.*, p. 151.

21. Shih ed., *op. cit.* (n. 9), pp. 416–418.

22. Teng and Fairbank, *op. cit.*, pp. 227–229.

23. Hu Shih, "Our Attitude toward Modern Western Civilization" (1926), de Bary et al., comp., *Sources of Chinese Tradition* (New York, 1960), pp. 853–854.

24. See Lu Hsün, "A Madman's Diary" (1918), *Selected Works* (Peking, 1956), I, 8–21; Ch'en Tu-hsiu, "The Basic Intellectual Differences between Eastern and Western Nations," *Ch'ing-nien tsa-chih*, I:4 (December, 1915); Li Ta-chao, "An Economic Interpretation of the Causes for Recent Chinese Intellectual Changes," *Hsin ch'ing-nien*, VII:2 (January, 1920).

25. Cf. Levenson, *Confucian China and Its Modern Fate*, pp. 134–145.

26. Cf. *passim*, Teng and Fairbank, *op. cit.*; Shih ed., *op. cit.*; de Bary et al., *op. cit.*

27. See Feng Kuei-fen, "On the Manufacture of Foreign Weapons" (1860); Li Hung-chang's recommendation of Western military technique in 1863; Tso Tsung-t'ang's reform plan of 1866; and the memorial to the T'ung-wen Kuan for the addition of an astronomy section (1866).

28. Chang Chih-tung, *China's Only Hope*, p. 93–94; K'ang Yu-wei, "Memorial on Promoting the Translation of Japanese Books and the Establishment of a Translation Bureau at the Capital" (1898), Chang Ching-lu ed., *Chung-kuo ch'u-pan shih-liao pu-pien* (Peking, 1957), p. 50.

29. De Bary et al., *op. cit.*, p. 678.

30. Li Hung-chang's memorial of December 10, 1874 in Teng and Fairbank, *op. cit.*, pp. 119–120; Chang Chih-tung's memorial of August, 1895 in *ibid.*, p. 129; and Liu K'un-i's secret proposal of July, 1895 in *ibid.*, pp. 127–128.

31. Shih ed., *op. cit.*, p. 105.

32. Teng and Fairbank, *op. cit.*, p. 68.

33. *Ibid.*, pp. 55, 48.

34. Shih ed., *op. cit.*, pp. 278–282.

35. De Bary et al., *op. cit.*, p. 735.

36. Shih ed., *op. cit.*, p. 367.

37. *Ibid.*, p. 432.

38. Quoted in Levenson, *Liang Ch'i-ch'ao and the Mind of Modern China*, p. 127 n.

39. Cf. Chün-tu Hsüeh, *Huang Hsing and the Chinese Revolution* (Stanford, 1961), p. 95, for sampling of newspaper editorials.

40. Cf. Chang Ching-lu, *Chung-kuo chin-tai ch'u-pan shih-liao* (Shanghai, 1954), I, 174–180, for a list of pre-1905 books, mainly Japanese and translations from Japanese, which influenced the revolutionary nationalists.

41. Hsüeh, *op. cit.*, p. 10.

42. Shih ed., *op. cit.*, pp. 665, 559.

43. See Liang in "The Influence of the Russian Revolution," *Hsin-min ts'ung-pao*, Nos. 13 and 14, used the post-1905 model of revolutionary Russia negatively, as a warning to prod for Chinese constitutional reform.

44. *Min pao*, photostat edition (Peking, 1957), No. 2 (May [sic], 1906), No. 3 (April, 1906), No. 4 (May, 1906), No. 6 (July, 1906), No. 7 (September, 1906), and No. 10 (December, 1906).

45. *Ibid.*, No. 10 (December, 1906).

46. *Ibid.*, No. 11 (January, 1907), No. 15 (July, 1907), No. 16 (September, 1907), No. 17 (October, 1907).

47. *Ibid.*, No. 3 (April, 1906), No. 12 (March, 1907).

48. *Tung-fang tsa-chih*, XIV:4 (April, 1917), 216; *Hsin ch'ing-nien*, III:2 (April, 1917).

49. *Ibid.*

50. Sun Hao-hsüan, "The Rise of a Great People," *Tsing-hua Collegiate Journal*, III:1 (November, 1917), 34–36.

51. Cf. the changing tone of two articles by the same author, Kao Lao, in that magazine: "The Course of the Great Russian Revolution," *Tung-fang tsa-chih*, XIV:5 (May, 1917), 35–42; and "The Situation in Russia since the Revolution," *ibid.*, XIV:12 (December, 1917), 15.

52. *Ibid.*, XV:1 (January, 1918), 41–42.

53. See "Present-Day Party Alignment in Russia," *ibid.*, XV:2 (February, 1918), 61–64; a short biography of Lenin, *ibid.*, XV:3 (March, 1918), 29–34; "Development of the Russian Socialist Movement," *ibid.*, XV:4 (April, 1918), 61–65; "Development of the Ukrainian Question," *ibid.*, XV:5 (May, 1918), 66–71; "The Problem of Land Distribution in Russia," *ibid.*, XV:9 (September, 1918), 43–50 and XV:12 (December, 1918), 47–52; "Bolshevik Thought and Its Failure," *ibid.*, XVI:5 (May, 1919), 29–42.

54. Chün Shih, Bolshevik Thought and Methods for Its Prevention," *ibid.*, XVI:6 (June, 1919), 1–4.

55. The following article appeared in that issue: "On Marxism," "Criticism of Marxism," "Marxist Studies," "A Short Biography of Marx," and Li Ta-chao's "My Marxist Viewpoint."

56. Tsou Lu, *Chung-kuo Kuomintang shih-kao* (Chungking, 1944), I, 304.

57. Teng and Fairbank, *op. cit.*, p. 265.

58. Cf. Chang ed., *Chung-kuo ch'u-pan shih-liao pu-pien*, p. 442 for a list of Marxist writings available in Chinese translation before 1917. Their apparent lack of popularity signified a pre-1917 Chinese sentiment that Marxism was irrelevant to backward China.

59. See Ch'en's "Appeal to Youth," *Ch'ing-nien tsa-chih*, I:1 (September, 1915), and "The Basic Intellectual Differences between Eastern and Western Nations," *ibid.*, I:4 (December, 1915); and Li's "Spring," *Hsin ch'ing-nien*, II:1 (September, 1916).

60. "The Russian Revolution and the Awakening of the Chinese People," *Hsin ch'ing-nien.* III:2 (April, 1917).

61. "A Comparison of the French Revolution and the Russian Revolution," Shih ed., *op. cit.*, p. 1202.

62. *Hsin ch'ing-nien*, V:5 (November, 1918).

63. Shih ed., *op. cit.*, p. 1251.

64. See Ch'en, "On Politics" (September, 1920), *ibid.*, pp. 1105–1116; Ch'en, "The Value of Commemorating National Independence" (October, 1920), *ibid.*, pp. 1117–1121; Li, "The Value of Historical Materialism in Viewing Contemporary History," *Hsin ch'ing-nien*, III:4 (December, 1920); Li, "The October Revolution and the Chinese People" (November, 1922), Shih ed., *op. cit.*, pp. 1215–1216; and Ch'en's argument for historical materialism (November, 1923), in Teng and Fairbank, *op. cit.*, pp. 249–251.

65. Shih ed., *op. cit.*, p. 1215.

66. Brandt et al., *A Documentary History of Chinese Communism*, p. 62.

67. *Ibid.*, pp. 63–65. Both manifestoes followed closely the 1920 theses on the national and colonial question, as well as the Zinoviev and Safarov speeches before the Congress of Toilers of the Far East, in early 1922.

68. *Ibid.*, pp. 71–72. This followed closely the these on the Eastern question of the Fourth Comintern Congress in 1922, as well as the resolution of the Executive Committee of the Comintern on the relations between the C.C.P. and the Kuomintang, and the E.C.C.I. directive to the Third Congress of the C.C.P.

69. *Ibid.*, pp. 74–77.

70. *Ibid.*, p. 96.

71. *Ibid.*, p. 122. This followed closely the E.C.C.I.'s resolutions on China, during the summer of 1927.

72. It is difficult to maintain a consistent line in this confusing situation. Cf. how Ch'ü Ch'iu-pai had to double-talk through it by proposing a "strategy" which seemed to cover all possibilities and yet emphasize none, in his *Chung-kuo ke-ming chih cheng-lun wen-t'i* (n.p., 1927), pp. 109–110.

73. Quoted in Benjamin Schwartz, *Chinese Communism and the Rise of Mao* (Cambridge, Mass., 1951), pp. 103–104.

74. Degras, *The Communist International, 1919–1943: Documents*, II, 437–738.

75. Brandt et al., *op. cit.*, p. 131.

76. J. P. Harrison, "The Li Li-san Line and the CCP in 1930," *China Quarterly*, No. 14 (April–June, 1963), p. 178.

77. Schwartz, *op. cit.*, p. 127.

78. *Ibid.*, pp. 50, 63–64, 84.

79. "Discussion concerning Socialism," *Hsin ch'ing-nien*, VIII:4 (December, 1920), quoted in Schwartz, *op. cit.*, p. 29.

80. "The Value of Commemorating National Independence," *Hsin ch'ing-nien*, VIII:3 (November, 1920), quoted in Schwartz, *op. cit.*, p. 29.

81. *Ibid.*, pp. 61–62.

82. Ch'en Tu-hsiu et al., *Wo-men ti cheng-chih i-chien shu* (n.p., n.d.), pp. 1–2, 8.

83. Li Ta-chao, *Li Ta-chao hsüan-chi* (Peking, 1962), p. 146.

84. *Ibid.*, p. 535.

85. Maurice Meisner, *Li Ta-chao and the Origins of Chinese Marxism* (University of Chicago, doctoral dissertation, 1962), pp. 293–294.

86. *Ibid.*, p. 303.

87. *Ibid.*, p. 273.

88. From the late 1920's to the early 1930's, in both China and Russia, there was much debate about the nature of Asiatic society and the oriental mode of production. For the controversy in China, cf. Benjamin Schwartz, "A Marxist Controversy on China," *Far Eastern Quarterly*, XIII (1953–54), 143–153; for the controversy in Russia, cf. Leo Yaresh's "The Problem of Periodization," in C. E. Black ed., *Rewriting Russian History*, (New York, 1962), pp. 49–54. The controversy centered on the non-Western characteristics of Asiatic society and the place of such Asiatic society within the universal Marxist process of history. It was a debate undertaken at the level of Marxist theory. To some extent, the Trotskyite, the Stalinist, and the Li Li-san ideas of China were affected by this theoretical controversy.

However, the development of the Maoist idea of China was not affected by this controversy. Not only was Mao, at this corresponding period, seemingly uninformed and definitely uninterested in the controversy. It is the argument of the following chapter that Mao would not approach Marxism from the perspective of theoretical concern, but would rather try to reconcile Marxist theory with his prior commitment to revolutionary practice. To the extent that I am concerned specifically with the Marxian, Leninist, and Maoist ideas of China, and not with the general history of the Marxist ideas of China, I shall not deal with that controversy and its related ideas of China.

Notes to Chapter V (pp. 107–140)

1. For the sources of this chapter, I have used the earliest available versions of Mao's speeches and writings. This was necessary to delineate the historical development of Mao's thought. These early versions have been compared with and supplemented by the later versions in the various official editions of Mao's selected works: *Mao Tse-tung hsüan-chi*, 1944 ed., Vol. II (Shansi-Chahar-Hopei Border Area, 1944); *Mao Tse-tung hsüan-*

chi, 1947 ed., 6 vols. (Shansi-Chahar-Hopei Border Area, 1947); *Mao Tse-tung hsüan-chi,* 1947 ed. supplement (Shansi-Chahar-Hopei Border Area, 1947); *Mao Tse-tung hsüan-chi,* 1951 ed., 4 vols. (Peking, 1951–1960). The standard English translations are based on the 1951 edition: *Selected Works,* 5 vols. (New York, 1954 ff.); *Selected Works of Mao Tse-tung,* Vol. IV (Peking, 1961); *Selected Military Writings of Mao Tse-tung* (Peking, 1963). The list of articles selected in each Chinese edition differs. A comparison of the early version with the later versions in the various editions indicates that there was not much revision or rewriting in the 1944 edition, the 1947 edition, and the supplement to the 1947 edition. There is a certain amount of revision and rewriting in the 1951 edition. Therefore, the 1951 edition and all English translations based on that edition are less reliable. These revisions and rewritings, though not fundamentally altering the content of Mao's thought, make his thought appear more systematic and consistent than it actually was. The writings and speeches of Mao for the early 1930's are not easily available. In this regard, the Ch'en Ch'eng Kiangsi soviet collection (*Shih-sou tzu-liao-shih kung-fei tzu-liao*), available in microfilms and photostats at the Hoover Institution, is a useful supplement. In addition, I have used S. R. Schram's excellent *The Political Thought of Mao Tse-tung* (New York, 1963). All translations have been checked against available English translations, and whenever possible improved.

2. *Ibid.,* pp. 96–97.

3. *Ibid.,* p. 170.

4. *Ibid.,* p. 95.

5. *Ibid.,* p. 105.

6. Cf. David Nivision, "The Problem of 'Knowledge' and 'Action' in Chinese Thought since Wang Yang-ming," *Studies in Chinese Thought,* pp. 112–141.

7. Cf. Mao's own account of his conversion in E. Snow, *Red Star over China* (New York, 1961), p. 155; and Schram's evaluation in *op. cit.,* p. 20.

8. It is generally agreed that Mao's control of the party was confirmed at the Tsun-i conference in early 1935. Cf. Schwartz's "Preface to the Third Printing" (1958) in *Chinese Communism and the Rise of Mao,* p. viii; Hsiao Tso-liang, *Power Relations within the Chinese Communist Movement, 1930–1934* (Seattle, 1961), pp. 159, 303; Howard L. Boorman, "Mao Tse-tung: the Lacquered Image," *China Quarterly,* No. 16 (October–December, 1963), pp. 22–23.

9. Excerpted from *Hunan li-shih tzu-liao,* No. 9 (1959) in Schram, *The Political Thought of Mao Tse-tung,* pp. 214–215.

10. *Ibid.,* p. 140.

11. Cf. the original version in *Chung-kuo nung-min,* No. 2 (February, 1926), pp. 1–13, with the revised version in *Hsüan-chi,* 1951 edition., I, 3–9.

12. *Chung-kuo nung-min,* p. 2. This entire passage was deleted from *Hsüan-chi,* 1951 edition I, 3.

13. This generalization is based upon a perusal of all relevant materials, in both microfilm and photostat forms, available in *Shih-sou tzu-liao-shih kung-fei tzu-liao,* as well as of the more limited samplings in the various editions of Mao's *Hsüan-chi.*

14. *Mao's China; Party Reform Documents, 1942–44* (Seattle, 1952), p. 245. Lacking the original Chinese version, I am using this English translation because it is based on an early 1940's version. The 1947 and 1951 editions of *Hsüan-chi* do not differ much from this version; and the content of the article fitted in very well with Mao's preoccupation of the 1927–1935 period.

15. "Rural Investigation Movement is a Most Important Task within the Expanding Area," *Hung-se Chung-hua*, No. 86 (June 17, 1933), 3; "The First Step in the Rural Investigation Movement," *ibid.*, No. 87 (June 20, 1933), 3; "Begin the Rural Investigation Movement in Accordance with the Unfolding Tendency and Characteristic of the Village Class Struggle," *ibid.*, No. 88 (June 23, 1933), 3; "The Initial Result of the Rural Investigation Movement," *Tou-cheng*, No. 24 (August 29, 1933), 4–12. All these are available in *Shih-sou tzu-liao-shih kung-fei tzu-liao*.

16. For this letter, I am using the version of the *Hsüan-chi*, 1947 edition. The version in the 1951 edition was excerpted and revised, and is therefore less reliable.

17. *Ibid.*, 1947 ed., Supplement, p. 91.

18. *Ibid.*, 1951 ed., I, 103.

19. "Letter of Mao Tse-tung to Yuan Kuo-p'ing concerning Direction for Mass Work" (dated March 6, but no year), available in *Shih-sou tzu-liao-shih kung-fei tzu-liao*. It was probably written during the early 1930's.

20. See "How to Undertake Rural Soviet Activities" in Chang Wen-t'ien and Mao Tse-tung, *Ch'u-hsiang su-wei-ai tsen-yang kung-tso* (n.p., 1934), pp. 1–39; "Soviet Activities in Ch'ang-kang Village, Hsing-kuo Hsien [Kiangsi]," *Tou-cheng*, No. 42 (January 12, 1934), 10–16; No. 43 (January 19, 1934), 15–20; and No. 44 (January 26, 1934), 16; "Soviet Activities in Ts'ai-ch'i Village, Shang-hang Hsien [Fukien]," *ibid.*, No. 45 (February 2, 1934), 15–16; No. 46 (February 9, 1934), 15–16; and No. 48 (February 23, 1934), 18–20. These are available in *Shih-sou tzu-liao-shih kung-fei tzu-liao*. Cf. also Mao Tse-tung, *Chih-yu su-wei-ai neng-kou chiu Chung-kuo* (Moscow, 1934). None of these is available in *Hsüan-chi*, 1951 edition. Elsewhere in the 1951 edition, the term "soviet area" often was revised to read either "Red area" or "revolutionary base area." The 1951 edition tried to de-emphasize Mao's dependence on the soviet model during the early and mid-1930's.

21. This shift was not yet evident in his December, 1935, article "On the Tactics of Fighting Japanese Imperialism," written immediately after the Long March. Cf. the *Hsüan-chi*, 1951 edition, I, 137–156.

22. Mao Tse-tung, *Chung-kuo ke-ming chan-cheng ti chan-lüeh wen-t'i* (n.p., 1943), pp. 1–3.

23. *Ibid.*, p. 9.

24. *Ibid.*, p. 7.

25. *Ibid.*, p. 14. In the revised *Hsüan-chi*, 1951 edition, I, 180, the following appeal to theory was inserted to precede the quoted sentence: "They call themselves Marxist-Leninists, but had actually not learned even an iota of Marxism-Leninism. Lenin said: 'The most essential thing in Marxism, the living soul of Marxism, is the concrete analysis of concrete conditions.' These comrades had forgotten exactly this point."

26. Mao Tse-tung, *Mao Tse-tung lun-wen chi* (Shanghai, 1937), p. 18.

27. *Ibid.*, p. 46. In *Hsüan-chi*, 1951 edition, I, 267, the italicized phrase was deleted.

28. *Hsüan-chi*, 1951 edition, I, 288 admitted that "On Contradiction" had been revised with material added and deleted. A. A. Cohen, "How Original is 'Maoism'?" *Problems of Communism*, X, No. 6 (November–December, 1961), pp. 35–36, argues that these two articles in their present form were not written in 1937, but in 1950 and 1952 respectively. D. J. Doolin and P. J. Golas in *"On Contradiction* in the Light of Mao Tse-tung's Essay on 'Dialectical Materialism',"* China Quarterly*, No. 19 (July–September, 1964), pp. 38–41, continued the same argument for "On Contradiction," but no longer mentioned "On Practice." S. R. Schram, in his introduction to *The Political Thought of Mao Tse-tung*, pp. 43–46, argued that the substance of these two articles dated back to 1937, although he granted that they might have been modified in their present versions. Schram, by citing Chang Ju-hsin, "Study and Master Mao Tse-tung's Theory and Practice," *Chieh-fang jih-pao* (February 18–19, 1942), showed that a version of "On Practice" existed before the start of the Sino-Japanese war. Neither side insisted that the 1951 edition is completely authentic. In terms of the content, I agree with Schram that the concern of these two articles could be traced back to 1937. But specifically, by comparing the level of sophistication in these two articles with the intellectual orientation of Mao in 1937, I would say that the 1951 edition of "On Practice" was not much revised. The emphasis on practice-oriented knowledge has been a persistent theme in Mao's thought. On the other hand, the 1951 edition of "On Contradiction" presents a theoretical sophistication more advanced than was revealed in Mao's subject-object contradiction of 1936, or in "On the New Stage" (1938), or in "On Dialectical Materialism" (1940). Therefore I would say that the present version of "On Contradiction" is unreliable.

29. *Hsüan-chi*, 1951 ed., I, 273, 279, 281, 283. In "On New Democracy" (January, 1940), Mao tried to apply this approach to an evaluation of the Three Principles of the People: "The old Three People's Principles were revolutionary in the old period, and reflected the historical particularism of the old period. But if one still wants to repeat the old stuff in the new period, . . . then he is a reactionary thing, ignorant of the times." In *Chieh-fang*, Nos. 98–99 (February 20, 1940), 34–35.

30. Mao Tse-tung, *Lun hsin chiai-tuan* ([Yenan], 1942 reprint of 1938 ed.), p. 101. The *Hsüan-chi*, 1951 edition, II, 521, is revised to read: "We should not study the words of Marxist-Leninist theory, but study it as the science of revolution. We should not only understand the conclusions about general laws which Marx, Engels, Lenin and Stalin derived from their extensive study of real life and revolutionary experience, but also study their standpoint and approach in viewing problems and solving them."

31. *Lun hsin chiai-tuan*, p. 102. The *Hsüan-chi*, 1951 edition, II, 522, is revised to read: "Communists are Marxist-internationalists, but Marxism must be integrated with the specific characteristics of our country and given a national form, before it can be put into practice. The great strength of Marxism-Leninism lies in its integration with the specific revolutionary practice of different countries. In the case of the C.C.P., it is a matter of

learning to apply the theory of Marxism-Leninism in the specific circumstances of China."

32. *Lun hsin chiai-tuan*, p. 102. The *Hsüan-chi*, 1951 edition, II, 522 is revised to read: "Our nation has a history of several thousand years, a history which has its specific characteristics and is full of treasures." The other sentence remained the same.

33. Cf. below, pp. 128–129.

34. In *Chieh-fang*, Nos. 98–99 (February 20, 1940), 22.

35. Translation from Doolin and Golas, "*On Contradiction* in the Light of Mao Tse-tung's Essay on 'Dialectical Materialism'," *op. cit.* (n. 28), p. 43.

36. *Chung-kuo ke-ming chan-cheng ti chan-lüeh wen-t'i*, p. 3. The *Hsüan-chi*, 1951 edition, I, 165, is revised to read: "They do not see that although we must cherish the Soviet experiences of war . . . we must also cherish the experience of China's revolutionary war."

37. *Lun hsin chiai-tuan*, pp. 34–35. The entire paragraph from which this quote is extracted was deleted from the *Hsüan-chi*, 1951 edition, II, 529–530. In its stead was placed a new paragraph, which still retained the contrast between the Western (specifically including Russian) experience of revolutionary movement from the cities to the countryside and the Chinese experience of revolutionary war from the countryside to the cities. Incidentally, this newly written paragraph was, in turn, deleted from the Moscow-sponsored English translation in *Selected Works*, II, 267.

38. Cf. below, pp. 120–121.

39. Mao tse-tung et al., *Kai-tsao hsüeh-hsi* (n.p. [1943]), p. 65.

40. These are the main speeches by Mao in connection with the *cheng-feng* movement: A February, 1942, revision of his May 5, 1941, speech, "The Reform of Our Studies"; the February 1, 1942, speech, "Reform in Learning, the Party and Literature"; the February 8, 1942, speech, "Oppose the Party's 'Eight-legged' Formalism"; and the May, 1942, opening and concluding talks before the Yenan Forum on Art and Literature.

41. "The Reform of Our Studies," in Mao, *op. cit.* (n. 39), p. 26. The *Hsüan-chi*, 1951 edition, III, 801 changed the italicized phrase to read: "in order to."

42. "Reform in Learning, the Party and Literature," in *Kai-tsao hsüeh-hsi*, p. 12.

43. *Ibid.*, p. 19.

44. Mao Tse-tung, *Lun lien-ho cheng-fu* (Chang-chia-k'ou, 1945), p. 83.

45. See "On Some Important Problems of the Party's Present Policy" (January, 1948), *Hsüan-chi*, 1951 ed., IV, 1267–1268; "A Circular on the Situation" (March, 1948), *ibid.*, pp. 1295–1296; "A Talk to the Editorial Staff of the *Shansi-Suiyuan Daily*" (April, 1948), *ibid.*, pp. 1320–1321; "On the People's Democratic Dictatorship" (June, 1949), *ibid.*, pp. 1484–1485.

46. "The Bankruptcy of the Idealist Conception of History," *ibid.*, pp. 1513, 1519.

47. Cf. above, p. 45 for the argument behind this sentence.

48. "The Bankruptcy of the Idealist Conception of History," *Hsüan-chi*, 1951 ed., IV, 1516.

49. *Hsüan-chi*, 1951 ed., I, 296.

50. *Ibid.*, pp. 295, 322.

51. Schram, *The Political Thought of Mao Tse-tung*, pp. 235–236.

52. *Communist China, 1955–1959; Policy Documents with Analysis* (Cambridge, Mass., 1962), p. 280.

53. *The Question of Agricultural Co-operation* (Peking, 1956), pp. 22 ff.

54. "The Bankruptcy of the Idealist Conception of History," *Hsüan-chi*, 1951 ed., IV, 1516.

55. *The Question of Agricultural Co-operation*, p. 9.

56. See Mao's 1936 interview with Edgar Snow, in Schram, *The Political Thought of Mao Tse-tung*, p. 256, and his 1940 insistence that the new democratic model is basically the same for all colonies and semicolonies, in *Chieh-fang*, Nos. 98–99 (February 20, 1940), p. 27.

57. A. M. Halpern, "The Foreign Uses of the Chinese Revolutionary Model," *China Quarterly*, No. 7 (July–September, 1961), pp. 1–16; D. S. Zagoria, *The Sino-Soviet Conflict, 1956–1961* (Princeton, 1962), pp. 266 ff.

58. *Hsüan-chi*, 1951 ed., I, 57; quoted in Cohen, "How Original is 'Maoism'?" *op. cit.* (n. 28), p. 38.

59. In *Chung-kuo nung-min*, No. 2 (February, 1926), p. 2.

60. *Ibid.*, p. 1. The awkward terms used in this quotation and in the chart taken from Mao's article represent literal translations of Mao's adaptations of Marxist concepts.

61. *Ibid.*, pp. 11–12.

62. *Ibid.*, p. 13.

63. All these points were deleted from the *Hsüan-chi*, 1951 edition, I, 3–9.

64. In Brandt et al., *A Documentary History of Chinese Communism*, p. 80. This version is based upon a compilation of various published 1927 texts in *Hsiang-tao, Chung-yang fu-k'an, Chinese Correspondence*, and *Revolutsionnyi Vostok*.

65. Brandt et al., *op. cit.*, p. 83. This passage was retained in the *Hsüan-chi*, 1947 edition, I, 7, but deleted from the 1951 edition, I, 17.

66. Brandt et al., *op. cit.*, p. 88.

67. *Ibid.*, p. 83.

68. *Ibid.*, p. 88.

69. *Hsüan-chi*, 1947 ed., Supplement, pp. 103–105. The wording in the *Hsüan-chi*, 1951 edition, I, 50–52, is slightly different.

70. *Hsüan-chi*, 1947 ed., Supplement, p. 54. The wording in the 1951 edition, I, 59, is slightly different.

71. *Hsüan-chi*, 1947 ed., Supplement, pp. 92–93. The version in the 1951 edition, I, 104–105, attempts to improve the consistency and the style of the 1947 version.

72. In *Hung-se Chung-hua*, No. 1 (December 11, 1931), 2. Available in *Shih-sou tzu-liao-shih kung-fei tzu-liao*.

73. "How to Undertake Rural Soviet Activities" in Chang and Mao, *Ch'u-hsiang su-wei-ai tsen-yang kung-tso*, p. 1.

74. Mao, *Chih-yu su-wei-ai neng-kou chiu Chung-kuo*, p. 22.

75. Mao, *Chung-kuo ke-ming chan-cheng ti chan-lüeh wen-t'i*, p. 17. The phraseology in *Hsüan-chi*, 1951 edition, I, 185, is slightly improved, and the last sentence ends more optimistically.

76. Cf. "On the Tactics of Fighting Japanese Imperialism" (December, 1935), *Hsüan-chi*, 1951 ed., I, 137; "The Present Tasks of China's Anti-

Japanese National United Front" (May, 1937), *Mao Tse-tung lun-wen chi,* p. 18.

77. Mao, *Chung-kuo ke-ming chan-cheng ti chan-lüeh wen-t'i,* p. 11.

78. *Mao Tse-tung lun-wen chi,* p. 33.

79. "The Urgent Tasks of the Chinese Revolution after the Establishment of the Joint Kuomintang-C.C.P. United Front," *ibid.,* p. 14. The phrasing in *Hsüan-chi,* 1951 edition, II, 358, is slightly different.

80. Mao, *Chung-kuo ke-ming chan-cheng ti chan-lüeh wen-t'i,* p. 11.

81. Cf. above, p. 116.

82. In *Lun ch'ih-chiu chan* (Yenan, 1938), p. 21, Mao Tse-tung differentiated China and Ethiopia; in Mao Tse-tung et al., *K'ang-Jih yu-chi chancheng ti i-pan wen-t'i* (Yenan, 1938), p. 11, he differentiated China and Morocco.

83. See *Lun ch'ih chiu chan,* p. 16.

84. *Lun hsin chiai-tuan,* pp. 15, 34.

85. *Ibid.,* p. 44.

86. *Ibid.,* p. 102.

87. Mao Tse-tung et al., *Chung-kuo ch'ing-yün wen-hsüan* (Yenan, 1940), pp. 13–14. All italicized passages are either deleted from or attenuated in *Hsüan-chi,* 1951 edition, II, 545–546.

88. According to *Hsüan-chi,* 1951 ed., II, 616, chapter 1 of the pamphlet on Chinese society was written by others, but revised by Mao; chapter 2, on the Chinese revolution, was written by Mao himself. Comparing the content of these two chapters with the development of Mao's thought in the late thirties, I have no reason to challenge that assertion. Since Mao supervised the writing of chapter 1, I will consider both chapters as evidence for Mao's idea of China in 1939.

89. Mao Tse-tung, *Chung-kuo ke-ming yü Chung-kuo Kung-ch'an-tang* ([Yenan], [1939]), p. 3. The italicized phrases were revised in *Hsüan-chi,* 1951 edition, II, 617. This certainly sounded more Marxist than in 1936, when Mao said: "The existence of mankind is organized into three major periods: the period of peaceful existence, the period of warring existence, and again the period of peaceful existence. We are now at the transitional point between the second and the third periods." *Chung-kuo ke-ming chancheng ti chan-lüeh wen-t'i,* p. 4. This passage has been deleted in *Hsüan-chi,* 1951 edition, I, 167.

90. *Chung-kuo ke-ming yü Chung-kuo Kung-ch'an-tang,* p. 3. Revised to read "remained sluggish in her economic, political and cultural development" in *Hsüan-chi,* 1951 edition, II, 618.

91. *Chung-kuo ke-ming yü Chung-kuo Kung-ch'an-tang,* p. 5.

92. *Ibid.,* p. 6.

93. *Ibid.* The *Hsüan-chi,* 1951 edition, II, 620, is revised to read: "It was not until the mid-nineteenth century, with the penetration of foreign capitalism, that great changes occurred within this society. As China's feudal society developed its commodity economy and possessed within itself the embryo of capitalism, even without the influence of foreign capitalism, China would have slowly developed into a capitalist society. The penetration of foreign capitalism acclerated this development." The 1951 edition tried to restore that internal dynamics to Chinese history which Mao in 1939 did not provide for premodern, feudal China.

94. *Chung-kuo ke-ming yü Chung-kuo Kung-ch'an-tang*, pp. 11-12.

95. *Ibid.*, pp. 20-21. Deleted from the *Hsüan-chi*, 1951 edition, II, 633, where the implication was much stronger that the entire landlord class was the enemy of the revolution.

96. *Chung-kuo ke-ming yü Chung-kuo Kung-ch'an-tang*, p. 22.

97. *Ibid.*, p. 23. The *Hsüan-chi*, 1951 edition, II, 635, reconstituted the petty bourgeoisie as the following: intelligentsia, small merchants, handicraftsmen, professionals. Mao's assessment of the revolutionary inclination of the petty bourgeoisie was more enthusiastic in 1939, than in the 1951 edition.

98. *Chung-kuo ke-ming yü Chung-kuo Kung-ch'an-tang*, pp. 26-27.

99. In *ibid.*, p. 29, Mao included the vagrants as a part of the proletariat. The *Hsüan-chi*, 1951 edition, II, 640-641, separated the two.

100. *Chung-kuo ke-ming yü Chung-kuo Kung-ch'an-tang*, p. 29.

101. In *Chieh-fang*, Nos. 98-99 (February 20, 1940), 23.

102. *Ibid.*, p. 26. Italicized passages are deleted in the 1951 edition, II, 666.

103. *Chieh-fang*, Nos. 98-99, p. 24.

104. *Ibid.*, p. 27.

105. *Ibid.*, The *Hsüan-chi*, 1951 edition, II, 668, deleted the two italicized sentences and substituted: "History has proved that the Chinese bourgeoisie is unable to fulfill this responsibility, which consequently must fall upon the shoulders of the proletariat."

106. *Chieh-fang*, Nos. 98-99, p. 28. The *Hsüan-chi*, 1951 edition, II, 671, changed the quote to read: "Under the leadership of the proletariat, the state operated enterprises of the new democratic republic are socialist in character and constitute the leading force in the entire economy; but this republic does not take over other capitalist private properties."

107. *Chieh-fang*, Nos. 98-99, p. 28. The *Hsüan-chi*, 1951 edition, II, 671, changed the quote to read: "the land of the landlords."

108. *Chieh-fang*, Nos. 98-99, p. 39. The *Hsüan-chi*, 1951 edition, II, 697-698 skillfully expanded this quote to read as follows (italics added to indicate additions to the 1940 version): "So far as national culture is concerned, *the guiding role is fulfilled by the communist ideology, and efforts should be made to disseminate socialism and communism among the working class and to educate, properly and methodically, the peasantry and other sections of the masses in socialism. But* the national culture is at present not yet a socialist culture. *New democratic politics, economy and culture all contain a socialist element, and not an ordinary but a decisive one at that, because they are under the leadership of the proletariat. But taken as a whole, the political, economic and cultural conditions are as yet not socialist but new democratic. For the Chinese revolution at the present stage, with its central task of combating foreign imperialism and domestic feudalism, is a bourgeois democratic revolution and not yet a socialist revolution aiming to overthrow capitalism. In the sphere of national culture,* it is wrong to assume that the national culture as a whole at present is or should be a socialist national culture. . . . *As there is a socialist factor in our politics and economy, so there will be a socialist factor in our national culture by way of reflection; but taking our society as a whole,* we have not yet *achieved* this kind of *wholly socialist* politics and economy, therefore cannot yet have this kind of *wholly socialist* national culture."

109. Compared with the *Hsüan-chi*, 1951 edition, Vol. II, the original

versions of these two pamphlets emphasized more the immobility of the feudal stage of Chinese history, the dependence upon the external dynamics of imperialism to lead feudal China into her semicolonial, semifeudal period, the separation of the democratic and socialist stages of China's revolution, the broad basis of the new democratic united front in which practically all classes, except the big landlords and the compradore-capitalists, could be included.

110. In *Mao's China: Party Reform Documents, 1942–44*, pp. 247–248. The *Hsüan-chi*, 1951 edition, III, 810, reads as follows: "Chinese society is one with two heads and a large middle; the proletariat and the landlords and big capitalists are the minorities; the broadest masses are the peasantry, the urban petty bourgeoisie and other intermediate classes."

111. In Schram, *The Political Thought of Mao Tse-tung*, p. 223. The sentence was deleted from the *Hsüan-chi*, 1951 edition, III, 857.

112. In "On Coalition Government," Mao said: "We communists advocate the establishment of a coalition government, because at present there is no democratic electorate system, and a coalition is necessary for unity against Japan. But what happens in the future, when there will be a democratic electorate system . . . ? In China, there appeared early a C.C.P. representing not only the proletariat . . . , but also simultaneously the broadest peasantry, petty bourgeoisie, intellectuals and other democratic elements. . . . Therefore the situation is entirely different. Any government which excludes the communist party can accomplish no good—this is the fundamental characteristic of a China entering the new democratic stage of history." *Lun lien-ho cheng-fu*, p. 42. This entire paragraph was deleted from the *Hsüan-chi*, 1951 edition, III, 1063.

113. *Lun lien-ho cheng-fu*, p. 30.

114. *Ibid.*, p. 34. In the *Hsüan-chi*, 1951 edition, III, 1056, the phrase is changed to read: "a state of the united front of democratic alliance based on the overwhelming majority of the people, under the leadership of the working class."

115. *Lun lien-ho cheng-fu*, pp. 3–4. The entire passage was deleted from the *Hsüan-chi*, 1951 edition, III, 1032.

116. In "On the Chungking Negotiations" (October, 1945), Mao said: "The general trend of China's development is certainly for the better, not for the worse. The world is progressing, the future is bright and no one can change this general trend of history." *Hsüan-chi*, 1951 ed., IV, 1162.

117. "Talk with the American Correspondent Anna Louise Strong," *ibid.*, 1951 ed., IV, 1191.

118. "Greet the New High Tide of the Chinese Revolution," *ibid.*, 1951 ed., IV, 1210–1211.

119. *Ibid.*, p. 1211.

120. "The Present Situation and Our Tasks," *ibid.*, 1951 ed., IV, 1259–1260.

121. "Speech at a Conference of Cadres in the Shansi-Suiyuan Liberated Area" (April, 1948), *ibid.*, 1951 ed., IV, 1311.

122. Cf. "On the Question of the National Bourgeoisie and the Enlightened Gentry" (March, 1948), *ibid.*, 1951 ed., IV, 1285–1286; "Proclamation of the Chinese People's Liberation Army" (April, 1949), *ibid.*, 1951 ed., IV, 1459–1461.

123. *Ibid.,* 1951 ed., IV, 1480–1481.

124. *Ibid.,* 1951 ed., IV, 1482.

125. "The Question of Agricultural Cooperation," *Communist China, 1955–59,* p. 101.

126. *Ibid.,* In "On the Correct Handling of Contradictions among the People," Mao said: "In discussing our path of industrialization, I am concerned here principally with the relationship between the growth of heavy industry, light industry and agriculture. Heavy industry is the core of China's economic construction. This must be affirmed. But, at the same time, full attention must be paid to the development of agriculture and light industry. As China is a great agricultural country, with over eighty per cent of its population in the villages, its industry and agriculture must be developed simultaneously. Only then will industry have raw materials and a market, and only so will it be possible to accumulate fairly large funds for the building of a powerful heavy industry. . . . With the development of agriculture and light industry, heavy industry will be assured of its market and funds, and thus grow faster." *Ibid.,* pp. 293–294.

127. "The Question of Agricultural Cooperation," *ibid.,* p. 104.

128. In "On the Correct Handling of Contradictions among the People," Mao said: "The superstructure . . . has played a positive role in facilitating the victory of socialist transformation and establishment of a socialist organization of labor. . . . But survivals of bourgeois ideology, bureaucratic ways of doing things in our state organs, and flaws in certain links in our state institutions stand in contradiction to the economic base of socialism. We must continue to resolve such contradictions in the light of specific conditions." *Ibid.,* p. 281.

129. Cf. above, p. 120.

130. Editorial notes by Mao to "Socialist Upsurge in the Countryside" (December, 1955), in Schram, *The Political Thought of Mao Tse-tung,* p. 251. Elsewhere, Mao claimed: "The point is that in the latter half of 1955 the situation in China underwent a fundamental change." In *Communist China, 1955–59,* p. 118.

131. Mao Tse-tung, *Ti-kuo chu-i ho i-ch'ieh fan-tung p'ai tu-shih chih lao-hu* (Peking, 1958), pp. 24–25.

132. In *Ventures,* V:1 (Winter, 1965), p. 35.

133. "Introducing A Co-operative," *Peking Review,* I, No. 15 (June 10, 1958), 6.

Bibliography

The following is a list of the works I consulted for this study. Some titles are directly related to the topic of the Marxist ideas of China, but more of them provide the historical background of the Marxist ideas of China. The titles are arranged according to the following subheadings: Methodological Aids; Works of Marx, Engels, Lenin, and Mao; The European Background; Western Marxism; The Russian Background; Russian Marxism; The Chinese Background; and Chinese Communism.

METHODOLOGICAL AIDS

Bendix, Reinhard. *Max Weber; An Intellectual Portrait*, Anchor ed. (Garden City, N. Y., 1962).

Bramson, Leon. *The Political Context of Sociology* (Princeton, 1961).

Collingwood, R. G. *An Essay in Philosophical Method* (Oxford, 1933).

———. *An Essay on Metaphysics* (Oxford, 1940).

Dray, William. *Laws and Explanation in History* (London, 1957).

Levenson, Joseph R. "'History' and 'Value': The Tensions of Intellectual Choice in Modern China," *Studies in Chinese Thought,* ed. A. F. Wright (Chicago, 1953), pp. 146–194.

Mannheim, Karl. *Essays on Sociology and Social Psychology,* ed. P. Kecskemeti (London, 1953).

———. *Essays on the Sociology of Knowledge* (New York, 1952).

———. *Ideology and Utopia: An Introduction to the Sociology of Knowledge,* tr. L. Wirth and E. Shils, Harvest ed. (New York, n.d.).

Merton, Robert K. *Social Theory and Social Structure,* rev. and enl. ed. (Glencoe, Ill., 1957).

Shils, Edward. "The Intellectuals and the Powers: Some Perspectives for Comparative Analysis," *Comparative Studies in Society and History,* I (1958–1959), 5–22.

Vico, Giambattista. *The New Science,* tr. T. G. Bergin and M. H. Fisch, Anchor ed. (New York, 1961).

Weber, Max. *From Max Weber: Essays in Sociology,* tr., ed. with introd. H. H. Gerth and C. W. Mills (New York, 1946).

———. *The Theory of Social and Economic Organization,* tr. A. M. Henderson and T. Parsons, introd. T. Parsons (New York, 1947).

Whitehead, Alfred North. *Adventures of Ideas,* Pelican ed. (London, 1942).

WORKS OF MARX, ENGELS, LENIN, AND MAO

Rubel, Maximilien. *Bibliographie des Oeuvres de Karl Marx* (Paris, 1956).
Marx, Karl. *Articles on India*, 2d Indian ed., introd. R. P. Dutt (Bombay, 1951).
————. *Capital, A Critique of Political Economy*, Vol. I: *The Process of Capitalist Production*, tr. from 3d German ed. S. Moore and E. Aveling, ed. F. Engels, rev. and amplified according to 4th German ed. E. Untermann (Chicago, 1909). Vol. II: *The Process of Circulation of Capital*, ed. F. Engels, tr. from 2d German ed. E. Untermann (Chicago, 1909). Vol. III: *The Process of Capitalist Production as a Whole*, ed. F. Engels, tr. from 1st German ed. E. Untermann (Chicago, 1909).
————. *A Contribution to the Critique of Political Economy*, tr. from 2d German ed. N. I. Stone (Chicago, 1904).
————. *Grundrisse der Kritik der politischen Ökonomie (Rohentwurf)*, *1857–1858* (Berlin, 1953).
————. *A History of Economic Theories from the Physiocrats to Adam Smith*, ed. K. Kautsky, tr. T. McCarthy, 1st ed. (New York, 1952).
————. *Marx on China, 1853–1860: Articles from the New York Daily Tribune*, introd. and notes D. Torr (London, 1951).
————. *Selected Writings in Sociology and Social Philosophy*, ed. with introd. and notes T. B. Bottomore and M. Rubel, tr. M. Rubel (London, 1956).
————. *Theories of Surplus Value; A Selection from Theorien über der Mehrwert*, ed. K. Kautsky, tr. G. A. Bonner and E. Burns (London, 1951).
Marx, Karl, and Friedrich Engels. *Arkhiv Marksa i Engelsa*, ed. V. Adoratskii and M. B. Mitin (Moscow, 1933–55), 13 vols.
————. *Aus dem literarischen Nachlass von Karl Marx, Friedrich Engels und Ferdinand Lassalle*, ed. F. Mehring (Stuttgart, 1902).
————. *Ausgewählte Briefe*, ed. V. Adoratskii (Zürich, 1934).
————. *Briefe an A. Bebel, W. Liebknecht, K. Kautsky und andere*, Vol. I: *1870–1886*, ed. V. Adoratskii (Moscow and Leningrad, 1933).
————. *The Civil War in the United States*, ed. R. Enmale, 2d ed. (New York, 1940).
————. *Historisch-kritische Gesamtausgabe, Werke, Schriften, Briefe*, Series I, 7 vols.; Series III, 4 vols., ed. D. Riazanov and V. Adoratskii (Moscow, 1927 ff.).
————. *Letters to Americans, 1848–1895: A Selection*, tr. L. E. Mins (New York, 1953).
————. *Manifesto of the Communist Party*, authorized English tr., ed. and annot. F. Engels (New York, 1932).
————. *Revolution and Counter-revolution; or Germany in 1848*, ed. E. M. Aveling (London, 1896).
————. *Revolution in Spain* (New York, 1939).
————. *The Russian Menace to Europe; A Collection of Articles, Speeches, Letters and News Dispatches*, selected and ed. P. W. Blackstock and B. F. Hoselitz (Glencoe, Ill., 1952).
————. *Selected Correspondence, 1846–1895*, tr. with explanatory notes D. Torr (New York, 1942).

——. *Sochineniia*, ed. V. Adoratskii (Moscow, 1928–1934), 12 vols.

Engels, Friedrich. *Aus der Frühzeit des Marxismus: Engels' Briefwechsel mit Kautsky*, ed. with explanatory notes K. Kautsky (Prague, 1935).

——. *The Condition of the Working-Class in England in 1844*, with the 1892 preface, tr. F. K. Wischnewetzky (London, 1892).

——. *Dialectis of Nature*, tr. C. Dutt, preface and notes by J. B. S. Haldane (New York, 1940).

——. *Herr Eugen Dühring's Revolution in Science*, tr. E. Burns, ed. C. P. Dutt (New York, 1939).

——. *Ludwig Feuerbach and the Outcome of Classical German Philosophy*, ed. C. P. Dutt (New York, 1941).

——. *The Origin of the Family, Private Property and the State* (New York, 1942).

——. *The Peasant War in Germany*, tr. M. J. Olgin (New York, 1926).

——. *Socialism, Utopian and Scientific*, tr. E. Aveling, introd. F. Engels, 4th ed. (London, 1918).

Spravochnik k II i III Izdaniiam Sochineniia V. I. Lenina (Moscow, and Leningrad, 1935).

Alfavitnyi Ukazatel Proizvedenii V. I. Lenina; Voshedshikh v IV Izdanie Sochinenii (Leningrad, 1951).

Lenin, V. I. *Collected Works of V. I. Lenin* (New York, 1927–1932), Vols. IV, XIII, XVIII, XIX, XX, XXI.

——. *Leninskii Sbornik*, ed. L. Kamenev, N. Bukharin, and V. Adoratskii (Moscow, 1924–33), 23 vols.

——. *O Kitae* (Moscow and Leningrad, 1926).

——. *Selected Works*, ed. J. and A. Fineberg, I. Levin (New York, 1935), 12 vols.

——. *Sochineniia*, 2nd ed. (Moscow and Leningrad, 1926–1932), 30 vols.

——. *Sochineniia*, 4th ed. (Moscow, 1941 ff.), 35 vols.

Columbia University. *Guide to the Writings of Mao Tse-tung in the East Asiatic Library* (New York, 1951).

Mao Tse-tung. "Analysis of the Classes in Chinese Society," *Chung-kuo nung-min*, No. 2 (February, 1926), pp. 1–13.

——. *Chih-yu su-wei-ai neng-kou chiu Chung-kuo* (Moscow, 1934).

——. *Ching-chi chien-she yü ch'a-t'ien yün-tung* (Moscow, 1934).

——. *Chung-kuo ke-ming chan-cheng ti chan-lüeh wen-t'i* (n.p., 1943).

——. *Chung-kuo ke-ming yü Chung-kuo Kung-ch'an-tang* ([Yenan], [1939]).

——. *Comrade Mao Tse-tung on "Imperialism and All Reactionaries Are Paper Tigers"* (Peking, 1958).

——. *Hsin min-chu chu-i lun* (Yenan, 1940).

——. "Introducing a Co-operative," *Peking Review*, I:15 (June 10, 1958), 6.

——. *Kai-tsao hsüeh-hsi* (n.p., [1943]).

——. *K'ang-Jih yu-chi chan-cheng ti chan-lüeh wen-t'i* (Hankow, 1938).

——. *Kuan-yü mu-ch'ien kuo-chi hsing-shih yü Chung-kuo k'ang-chan ti t'an-hua* (n.p., n.d.).

——. *Lun ch'ih-chiu chan* (Yenan, 1938).

——. *Lun hsin chiai-tuan* ([Yenan], 1942 reprint of 1938 ed.).

——. *Lụn lien-ho cheng-fu* (Chang-chia-k'ou, 1945).

———. *Mao chu-hsi tsai Su-lien ti yen-lun* (Peking, 1957).

———. *Mao Tse-tung hsüan-chi*, 1944 ed. (Shansi-Chahar-Hopei Border Area, 1944), Vol. II; 1947 ed. (Shansi-Chahar-Hopei Border Area, 1947), 6 vols.; 1947 ed., Supplement (Shansi-Chahar-Hopei Border Area, 1947); 1951 ed. (Peking, 1951–60), 4 vols.

———. *Mao Tse-tung lun-wen chi* (Shanghai, 1937).

———. *Mao Tse-tung tzu-chuan* (Shanghai, 1937).

———. "On Dialectical Materialism; A Fragment," tr. and annotated by C. S. Chao, *Studies in Soviet Thought*, III (December, 1963), 270–277.

———. *On the Correct Handling of Contradictions among the People* (Peking, 1957).

———. "Opening Address to the Eighth National Congress" (September 15, 1956), *People's China*, No. 19 (October 1, 1956), pp. 4–6.

———. *The Question of Agricultural Cooperation* (Peking, 1956).

———. "Report to the Party Plenum" (June 6, 1950), *People's China*, II:1 (July 1, 1950), 4–6.

———. *Selected Works* (New York, 1954 ff.), 5 vols.

———. *Selected Works of Mao Tse-tung*, 1st ed. (Peking, 1961), Vol. IV.

———. *Selected Military Writings of Mao Tse-tung* (Peking, 1963).

———. *Ti-kuo chu-i ho i-ch'ieh fan-tung p'ai tu-shih chih lao-hu* (Peking, 1958).

———. *Tsai Yenan wen-i-tso t'an-hui shang ti chiang-hua* ([Yenan], 1943).

———. *Une Etude de l'Education physique*, tr. and ed. S. R. Schram (Paris, 1962).

———. et al. *Chung-kuo ch'ing-yün wen-hsuan* (Yenan, 1940).

———. et al. *Dr. Sun Yat-sen: Commemorative Articles and Speeches* (Peking, 1957).

———. et al. *K'ang-Jih chiu-kuo chih-nan* (Shanghai, 1937).

Shih-sou tzu-liao-shih kung-fei tzu-liao (microfilm and photostat at Hoover Institute, Stanford, Calif.).

THE EUROPEAN BACKGROUND

Arendt, Hannah. *The Human Condition* (Chicago, 1958).

———. *On Revolution* (New York, 1963).

Baillie, John. *The Belief in Progress* (London, 1950).

Barber, Elinor G. *The Bourgeoisie in Eighteenth-Century France* (Princeton, 1955).

Barthold, V. V. *Istoriia Izucheniia Vostoka v Evrope i v Rossii*, 2d ed. (London, 1925).

Bauer, Otto. *Die Nationalitätenfrage und die Sozialdemokratie* (Vienna, 1909).

Becker, Carl. *Heavenly City of the Eighteenth-Century Philosophers* (New York, 1932).

Bernier, François. *Voyages de François Bernier* (Paris, 1830), 2 vols.

Boxer, C. R. "Some Aspects of Western Historical Writing on the Far East, 1500–1800," *Historians of China and Japan*, ed. W. G. Beasley and E. G. Pulleyblank (London and New York, 1961), pp. 307–327.

Bruford, W. H. *Germany in the Eighteenth Century; The Social Background of the Literary Revival* (Cambridge, England, 1935).
Buber, Martin. *Paths in Utopia*, tr. R. F. C. Hull, introd. E. Fischoff (New York, 1950).
Bury, J. B. *The Idea of Progress; An Enquiry into Its Origin and Growth* (New York, 1923).
Cassirer, Ernst. *The Myth of the State*, Anchor ed. (New York, 1955).
———. *The Philosophy of the Enlightenment*, tr. F. C. A. Koelln and J. P. Pettegrove (Boston, 1955).
Clapham, J. H. *The Economic Development of France and Germany, 1815–1914*, 4th ed. (Cambridge, England, 1936).
Clark, Robert T., Jr. *Herder; His Life and Thought* (Berkeley, 1955).
Collingwood, R. G. *The Idea of History* (Oxford, 1946).
———. *The Idea of Nature* (Oxford, 1945).
Croce, B. *What Is Living and What Is Dead of the Philosophy of Hegel*, tr. from 3d ed. D. Ainslie (London, 1915).
Dawson, Christopher. *Progress and Religion: an Historical Enquiry* (London, New York, 1933).
Dawson, R. "Western Conceptions of Chinese Civilization," *The Legacy of China*, ed. R. Dawson (Oxford, 1964), pp. 1–27.
Elton, G. *The Revolutionary Idea in France, 1789–1871*, 2d ed. (London, 1937).
Ergang, R. R. *Herder and the Foundations of German Nationalism* (New York, 1931).
Findlay, J. N. *Hegel; A Re-Examination* (London, 1958).
Frankel, Charles. *The Faith of Reason; The Idea of Progress in the French Enlightenment* (New York, 1948).
Grégoire, Franz. *Etudes hégéliennes. Les Points capitaux du Système* (Louvain and Paris, 1958).
Guy, Basil. "The French Image of China before and after Voltaire," *Travaux sur Voltaire et le dix-huitième Siècle*, ed. T. Besterman (Geneva, 1963), Vol. XXI.
Hamerow, Theodore S. *Restoration, Revolution, Reaction: Economics and Politics in Germany, 1815–1871* (Princeton, 1958).
Hazard, Paul. *The European Mind (1680–1715)*, tr. J. L. May, Meridian ed. (Cleveland and New York, 1963).
———. *European Thought in the Eighteenth Century*, tr. J. L. May (London, 1954).
Hegel, G. W. F. *Lectures on the Philosophy of History*, tr. J. Sibree (London, 1894).
Herder, J. G. *Outlines of a Philosophy of the History of Man*, tr. T. Churchill (London, 1800).
Hudson, G. F. *Europe and China; A Survey of Their Relation from the Earliest Times to 1800* (London, 1931).
Hughes, H. Stuart. *Consciousness and Society; the Reorientation of European Society, 1890–1930* (New York, 1958).
Hyppolite, Jean. *Genèse et Structure de la Phénoménologie de l'Esprit de Hegel* (Paris, 1946).
———. *Introduction à la Philosophie de l'Histoire de Hegel* (Paris, 1948).
———. *Logique et Existence; Essai sur la Logique de Hegel* (Paris, 1953).

Jones, Richard. *An Essay on the Distribution of Wealth and on the Sources of Taxation* (London, 1831).

———. *Literary Remains, consisting of Lectures and Tracts on Political Economy*, ed. W. Whewell (London, 1859).

Koebner, R. "Despot and Despotism: Vicissitudes of a Political Term," *Journal of the Warburg and Courtauld Institutes*, XIV (1951), 275 ff.

Kohn, Hans. *The Idea of Nationalism* (New York, 1944).

Kohn-Bramstedt, Ernst. *Aristocracy and the Middle Classes in Germany; Social Types in German Literature, 1830–1900*, foreword by G. P. Gooch (London, 1937).

Krieger, Leonard. *The German Idea of Freedom: History of a Political Tradition* (Boston, 1957).

Kroner, Richard. *Kant's Weltanschauung*, tr. J. E. Smith (Chicago, 1956).

Lach, Donald F. "China and the Era of the Enlightenment," *Journal of Modern History*, XIV (1942), 209–223.

———. *Contribution of China to German Civilization, 1648–1740* (Chicago, 1941).

Laski, Harold. *The Rise of Liberalism* (New York, 1936).

Leibniz, G. W. *The Preface to Novissima Sinica*, commentary and tr. D. F. Lach (Honolulu, 1957).

Löwith, Karl. *Meaning in History* (Chicago, 1949).

Lovejoy, A. O. *Essays in the History of Ideas*, Capricorn ed. (New York, 1960).

Marcuse, Herbert. *Reason and Revolution; Hegel and the Rise of Social Theory*, 2d ed. (London, 1955).

Mason, Mary G. *Western Concepts of China and the Chinese, 1840–1876* (New York, 1939).

Maverick, Lewis A. *China a Model for Europe* (San Antonio, Texas, 1946), 2 vols.

Merz, T. *History of European Thought in the Ninteenth Century* (Edinburgh, 1896–1914), 4 vols.

Mills, John Stuart. *Principles of Political Economy* (Boston, 1848).

Montesquieu. *Oeuvres complètes de Montesquieu*, ed. A. Masson (Paris, 1950–1955), 3 vols.

Mornet, D. *Les Origines intellectuelles de la Révolution française, 1715–1787* (Paris, 1933).

Mueller, G. E. "The Hegel Legend of 'Thesis-Antithesis-Synthesis'," *Journal of the History of Ideas*, XIX (1958), 411–414.

Namier, Lewis B. *1848: The Revolution of the Intellectuals* (Oxford, 1946).

Pinot, V. *La Chine et la Formation de l'Esprit philosophique en France, 1640–1740* (Paris, 1932).

Plamenatz, John. *The Revolutionary Movement in France, 1815–1871* (London, 1952).

Quesnay, François. *Oeuvres économiques et philosophiques de François Quesnay*, ed. with introd. A. Oncken (Frankfurt and Paris, 1888).

Reichwein, A. *China and Europe: Intellectual and Artistic Contacts in the Eighteenth Century*, tr. J. C. Powell (London, 1925).

Robertson, Priscilla. *Revolutions of 1848: A Social History* (Princeton, 1952).

Rose, E. "China as a Symbol of Reaction in Germany, 1830–1880," *Comparative Literature*, III (1951–1952), 57–76.

Rowbotham, Arnold H. "A Brief Account of the Early Development of Sinology," *Chinese Social and Political Science Review*, VII (1923), 113–138.

———. "China and the Age of Enlightenment in Europe," *Chinese Social and Political Science Review*, XIX (1935), 176–201.

———. *Missionary and Mandarin; The Jesuits at the Court of China* (Berkeley, 1942).

Ruggiero, Guido de. *History of European Liberalism* (London, 1927).

Sampson, R. V. *Progress in the Age of Reason; The Seventeenth Century to the Present Day* (London, 1956).

Schulin, Ernst. *Die weltgeschichtliche Erfassung des Orients bei Hegel und Ranke* (Göttingen, 1958).

Sée, Henri. *Economic and Social Conditions in France during the Eighteenth Century*, tr. E. H. Zeydel (New York, 1927).

Seldon, E. S. *China in German Poetry from 1773 to 1883* (Berkeley, 1942).

Smith, Adam. *An Enquiry into the Nature and Causes of the Wealth of Nations*, 5th ed. (New York, 1937).

Stace, W. T. *The Philosophy of Hegel: A Systematic Exposition*, Dover ed. (New York, 1955).

Stelling-Michaud, P. S. "Le Mythe du Despotisme oriental," *Schweizer Beiträge zur Allgemeinen Geschichte*, XVIII–XIX (1960–1961), 328–346.

Tuveson, E. C. *Millennium and Utopia; A Study in the Background of the Idea of Progress* (Berkeley, 1949).

Venturi, Franco. "Oriental Despotism," *Journal of the History of Ideas*, XXIV (1963), 133–142.

Voltaire. *The Age of Louis XIV and Other Selected Writings*, tr. and abridged with introd. J. H. Brumfitt (New York, 1963).

Weldon, T. D. *Kant's Critique of Pure Reason*, 2d ed. (Oxford, 1958).

Whitehead, Alfred North. *Science and the Modern World* (New York, 1925).

Willey, Basil. *The Eighteenth Century Background* (New York, 1940).

Wilson, Edmund. *To the Finland Station: A Study in the Writing and Acting of History*, Anchor ed. (Garden City, N.Y., n.d.).

Zilsel, E. "The Genesis of the Concept of Scientific Progress," *Journal of the History of Ideas*, VI (1945), 325–349.

WESTERN MARXISM

Acton, H. B. *The Illusion of the Epoch: Marxism-Leninism as a Philosophical Creed* (Boston, 1957).

Adams, H. P. *Karl Marx in His Earlier Writings* (London, 1940).

Axelos, K. *Marx, Penseur de la Technique de l'Aliénation de l'Homme à Conquête du Monde* (Paris, 1961).

Bell, Daniel. "Two Roads from Marx," *The End of Ideology*, by D. Bell (Glencoe, Ill., 1960), pp. 335–368.

Berlin, Isaiah. *Karl Marx; His Life and Environment*, Galaxy ed. (New York, 1959).

Bestor, Arthur E., Jr. "Evolution of the Socialist Vocabulary," *Journal of the History of Ideas*, IX (1948), 259–302.

Bloom, Solomon F. *The World of Nations; A Study of the National Implications in the Work of Karl Marx* (New York, 1941).

Bober, M. M. *Karl Marx's Interpretation of History*, 2d rev. ed. (Cambridge, Mass., 1948).

Böhm-Bawerk, Eugen von. *Karl Marx and the Close of His System: and Böhm-Bawerk's Criticism of Marx by Rudolph Hilferding*, ed. with introd. P. M. Sweezy (New York, 1949).

Bukharin, N. *Historical Materialism: A Systematic Sociology*, authorized tr. from 3d ed. (New York, 1925).

Carr, E. H. *Karl Marx; A Study in Fanaticism* (London, 1934).

Cole, G. D. H. *A History of Socialist Thought* (London and New York, 1955–1960), 5 vols. in 7 parts.

Cornforth, M. *Dialectical Materialism* (London, 1952–1954), 3 vols.

Cornu, Auguste. *Karl Marx; de l'Hégélianisme au Matérialisme historique* (Paris, 1934).

———. *Karl Marx et Friedrich Engels* (Paris, 1955–1958), 2 vols.

Croce, B. *Historical Materialism and the Economics of Karl Marx*, tr. C. M. Meredith (New York, 1914).

Daniels, R. V. *The Nature of Communism* (New York, 1962).

Federn, Karl. *The Materialist Conception of History* (London, 1939).

Gregoire, Franz. *Aux Sources de la Pensée de Marx, Hegel, Feuerbach* (Louvain and Paris, 1947).

Hammon, Oscar. "The Spectre of Communism in the 1840's," *Journal of the History of Ideas*, XIV (1953), 404–420.

Hook, Sidney. *From Hegel to Marx; Studies in the Intellectual Development of Karl Marx* (New York, 1950).

———. *Towards the Understanding of Karl Marx* (New York, 1933).

Hoselitz, B. F. "Karl Marx on Secular Economic and Political Development," *Comparative Studies in Society and History*, VI (1963–1964), 142–163.

International Workingmen's Association. *The First International; Minutes of the Hague Congress of 1872 with Related Documents*, ed. and tr. H. H. Gerth (Madison, Wis., 1958).

Kautsky Karl. *The Economic Doctrine of Karl Marx*, tr. H. J. Stenning (London, 1936).

———. *Ethics and the Materialist Conception of History*, tr. J .B. Askew, 4th rev. ed. (Chicago, 1918).

Krieger, Leonard. "Marx and Engels as Historians," *Journal of the History of Ideas*, XIV (1953), 381–403.

Laski, Harold. *Communist Manifesto, Socialist Landmark; A New Appreciation written for the Labour Party together with the Original Text and Prefaces* (London, 1948).

Lichtheim, George. "Marx and 'the Asiatic Mode of Production'," *Far Eastern Affairs: No. 3*, ed. G. F. Hudson (Carbondale, Ill., 1963), pp. 86–112.

———. *Marxism: A Historical and Critical Study* (New York, 1961).

Mayer, Gustav. *Friedrich Engels: A Biography*, tr. G. and H. Highet, ed. R. H. S. Crossman (London, 1936).

Mehring, Franz. *Karl Marx; the Story of His Life*, tr. E. Fitzgerald (London, 1936).

Meisner, Maurice. "The Despotism of Concepts: Wittfogel and Marx on China," *China Quarterly*, No. 16 (October–December, 1963), pp. 99–111.

Meyer, Alfred G. *Marxism: the Unity of Theory and Practice* (Cambridge, Mass., 1954).

Mitrany, David. *Marx against the Peasants* (London, 1951).

Monnerot, Jules. *Sociology and Psychology of Communism*, tr. J. Degras and R. Rees (Boston, 1953).

Naquet, P. Vidal. "Histoire et Idéologie: Karl Wittfogel et le Concept de 'Mode de Production asiatique'," *Annales: Economies, Sociétés, Civilisations*, XIX (1964), 531–549.

Nicolaievsky, B., and O. Maenchen-Helfen. *Karl Marx: Man and Fighter*, tr, G. David and E. Mosbacher (London, 1936).

Plamenatz, John. *German Marxism and Russian Communism* (London, 1954).

Popitz, Heinrich. *Der entfremdete Mensch: Zeitkritik und Geschichtsphilosophie des jungen Marx* (Basel, 1953).

Rostow, W. W. *The Stages of Economic Growth: A Non-Communist Manifesto* (Cambridge, England, 1960).

Rühle, Otto. *Karl Marx; His Life and Work*, tr. E. and C. Paul (New York, 1929).

Schlesinger, R. *Marx, His Time and Ours* (London, 1951).

Schumpeter, Joseph A. *Capitalism, Socialism, and Democracy*, 3d ed. (New York, 1950).

Schwarzschild Leopold. *Karl Marx, the Red Prussian*, Universal Library ed. (New York, n.d.).

Sée, Henri. *The Economic Interpretation of History*, tr. and introd. M. M. Knight (New York, 1929).

Stekloff, G. M. *History of the First International*, tr. E. and C. Paul (New York, 1928).

Sweezy, Paul M. *The Theory of Capitalist Development; Principles of Marxian Political Economy* (New York, 1942).

Tucker, Robert C. *Philosophy and Myth in Karl Marx* (New York, 1961).

Ulam, Adam B. *The Unfinished Revolution: An Essay on the Sources of Influences of Marxism and Communism* (New York, 1960).

Wittfogel, Karl A. "The Marxist View of China," *China Quarterly*, No. 11 (July–September, 1962), pp. 1–20; No. 12 (October–December, 1962), pp. 154–169.

———. "The Ruling Bureaucracy of Oriental Despotism," *Review of Politics*, XV (1953), 350–359.

THE RUSSIAN BACKGROUND

Adams, Arthur E. "The Character of Pestel's Thought," *American Slavic and E. European Review*, XII (1953), 153–161.

Arsenev, K., et al. *Intelligentsiia v Rossii: Sbornik Statei* (St. Petersburg, 1910).

Avakumovic, I. "A Statistical Approach to the Revolutionary Movement in Russia, 1878–1887," *American Slavic and E. European Review*, XVIII (1959), 182–186.

Barghoorn, Frederick C. "Nihilism, Utopia, and Realism in the Thought of Pisarev," *Russian Thought and Politics*, ed. H. McLean *et al.* (Cambridge, Mass., 1957), pp. 225–235.

————. "Some Russian Images of the West," *The Transformation of Russian Society*, ed. C. E. Black (Cambridge, Mass., 1960), pp. 574–587.

Becker, Christopher. "*Raznochintsy:* The Development of the Word and of the Concept." *American Slavic and E. European Review,* XVIII (1959), 63–74.

Bedford, C. H. "Dmitry Merezhkovsky, the Intelligentsia, and the Revolution of 1905," *Canadian Slavonic Papers,* ed. G. S. N. Luckyj (Toronto, 1958), III, 27–42.

Belinsky, V. G. *Selected Philosophical Works* (Moscow, 1956).

Beloff, Max. "Russia," *The European Nobility in the Eighteenth Century,* ed. A. Goodwin (London, 1953), pp. 172–189.

Berdiaev, Nicholas. *The Russian Idea* (New York, 1947).

Berlin, Isaiah. "A Marvelous Decade," *Encounter,* IV:21 (June, 1955), 27–39; V:26 (November, 1955), 21–29; V:27 (December, 1955), 22–43; VI:5 (May, 1956), 20–34.

Bill, Valentine T. *The Forgotten Class; The Russian Bourgeoisie from the Earliest Beginning to 1900* (New York, 1959).

Billington, James H. "The Intelligentsia and the Religion of Humanity," *American Historical Review,* LXV (1959–1960), 807–821.

————. *Mikhailovsky and Russian Populism* (Oxford, 1958).

Black, Cyril E., H. Seton-Watson and N. V. Riasanovsky. "Discussion: The Nature of Imperial Russian Society," *Slavic Review,* XX (1961), 565–600.

Bodde, Derk. *Tolstoy and China* (Princeton, 1950).

Bowman, Herbert E. "Intelligentsia in Nineteenth-Century Russia," *Slavic and E. European Journal,* XV (1957), 5–21.

————. "Revolutionary Elitism in Černyševsky," *American Slavic and East European Review,* XIII (1954), 185–199.

————. *Vissarion Belinski, 1811–1848; A Study in the Origins of Social Criticism in Russia* (Cambridge, Mass., 1954).

Bruford, W. H. *Chekhov and His Russia: A Sociological Study* (London, 1947).

Byrnes, Robert F. "Pobedonostsev on the Instruments of Russian Government," *Continuity and Change in Russian and Soviet Thought,* ed. E. J. Simmons (Cambridge, Mass., 1955), pp. 113–128.

Cahen, G. *Histoire des Relations de la Russie avec la Chine sous Pierre le Grand* (Paris, 1914).

Cherniavsky, Michael. "Khan or Basileus: An Aspect of Russian Medieval Political Theory," *Journal of the History of Ideas,* XX (1959), 459–476.

Chernyshevsky, N. G. *Selected Philosophical Works* (Moscow, 1953).

————. *What Is To Be Done?,* tr. B. R. Tucker, Vintage ed. (New York, 1961).

Daniels, R. V. "Intellectuals and the Russian Revolution," *American Slavic and E. European Review,* XX (1961), 270–278.

Dobroliubov, N. A. *Selected Philosophical Essays* (Moscow, 1956).

Dostoevsky, F. M. *The Diary of a Writer,* tr. and annot. B. Brazol (New York, 1949), 2 vols.

Elkin, B. I. "The Conflict between East and West; A Philosophical and Historical Approach," *Slavonic and E. European Review,* XXVII:69 (May 1949), 579–592.

Fedotov, G. P. *The Russian Religious Mind,* Torchbook ed. (New York, 1960).

Feldmesser, Robert A. "Social Classes and Political Structure," *The Transformation of Russian Society,* ed. C. E. Black (Cambridge, Mass., 1960), pp. 235–252.

Fischer, George. "The Intelligentsia and Russia," *The Transformation of Russian Society,* ed. C. E. Black (Cambridge, Mass., 1960), pp. 253–274.

———. "The Russian Intelligentsia and Liberalism," *Russian Thought and Politics,* ed. H. McLean et al., (Cambridge, Mass., 1957), p. 317–336.

———. *Russian Liberalism; From Gentry to Intelligentsia* (Cambridge, Mass., 1958).

Gerschenkron, Alexander. *Economic Backwardness in Historical Perspective* (Cambridge, Mass., 1962).

———. "The Problem of Economic Development in Russian Intellectual History of the Nineteenth Century," *Continuity and Change in Russian and Soviet Thought,* ed. E. J. Simmons (Cambridge, Mass., 1955), pp. 11–39.

Gurko, V. I. *Features and Figures of the Past; Government and Opinion in the Reign of Nicholas II,* ed. J. Sterling et al., tr. L. Matveev (Stanford, 1939).

Haimson, L. H. "The Parties and the State: The Evolution of Political Attitudes," *The Transformation of Russian Society,* ed. C. E. Black (Cambridge, Mass., 1960), pp. 110–145.

Hans, N. A. *History of Russian Educational Policy (1701–1917)* (London, 1931).

Hare, Richard. *Pioneers of Russian Social Thought* (London, 1951).

———. *Portraits of Russian Personalities between Reform and Revolution* (London, 1959).

Haumant, Emile. *La Culture française en Russie (1700–1900)* (Paris, 1910).

Herzen, Alexander. *From the Other Shore; and The Russian People and Socialism,* introd. I. Berlin (London, 1956).

———. *Selected Philosophical Works* (Moscow, 1956).

Ivanov-Razumnik, R. V. *Istoriia russkoi obshchestvennoi Mysli* (St. Petersburg, 1911–14), 2 vols.

Izhboldin, B. S. "The Eurasian Movement," *Russian Review,* V (1946), 64–73.

Kaplan, Frederick I. "Russian Fourierism of the 1840's: A Contrast to Herzen's Westernism," *American Slavic and East European Review,* XVII (1958), 161–172.

Karpovich, Michael. "Two Types of Russian Liberalism: Maklakov and Milliukov," *Continuity and Change in Russian and Soviet Thought,* ed. E. J. Simmons (Cambridge, Mass., 1955), pp. 129–143.

Khomiakov, A. S. *Polnoe Sobranie Sochinenii,* Vols. V–VII: *O vsemirnoi Istorii* (Moscow, 1904–1906).

Kliuchevskii, V. O. *A History of Russia,* tr. C. J. Hogarth (New York, 1960), 5 vols.

Kohn, Hans. "Dostoyevsky and Danilevsky: Nationalist Messianism," *Continuity and Change in Russian and Soviet Thought,* ed. E. J. Simmons (Cambridge, Mass., 1955), pp. 500–515.

———. *The Mind of Modern Russia,* Torchbook ed. (New York, 1962).

————. *Pan-Slavism; Its History and Ideology*, 2d rev. ed., Vintage ed. (New York, 1960).

Kornilov, Alexander. *Modern Russian History*, tr. A. S. Kaun (New York, 1943).

————. *Obshchestvennoe Dvizhenie pri Aleksandr II (1855–1881)* (Moscow, 1909).

Koyré, Alexandre. *Etudes sur l'Histoire de la Pensée philosophique en Russie* (Paris, 1950).

————. *La Philosophie et le Problème national en Russie au Début du XIXe Siècle* (Paris, 1929).

Lampert, E. *Studies in Rebellion* (New York, 1957).

Laue, Theodore H. von. *Sergei Witte and the Industrialization of Russia* (New York, 1963).

Lednicki, Waclaw. *Russia, Poland and the West; Essay in Literary and Cultural History* (New York, n.d.).

Leontiev, K. N. *Sobranie Sochinenii*, Vols. V–VII: *Vostok, Rossiia i Slavianstvo* (Moscow, 1912).

Losskii, N. O. *History of Russian Philosophy* (London, 1952).

Malia, Martin. *Alexander Herzen and the Birth of Russian Socialism, 1812–1855* (Cambridge, Mass., 1961).

————. "Schiller and the Early Russian Left," *Russian Thought and Politics*, ed. H. McLean *et al.* (Cambridge, Mass., 1957), pp. 169–200.

————. "What Is the Intelligentsia?" *Daedalus* (Summer, 1960), pp. 441–458.

Malozemoff, Andrew. *Russian Far Eastern Policy, 1881–1904* (Berkeley, 1958).

Masaryk, Thomas G. *The Spirit of Russia*, tr. E. and C. Paul, 2d ed. (London and New York, 1955), 2 vols.

Mazour, Anatole. *The First Russian Revolution* (Berkeley, 1937).

Meijer, J. M. *Knowledge and Revolution: The Russian Colony in Zuerich (1870–1873); A Contribution to the Study of Populism* (Assen, the Netherlands, 1955).

Mendel, Arthur P. *Dilemmas of Progress in Tsarist Russia: Legal Marxism and Legal Populism* (Cambridge, Mass., 1961).

Miliukov, Paul N. "Eurasianism and Europeanism in Russian History," *Festschrift Th. G. Masaryk zum 80. Geburtstage* (Bonn, 1930), I, 225–236.

————. *Le Mouvement intellectual russe*, tr. J. W. Bienstock (Paris, 1918).

————. *Ocherki po Istorii russkoi Kultury*, Jubilee ed. (Paris, 1930).

Mirsky, D. S. *A History of Russian Literature*, ed. F. J. Whitfield, Vintage ed. (New York, 1958).

Nahirny, Vladimir C. "The Russian Intelligentsia: From Men of Ideas to Men of Convictions," *Comparative Studies in Society and History*, IV (1961–62), 403–435.

Obshchestvennoe Dvizhenie v Rossii v Nachalie XX-go Vieka, ed. L. Martov *et al.* (St. Petersburg, 1909), Vol. I.

Ovsianiko-Kulikovskii, D. N. *Sobranie Sochinenii*, Vols. VII–IX: *Istoriia russkoi Intelligentii*, 6th ed. (Moscow, 1923–1924).

Parry, Albert. *Russian Missionaries in China, 1689–1917* (Berkeley, 1940).

Petrovich, Michael B. *The Emergence of Russian Pan-Slavism, 1856–1870* (New York, 1956).

Pipes, Richard. "The Historical Evolution of the Russian Intelligentsia," *Daedalus* (Summer, 1960), pp. 487–502.

———, ed. *Karamzin's Memoir on Ancient and Modern Russia; A Translation and Analysis* (Cambridge, Mass., 1959).

———. "Max Weber on Russia," *World Politics*, VII (1954–1955), 371–401.

Pisarev, D. *Selected Philosophical, Social and Political Essays* (Moscow, 1958).

Pollard, Alan P. "The Russian Intelligentsia: The Mind of Russia," *California Slavic Studies*, III (Berkeley, 1964), 1–32.

Radishchev, A. *A Journey from St. Petersburg to Moscow*, tr. L. Wiener, ed. with introd. R. Thaler (Cambridge, Mass., 1958).

Raeff, Marc. *Michael Speransky, Statesman of Imperial Russia, 1772–1839* (The Hague, 1957)

———. "The Russian Autocracy and Its Officials," *Russian Thought and Politics*, ed. H. McLean *et al.* (Cambridge, Mass., 1957), pp. 77–91.

———. "Some Reflections on Russian Liberalism," *Russian Review*, XVIII (1959), 218–230.

Reeves, Helen S. "Utopian Socialism in Russian Literature: 1840's–1860's," *American Slavic and East European Review*, XVIII (1959), 374–393.

Riasanovsky, N. V. "Fourierism in Russia," *American Slavic and East European Review*, XII (1953), 289–302.

———. *Nicholas I and Official Nationality in Russia, 1825–1855* (Berkeley, 1959).

———. "Russia and Asia: Two Nineteenth-Century Russian Views," *California Slavic Studies*, I (Berkeley, 1960), 170–181.

———. *Russia and the West in the Teaching of the Slavophiles* (Cambridge, Mass., 1952).

Roberts, H. L., M. Raeff, and M. Szeftel. "Discussion: Russia and the West," *Slavic Review*, XXIII (1964), 1–30.

Robinson, Geroid T. *Rural Russia under the Old Regime* (New York, 1932).

Rogger, Hans. "The Formation of the Russian Right, 1900–1906," *California Slavic Studies*, III (Berkeley, 1964), 66–94.

———. *National Consciousness in Eighteenth-Century Russia* (Cambridge, Mass., 1960).

———. "Nationalism and the State: A Russian Dilemma," *Comparative Studies in Society and History*, IV (1961–1962), 253–264.

Romanovich-Slavatinskii, A. *Dvorianstvo v Rossii ot Nachala XVIII Vieka do Otmieny kriepostnogo Prava*, 2d ed. (Kiev, 1912).

Sarkisyanz, E. "Russian Attitudes toward Asia," *Russian Review*, XIII (1954), 245–254.

———. *Russland und der Messianismus des Orients: Sendungsbewusstsein und politischer Chiliasmus des Ostens* (Tübingen, 1955).

Schapiro, Leonard. "The *Vekhi* Group and the Mystique of the Revolution," *Slavonic and East European Review*, XXXIV (1955), 56–76.

Schelting, Alexander von. *Russland und Europa im russischen Geschichtsdenken* (Bern, 1948).

Schwartz, Harry. *Russia's Soviet Economy*, 2d ed. (Engelwood Cliffs, N. J., 1954).

Seton-Watson, Hugh. *The Decline of Imperial Russia, 1855–1914* (New York, 1952).

Sliozberg, G. B. *Dorevoliutsionnyi Stroi Rossii* (Paris, 1933).

Spector, Ivar. *The First Russian Revolution; Its Impact on Asia* Spectrum ed. (Engelwood Cliffs, N. J., 1962).

Stanton, J. W. "Russian Embassies to Peking during the Eighteenth Century," *University of Michigan Historical Essays*, ed. A. E. R. Boak (Ann Arbor, 1937), pp. 97–112.

Stepun, Fedor. "The Russian Intelligentsia and Bolshevism," *Russian Review*, XVII (1958), 263–277.

Thaden, E. C. "The Beginnings of Romantic Nationalism in Russia," *American Slavic and E. European Review*, XIII (1954), 500–521.

Thaler, Roderick P. "Radiščev, Britain, and America," *Russian Thought and Politics*, ed H. McLean *et al.* (Cambridge, Mass., 1957), pp. 59–75.

Tidmarsh, Kyril. "Lev Tikhomirov and a Crisis in Russian Radicalism," *Russian Review*, XX (1961), 45–63.

Tkachev, P. N. *Izbrannie Sochineniia na sotsialno-politicheskie Temy*, ed. B. P. Kozmin (Moscow, 1922–1923).

Tompkins, S. T. *The Russian Intelligentsia* (Norman, Okla., 1957).

Tucker, Robert C. "The Image of Dual Russia," *The Transformation of Russian Society*, ed. C. E. Black (Cambridge, Mass., 1960), pp. 587–605.

Venturi, Franco. *Roots of Revolution; A History of the Populist and Socialist Movements in Nineteenth-Century Russia*, tr. F. Haskell (New York, 1960).

Viekhi: Sbornik Statei o russkoi Intelligentsii, by N. A. Berdiaev *et al.*, 3d ed. (Moscow, 1909).

Wallace, D. Mackenzie. *Russia on the Eve of War and Revolution*, ed. and introd. C. E. Black, Vintage ed. (New York, 1961).

Wildman, A. K. "The Russian Intelligentsia of the 1890's," *American Slavic and East European Review*, XIX (1960), 157–179.

Zenkovskii, V. V. *A History of Russian Philosophy*, tr. G. L. Kline (New York, 1953), 2 vols.

———. *Russian Thinkers and Europe*, tr. G. S. Bodde (Ann Arbor, 1953).

Zetlin, Mikhail. *The Decembrists*, tr. G. Panin, preface by M. Karpovich (New York, 1958).

RUSSIAN MARXISM

Akademiia Nauk SSSR. Institut Vostokovedeniia. *Lenin i Vostok; Sbornik Statei* (Moscow, 1960).

Baron, S. H. *Plekhanov: The Father of Russian Marxism* (Stanford, 1963).

———. "Plekhanov's Russia: The Impact of the West upon an 'Oriental' Society," *Journal of the History of Ideas*, XIX (1958), 388–404.

Berdiaev, Nicholas. *The Origin of Russian Communism*, tr. R. M. French, 2d ed. (London, 1955).

Boersner, D. *The Bolsheviks and the National and Colonial Question (1917–1928)* (Geneva, 1957).

Bukharin, N. "Imperialism and Communism," *Foreign Affairs*, XIV (1936), 563–577.

——. *Imperialism and World Economy* (New York, 1929).

——, et al. *Marxism and Modern Thought*, tr. R. Fox (London, 1935).

Bunyan, J., and H. H. Fisher. *The Bolshevik Revolution, 1917–1918; Documents and Materials* (Stanford, 1961).

Carr, E. H. *A History of Soviet Russia* (New York, 1950 ff.), 5 vols.

Dan, F. I. *Proiskhozdenie Bolshevizma* (New York, 1946).

Daniels, R. V. "Lenin and the Russian Revolutionary Tradition," *Russian Thought and Politics*, ed. H. McLean et al. (Cambridge, Mass., 1957), pp. 339–353.

——. "The State and the Revolution; A Case Study in the Genesis and Transformation of Communist Ideology," *American Slavic and E. European Review*, XII (1953), 22–43.

Degras, Jane, ed. *The Communist International; Documents, 1919–1943* (London and New York, 1956–60), 2 vols.

——, ed. *Soviet Documents on Foreign Policy* (New York, 1951), 3 vols.

Deutscher, I. *The Prophet Armed; Trotsky: 1879–1921* (New York, 1954).

——. *The Prophet Unarmed; Trotsky: 1921–1929* (New York, 1959).

——. *Stalin; A Political Biography* (New York, 1949).

Eudin, Xenia J., and R. C. North. *Soviet Russia and the East: 1920–1927; A Documentary Survey* (Stanford, 1957).

Fischer, Louis. *The Soviets in World Affairs, 1917–1929*, 2d ed. (Princeton, 1951), 2 vols.

Freymond, J. *Lenine et l'Impérialisme* (Lausanne, 1951).

Froelich, P. *Rosa Luxemburg; Her Life and Work*, tr. by E. Fitzgerald (London, 1940).

Gankin, Olga, and H. H. Fisher. *The Bolsheviks and the World War: The Origins of the Third International* (Stanford, 1940).

Gay, P. *The Dilemma of Democratic Socialism; Eduard Bernstein's Challenge to Marx* (New York, 1952).

Goodman, E. R. *The Soviet Design for a World State* (New York, 1960).

Haimson, L. H. *The Russian Marxists and the Origins of Bolshevism* (Cambridge, Mass., 1955).

Haithcox, John P. "The Roy-Lenin Debate on Colonial Policy: A New Interpretation," *Journal of Asian Studies*, XXIII (1963–1964), 93–101.

Hammond, T. T. *Lenin on Trade Unions and Revolution, 1893–1917* (New York, 1957).

——. "Leninist Authoritarianism before the Revolution," *Continuity and Change in Russian and Soviet Thought*, ed. E. J. Simmons (Cambridge, Mass., 1955), pp. 144–156.

Hilferding, Rudolf. *Das Finanzkapital: eine Studie über die jüngste Entwicklung des Kapitalismus*, 2d ed. (Vienna, 1910).

Hobson, J. A. *Imperialism; A Study*, 3d ed. rev. (London, 1938).

Hovde, B. J. "Socialist Theories of Imperialism prior to the Great War," *Journal of Political Economy*, XXXVI (1928), 569–591.

Joll, J. *The Second International, 1889–1914* (New York, 1956).

Kelsen, H. *The Political Theory of Bolshevism; A Critical Analysis* (Berkeley, 1948).

Kruger, Daniel H. "Hobson, Lenin, and Schumpeter on Imperialism," *Journal of the History of Ideas*, XVI (1955), 252–259.

Krupskaya, N. K. *Memories of Lenin*, tr. from 2d ed. E. Verney (New York, 1933), 2 vols.

Langer, William. "A Critique of Imperialism," *Foreign Affairs*, XIV (1935), 102–119.

Von Laue, T. H. *Why Lenin? Why Stalin? A Reappraisal of the Russian Revolution, 1900–1930* (Philadelphia, 1964).

Lazitch, B. *Lenine et le IIIᵉ Internationale*, preface by A. Aron (Neuchatel, 1951).

Lenin i Vostok; Sbornik Statei, 2d ed. (Moscow, 1925).

Low, A. D. *Lenin on the Question of Nationality* (New York, 1958).

Luxemburg, Rosa. *The Accumulation of Capital*, tr. A. Schwarzchild, introd. J. Robinson (New Haven, 1951).

Mehnert, Klaus. *Stalin versus Marx: the Stalinist Historical Doctrine* (New York, 1952).

Meyer, A. G. *Leninism* (Cambridge, Mass., 1957).

Novyi Vostok, ed. M. Pavlovich (1922–1927).

Page, Stanley W. *Lenin and World Revolution* (New York, 1959).

Pipes, Richard. *The Formation of the Soviet Union: Communism and Nationalism, 1917–1923* (Cambridge, Mass., 1954).

———. "Russian Marxism and Its Populist Background: The Late Nineteenth Century," *Russian Review*, XIX (1960), 316–337.

———. *Social Democracy and the St. Petersburg Movement, 1885–1897* (Cambridge, Mass., 1963).

Plekhanov, G. V. *Sochineniia*, ed. D. Riazanov (Moscow, 1923–27), 24 vols.

Polevoi, IU. Z. *Zarozhdenie Marksizma v Rossii 1883–1894 GG.* (Moscow, 1959).

Rochester, A. *Lenin on the Agrarian Question* (New York, 1942).

Schapiro, Leonard. *The Communist Party of the Soviet Union* (London and New York, 1959).

———. *The Origin of the Communist Autocracy* (London, 1955).

Schumpeter, Joseph A. *Imperialism; Social Classes*, Meridian ed. (New York, 1955).

Schwarz, Solomon M. "Populism and Early Russian Marxism on Ways of Economic Development of Russia," *Continuity and Change in Russian and Soviet Thought*, ed. E. J. Simmons (Cambridge, Mass., 1955), pp. 40–62.

Shub, David. *Lenin; A Biography* (Garden City, N. Y., 1948).

Smith, David G. "Lenin's 'Imperialism': A Study in the Unity of Theory and Practice," *Journal of Politics*, XVII (1955), 546–569.

Stalin, J. V. *Marxism and the National Question* (New York, 1942).

———. *Marxism and the National-Colonial Questions* (New York, 1935).

Stranjakovitch, B. *Lénine et le IIIᵉ Internationale* (Geneva, 1950).

Treadgold, Donald W. *Lenin and His Rivals; The Struggle for Russia's Future, 1898–1906* (New York, 1955).

Trotsky, L. *The First Five Years of the Communist International,* tr. J. G. Wright (New York, 1945–53) 2 vols.
——. *Lenin* (New York, 1925).
——. *The Permanent Revolution,* 1st Indian ed. (Calcutta, 1947).
Varga, E., and L. Mendelsohn, ed. *New Data for V. I. Lenin's "Imperialism, the Highest Stage of Capitalism"* (New York, n.d.).
Wetter, Gustave. *Dialectical Materialism: A Historical and Systematic Survey of Philosophy in the Soviet Union,* tr. P. Heath (New York, 1959).
Winslow, E. M. *The Pattern of Imperialism; A Study in the Theories of Power* (New York, 1948).
Wolfe, Bertram D. *Three Who Made a Revolution* (New York, 1948).
Yaresh, Leo. "The Problem of Periodization," *Rewriting Russian History,* ed. C. E. Black, 2d ed. rev. (New York, 1962), pp. 34–77.

THE CHINESE BACKGROUND

Biggerstaff, K. *The Earliest Modern Government Schools in China (1861–1894)* (Ithaca, N. Y., 1961).
——. "The Secret Correspondence of 1867–1868," *Journal of Modern History,* XXII (1950), 122–136.
——. "The T'ung Wen Kuan," *Chinese Social and Political Science Review,* XVIII (1934), 307–340.
Boardman, E. P. *Christian Influence upon the Ideology of the Taiping Rebellion, 1851–1864* (Madison, Wis., 1952).
Bodde, Derk. "Harmony and Conflict in Chinese Philosophy," *Studies in Chinese Thought,* ed. A. F. Wright (Chicago, 1953), pp. 19–80.
Brière, O. *Fifty Years of Chinese Philosophy, 1898–1950,* tr. L. G. Thompson (London, 1956).
Britton, Rosswell S. *The Chinese Periodical Press, 1800–1912* (Shanghai, 1933).
Cameron, Meribeth E. *The Reform Movement in China, 1898–1912* (Stanford, 1931).
Chan Wing-tsit. *Religious Trends in Modern China* (New York, 1953).
Chang Chih-tung. *China's Only Hope,* tr. S. I. Woodbridge (New York, 1900).
Chang Ching-lu, ed. *Chung-kuo chin-tai ch'u-pan shih-liao* (Shanghai, 1954), 2 vols.
——, ed. *Chung-kuo hsien-tai ch'u-pan shih liao* (Shanghai, 1954–56) 3 vols.
——, ed. *Chung-kuo ch'u-pan shih-liao pu-pien* (Peking, 1957).
Chang Chung-li. *The Chinese Gentry; Studies on Their Role in Nineteenth-Century Chinese Society,* introd. F. Michael (Seattle, 1955).
Chang Hsi-t'ung. "The Earliest Phase of the Introduction of Western Political Science into China," *Yenching Journal of Social Studies,* I (1950), 1–29.
Chang T'ien-tsu. *Sino-Portuguese Trade, 1514–1644; A Synthesis* (Leiden, 1934).

Ch'en, Gideon. *Lin Tse-hsü* (Peking, 1934).

———. *Tseng Kuo-fan* (Peking, 1935).

———. *Tso Tsung-t'ang* (Peking, 1938).

Ch'en, Jerome. *Yuan Shih-k'ai, 1859–1916* (Stanford, 1961).

Ch'en Teng-yüan. "Hsi-hsüeh lai Hua shih kuo-jen chih wu-tuan t'ai-tu," *Tung-fang tsa-chih*, XXVII (1930), 61–76.

Ch'ien Mu. *Chung-kuo chin san-pai nien hsüeh-shu shih*, 2 vols. (Shanghai, 1937).

Chih, André. *L'Occident "chrétien" vu par les Chinois, vers la Fin du XIXᵉ Siècle (1870–1900)*, (Paris, 1962).

Chow Tse-tsung. "The Anti-Confucian Movement in Early Republican China," *The Confucian Persuasion*, ed. A. F. Wright (Stanford, 1960), pp. 288–312.

———. *The May Fourth Movement; Intellectual Revolution in Modern China* (Cambridge, Mass., 1960).

Ch'ü T'ung-tsu. "Chinese Class Structure and Its Ideology," *Chinese Thought and Institutions*, ed. J. K. Fairbank (Chicago, 1957), pp. 235–250.

Ch'uan Han-sheng. "Ch'ing-mo fan-tui Hsi-hua ti yen-lun," *Ling-nan hsueh-pao*, V (1936), 122–166.

Clubb, O. Edmund. *Twentieth-Century China* (New York, 1964).

Cohen, P. A. "The Anti-Christian Tradition in China," *Journal of Asian Studies*, XX (1960–1961), 169–180.

De Bary, W. Theodore, Chan Wing-tsit, and Burton Watson, comp. *Sources of the Chinese Tradition* (New York, 1960).

De Francis, John. *Nationalism and Language Reform in China* (Princeton, 1950).

Eberhard, W. *Conquerors and Rulers; Social Forces in Medieval China* (Leiden, 1952).

Eisenstadt, S. N. "The Study of Oriental Despotism as Systems of Total Power," *Journal of Asian Studies*, XVII (1958), 435–446.

Fairbank, John K. "Synarchy under the Treaties," *Chinese Thought and Institutions*, ed. J. K. Fairbank (Chicago, 1957), pp. 204–231.

———. *Trade and Diplomacy on the China Coast; the Opening of the Treaty Ports, 1842–1854* (Cambridge, Mass., 1953).

———, and Ssu-yü Teng. *Ch'ing Administration; Three Studies* (Cambridge, Mass., 1960).

Fei Hsiao-tung. *China's Gentry; Essays in Rural-Urban Relations*, rev. and ed. M. P. Redfield (Chicago, 1953).

Fei Min. *Chung-kuo chin-tai ssu-hsiang fa-chan chien-shih* (Shanghai, 1949).

Feuerwerker, Albert. *China's Early Industrialization; Sheng Hsuan-huai (1844–1916) and Mandarin Enterprise* (Cambridge, Mass., 1958).

Franke, Wolfgang. *The Reform and Abolition of the Traditional Chinese Examination System* (Cambridge, Mass., 1960).

Feng Yu-lan. *A History of Chinese Philosophy*, tr. D. Bodde (Princeton, 1952–53), 2 vols.

Hackett, Roger F. "Chinese Students in Japan, 1900–1910," Harvard University Regional Studies, *Papers on China*, III (May, 1949), 134–169.

Ho Ping-ti. "Aspects of Social Mobility in China, 1368–1911," *Comparative Studies in Society and History*, I (1958–59), 330–359.

Hou Wai-lu. *Chin-tai Chung-kuo ssu-hsiang hsüeh-shuo shih* (Shanghai, 1947).

Howard, R. K. "K'ang Yu-wei (1858–1927): His Intellectual Background and Early Thought," *Confucian Personalities*, ed. A. F. Wright and D. Twichett (Stanford, 1962), pp. 294–316.

Hsia, C. T. *A History of Modern Chinese Fiction, 1917–1957* (New Haven, 1960).

Hsin ch'ing-nien, ed. Ch'en Tu-hsiu (1915–1921).

Hsü, Immanuel C. Y. *China's Entrance into the Family of Nations: The Diplomatic Phase, 1858–1880* (Cambridge, Mass., 1960).

Hsüeh Chün-tu. *Huang Hsing and the Chinese Revolution* (Stanford, 1961).

——. "Sun Yat-sen, Yang Ch'u-yun, and the Early Revolutionary Movement in China," *Journal of Asian Studies*, XIX (1959–60), 307–318.

Hu Hua, ed. *Chung-kuo hsin ming-chu chu-i ke-ming shih ts'an-k'ao tzu-liao* (Shanghai, 1951).

Hu Sheng. *Imperialism and Chinese Politics* (Peking, 1955).

Hu Shih. *The Chinese Renaissance* (Chicago, 1934).

Hua Kang. *Wu-ssu yün-tung shih* (Shanghai, 1951).

Huang Sung-k'ang. *Lu Hsun and the New Culture Movement of Modern China* (Amsterdam, 1957).

Hucker, Charles O. "Confucianism and the Chinese Censorial System," *Confucianism in Action*, ed. D. S. Nivison and A. F. Wright (Stanford, 1959), pp. 182–208.

Hughes, E. R. *The Invasion of China by the Western World* (New York, 1938).

Hummel, A. W. ed. *Eminent Chinese of the Ch'ing Period (1644–1912)* (Washington, D.C.: U.S. Library of Congress, Orientalia Division, 1943), 2 vols.

Jansen, Marius B. *The Japanese and Sun Yat-sen* (Cambridge, Mass., 1954).

Jung Meng-yüan. "Kitaiskaia Pressa 1905 G. o russkoi Revoliutsii," *Voprosy Istorii*, No. 6 (1955), pp. 98–104.

K'ang Yu-wei. *Ta T'ung Shu: The One-World Philosophy of K'ang Yu-wei*, tr. with introd, and notes L. G. Thompson (London, 1958).

Kiang Wen-han. *The Ideological Background of the Chinese Student Movement* (New York, 1948).

Kracke, E. A., Jr. "The Changing Role of the Chinese Intellectual: An Introductory Note," *Comparative Studies in Society and History*, I (1958–59), 23–25.

Kuo Chan-po. *Chin wu-shih nien Chung-kuo ssu-hsiang shih* (Peking, 1935).

Latourette, K. S. *A History of Christian Missions in China* (New York, 1929).

Lee Shu-ching. "Intelligentsia of China," *American Journal of Sociology*, LII (1946–47), 488–497.

Levenson, Joseph R. *Confucian China and Its Modern Fate*. Vol. I: *The Problem of Intellectual Continuity* (Berkeley and Los Angeles, 1958); Vol. II: *The Problem of Monarchical Decay* (Berkeley and Los Angeles, 1964); Vol. III: *The Problem of Historical Significance* (Berkeley and Los Angeles, 1965).

——. *Liang Ch'i-ch'ao and the Mind of Modern China* (Cambridge, Mass., 1959)

———. "*T'ien Hsia* and *Kuo*, and the 'Transvaluation of Values'," *Far Eastern Quarterly*, XI (1951–52), 447–451.
Levy, Marion J., Jr. *The Family Revolution in Modern China* (Cambridge, Mass., 1949).
Li Chien-nung. *The Political History of China, 1840–1928*, tr. and ed. S. Y. Teng and J. Ingalls (Princeton, 1956).
Li Shu. "I-chiu-ling-wu nien O-kuo ke-ming ho Chung-kuo," *Li-shih yen-chiu*, II (1955), 1–17.
Liang Ch'i-ch'ao. *Intellectual Trends in the Ch'ing Period*, tr. I. C. Y. Hsü (Cambridge, Mass., 1959).
Liang Sou-ming. *Tung-Hsi wen-hua chi ch'i che-hsüeh* (Shanghai, 1922).
Lin Yutang. *A History of the Press and Public Opinion in China* (Chicago, 1936).
Liu Hsuan-min. "Russo-Chinese Relations up to the Treaty of Nerchinsk," *Chinese Social and Political Science Review*, XXII (1940), 391–440.
Liu Kwang-ching. "Early Christian Colleges in China," *Journal of Asian Studies*, XX (1960–61), 71–78.
Lu Hsün. *Selected Works* (Peking, 1956–1960), 4 vols.
MacNair, Harlee F. *China in Revolution* (Chicago, 1935).
Marcus, J. T. "Time and the Sense of History: West and East," *Comparative Studies in Society and History*, III (1960–1961), 123–139.
Marsh, R. M. *The Mandarins; The Circulation of Elites in China, 1600–1900* (New York, 1961).
Michael, Franz. "State and Society in Nineteenth-Century China," *World Politics*, VII (1954–1955), 419–433.
Min-pao, 1905–1910 (Peking, 1957), photostat ed. 4 vols.
Muramatsu Yuji. "Some Theme in Chinese Rebel Ideologies," *The Confucian Persuasion*, ed. A. F. Wright (Stanford, 1960), pp. 241–267.
Needham, Joseph. "Human Laws and Laws of Nature in China and the West," *Journal of the History of Ideas*, XII (1951), 3–30, 194–230.
Nivison, David S. "The Problem of 'Knowledge' and 'Action' in Chinese Thought since Wang Yang-ming," *Studies in Chinese Thought*, ed. A. F. Wright (Chicago, 1953), pp. 112–145.
———. "Protest against Conventions and Conventions of Protest," *The Confucian Persuasion*, ed. A. F. Wright (Stanford, 1960), pp. 177–201.
Pavlovsky, M. N. *Chinese Russian Relations* ([New York, 1949]).
Peake, Cyrus H. *Nationalism and Education in Modern China* (New York, 1932).
Perevertailo, A. S., ed. *Ocherki Istorii Kitaia v noveishee Vremia* (Moscow, 1959).
Powell, R. L. *The Rise of Chinese Military Power, 1895–1911* (Princeton, 1955).
Sakai, Robert K. "Ts'ai Yüan-pei as a Synthesizer of Western and Chinese Thought," Harvard University Regional Studies, *Papers on China*, III (May, 1949), 170–192.
Sansom, George B. *The Western World and Japan; A Study in the Interaction of European and Asiatic Cultures* (New York, 1949).
Scalapino, Robert A., and Harold Schiffrin. "Early Socialist Currents in the Chinese Revolutionary Movement: Sun Yat-sen versus Liang Ch'i-ch'ao," *Journal of Asian Studies*, XVIII (1958–1959), 321–342.

Scalapino, Robert A., and G. T. Yu. *The Chinese Anarchist Movement* (Berkeley, 1961)

Schiffrin, Harold. "Sun Yat-sen's Early Land Policy: The Origin and Meaning of 'Equalization of Land Rights'," *Journal of Asian Studies,* XVI (1956–57), 549–594.

Schwartz, Benjamin. "Ch'en Tu-hsiu and the Acceptance of the Modern West," *Journal of the History of Ideas,* XII (1951), 61–72.

———. *In Search of Wealth and Power: Yen Fu and the West* (Cambridge, Mass., 1964).

———. "The Intellectual History of China: Preliminary Reflections," *Chinese Thought and Institutions,* ed. J. K. Fairbank (Chicago, 1957), pp. 15–30.

Shih Chün, ed. *Chung-kuo chin-tai ssu-hsiang shih ts'an-k'ao tzu-liao chien-pien* (Peking, 1957).

Shih, Vincent Y. C. "The Ideology of the Taiping T'ien Kuo," *Sinologica,* III (1951), 1–15.

Shu Hsin-ch'eng. *Chin-tai Chung-kuo liu-hsüeh shih* (Shanghai, 1927).

Steiger, G. N. *China and the Occident; The Origin and Development of the Boxer Movement* (New Haven, 1927).

Sun, E-tu Zen, and J. de Francis. *Chinese Social History: Translations of Selected Studies* (Washington, D. C., 1956).

Sun Yat-sen. *Tsung-li ch'uan-chi,* ed. Hu Han-min (Shanghai, 1930).

Swisher, Earl. "Chinese Intellectuals and the Western Impact, 1838–1900," *Comparative Studies in Society and History,* I (1958–59), 26–37.

Tan, Chester. *The Boxer Catastrophe* (New York, 1955).

Teng Ssu-yü. *New Light on the History of the Taiping Rebellion* (Cambridge, Mass., 1950).

———. and J. K. Fairbank. *China's Response to the West; A Documentary Survey, 1839–1923* (Cambridge, Mass., 1954).

Tsien Tsuen-hsuin. "Western Impact on China through Translation," *Far Eastern Quarterly,* XIII (1953–1954), 305–327.

Tsing-hua Collegiate Journal (1917–1918).

Tsou Lu. *Chung-kuo Kuomintang shih-k'ao* (Chungking, 1944).

Tsui Shu-chin. "The Influence of the Canton-Moscow Entente upon Sun Yat-sen's Political Philosophy," *Chinese Social and Political Science Review,* XVIII (1934), 96–145, 177–209, 341–388.

Tsung Hyui-puh. "Chinese Translations of Western Literature," *Chinese Social and Political Science Review,* XII (1928), 369–378.

Tung-fang tsa-chih (1917–1920).

Van Slyke, L. P. "Liang Sou-ming and the Rural Reconstruction Movement," *Journal of Asian Studies,* XVIII (1958–59), 457–474.

Varg, P. A. *Missionaries, Chinese, and Diplomats; The American Protestant Movement in China, 1890–1952* (Princeton, 1958).

Waley, Arthur. *The Opium War through Chinese Eyes* (New York, 1958).

Wang, Y. C. "Intellectuals and Society in China, 1860–1949," *Comparative Studies in Society and History,* III (1960–1961), 394–426.

———. "The Intelligentsia in China," *Foreign Affairs,* XXXVI (1957–58), 315–329.

———. "Western Impact and Social Mobility in China," *American Sociological Review,* XXV (1960), 843–855.

Weber, Max. *The Religion of China: Confucianism and Taoism,* tr. and ed. H. H. Gerth (Glencoe, Ill., 1951).

Wilhelm, H. "The Problem of Within and Without, a Confucian Attempt in Syncretism," *Journal of the History of Ideas,* XII (1951), 48–60.

Wilhelm, R. "Intellectual Movements in Modern China," *Chinese Social and Political Science Review,* VIII (1924), 110–124.

Wittfogel, Karl A. "Chinese Society: An Historical View," *Journal of Asian Studies,* XVI (1956–57), 343–364.

———. *Oriental Despotism; A Comparative Study of Total Power* (New Haven, 1957).

———. "Oriental Society in Transition," *Far Eastern Quarterly,* XIV (1954–55), 469–478.

Wright, Arthur F. "The Study of Chinese Civilization," *Journal of the History of Ideas,* XXI (1960), 233–255.

Wright, Mary C. *The Last Stand of Chinese Conservatism; The T'ung-chih Restoration, 1862–1874* (Stanford, 1957).

———. "The Pre-Revolutionary Intellectuals of China and Russia," *China Quarterly,* No. 6 (1961), pp. 175–179.

Yamamoto, Tatsuro and Sumiko. "The Anti-Christian Movement in China, 1922–1927," *Far Eastern Quarterly,* XII (1952–53), 133–147.

Yang, C. K. "The Functional Relations between Confucian Thought and Chinese Religion," *Chinese Thought and Institutions,* ed. J. K. Fairbank (Chicago, 1957), pp. 269–290.

———. "Some Characteristics of Chinese Bureaucratic Behavior," *Confucianism in Action,* ed. D. S. Nivison and A. F. Wright (Stanford, 1959), pp. 134–164.

Yang Ming-chai. *P'ing Chung-Hsi wen-hua kuan* (Peking, 1924).

CHINESE COMMUNISM

Boorman, Howard L. "Mao Tse-tung: The Lacquered Image," *China Quarterly,* No. 16 (October–December 1963), pp. 1–55.

Brandt, C. *Stalin's Failure in China, 1924–1927* (Cambridge, Mass., 1958).

———, B. Schwartz and J. K. Fairbank. *A Documentary History of Chinese Communism* (Cambridge, Mass., 1952).

Chao Kuo-chün. *Agrarian Policy of the Chinese Communist Party, 1921–1959* (Bombay, 1960).

Ch'en Po-ta. *Lun Mao Tse-tung ssu-hsiang* (Peking, 1951).

———. *Mao Tse-tung on the Chinese Revolution,* tr. from 7th ed. of 1952 (Peking, 1953).

Ch'en Tu-hsiu. *Tu-hsiu wen-t'sun* (Shanghai, 1922).

———, et al. *Wo-men ti cheng-chih i-chien shu* (n.p., n.d.).

Ch'ü Ch'iu-pai. *Chung-kuo ke-ming chih cheng-lun wen-t'i* (n.p., 1927).

Chung-kuo Kung-ch'an-tang. *Eighth National Congress of the Communist Party of China* (Peking, 1956), 3 vols.

Cohen, A. A. "How Original is 'Maoism'?" *Problems of Communism,* X:6 (November–December, 1961), 34–42.

———. *The Communism of Mao Tse-tung* (Chicago, 1964).

Communist China, 1955–1959; Policy Documents with Analysis, foreword by R. R. Bowie and J. K. Fairbank (Cambridge, Mass., 1962).

Daniels, R. V. "The Chinese Revolution in Russian Perspective," *World Politics,* XIII (1960–1961), 210–230.

Doolin, D. J., and P. J. Golas. *"On Contradiction* in the Light of Mao Tse-tung's Essay on 'Dialectical Materialism',*" China Quarterly,* No. 19 (July–September 1964), pp. 38–46.

Erenburg, G. B. *Natsionalno-osvoboditelnoe Dvizhenie v Kitae (1918–1924)* (Moscow, 1950).

———. *Ocherki natsionalno-osvoboditelnoi Borby kitaiskogo Naroda v noveishee Vremia* (Moscow, 1951).

Fairbank, J. K., and E-tu Zen Sun. *Chinese Communist Publications: An Annotated Bibliography of Material in the Chinese Library at Harvard University* (Cambridge, Mass., 1949).

Feuerwerker, Albert. "China's History in Marxian Dress," *American Historical Review,* LXVI (1960–1961), 323–353.

———. "From 'Feudalism' to 'Capitalism' in Recent Historical Writing from Mainland China," *Journal of Asian Studies,* XVIII (1958–1959), 107–115.

———, and S. Cheng. *Chinese Communist Studies of Modern Chinese History* (Cambridge, Mass., 1961).

Gasster, Michael. "Some Recent Books on the Rise of Chinese Communism," *Slavic Review,* XXIII (1964), 333–342.

Griffith, William E. *The Sino-Soviet Rift* (Cambridge, Mass., 1963).

Halpern, A. M. "The Foreign Uses of the Chinese Revolutionary Model," *China Quarterly,* No. 7 (July–September, 1961), pp. 1–16.

Harrison, James P. "The Li Li-san Line and the CCP in 1930," *China Quarterly,* No. 14 (April–June, 1963), pp. 178–194; No. 15 (July–September, 1963), pp. 140–159.

Ho Kan-chih. *A History of the Modern Chinese Revolution* (Peking, 1959).

Holubnychy, Vsevolod. "Mao Tse-tung's Materialistic Dialectics," *China Quarterly,* No. 19 (July–September, 1964), pp. 3–37.

Hsiao, Tso-liang. *Power Relations within the Chinese Communist Movement, 1930–1934; A Study of Documents* (Seattle, 1961).

Hsüeh, Chün-tu. *The Chinese Communist Movement, 1921–37: An Annotated Bibliography of Selected Materials in the Chinese Collection of the Hoover Institute on War, Revolution and Peace,* Hoover Institute Bibliography Series No. 8 (Stanford, 1960).

Hu Chiao-mu. *Thirty Years of the Communist Party of China* (Peking, 1952).

Hu Hua, comp. *Chung-kuo hsin min-chu chu-i ke-ming shih* (Shanghai, 1950).

Hua Kang. *Chung-kuo min-tsu chieh-fang yün-tung shih* (Peking, 1951).

Hudson, G. F., R. Lowenthal, and R. MacFarquhar, documented and analyzed. *The Sino-Soviet Dispute* (New York, 1961).

International Conference on Sino-Soviet Bloc Affairs. *Unity and Contradiction; Major Aspects of Sino-Soviet Relations,* ed. K. London (New York, 1962).

Isaacs, Harold R. *The Tragedy of the Chinese Revolution*, rev. ed. (Stanford, 1951).

Johnson, C. A. *Peasant Nationalism and Communist Power* (Stanford, 1962).

Kapitsa, M. S. *Sovetsko-kitaiskie Otnosheniia* (Moscow, 1958).

Labedz, Leopold, ed. *Revisionism: Essays on the History of Marxist Ideas* (New York, 1962).

Laqueur, Z. "The Shifting Line of Soviet Orientology," *Problems of Communism*, V:2 (March–April, 1956), 20–26.

Leng Shao-chuan and Norman D. Palmer. *Sun Yat-sen and Communism* (New York, 1961).

Levenson, Joseph R. "The Past Made to Measure: History under Chairman Mao," *Soviet Survey*, No. 24 (April–June, 1958), pp. 32–37.

Li Ta-chao. *Li Ta-chao hsüan-chi* (Peking, 1962).

MacFarquhar, Roderick. *The Hundred Flowers Campaign and the Chinese Intellectuals* (New York, 1960).

McLane, Charles B. *Soviet Policy and the Chinese Communists, 1931–1946* (New York, 1958).

Mao's China; Party Reform Documents, 1942–44, tr. with introd. B. Compton (Seattle, 1952).

Meisner, Maurice. *Li Ta-chao and the Origins of Chinese Marxism* (University of Chicago doctoral dissertation, 1962).

Mu Fu-sheng. *The Wilting of the Hundred Flowers; the Chinese Intelligentsia under Mao* (New York, 1962).

Nivison, David S. "Communist Ethics and Chinese Tradition," *Journal of Asian Studies*, XVI (1956–1957), 51–74.

North, Robert C. *Kuomintang and Chinese Communist Elites* (Stanford, 1952).

———. *Moscow and Chinese Communists* (Stanford, 1953).

———. "Two Revolutionary Models: Russian and Chinese," *Communist Strategies in Asia*, ed. A. D. Barnett (New York, 1963), pp. 34–60.

———. and X. J. Eudin. *M. N. Roy's Mission to China; the Communist-Kuomintang Split of 1927* (Berkeley, 1963).

Roy. M. N. *Revolution and Counter-Revolution in China* (Calcutta, 1946).

Schram, Stuart R. "On the Nature of Mao Tse-tung's 'Deviation' in 1927," *China Quarterly*, No. 18 (April–June, 1964), pp. 55–66.

———. *The Political Thought of Mao Tse-tung* (New York, 1963).

Schran, Peter. "On the Rationality of the Great Leap Forward and Rural People's Communes," *Ventures*, V:1 (Winter, 1965), 31–38.

Schwartz, Benjamin. *Chinese Communism and the Rise of Mao* (Cambridge, Mass., 1951).

———. "Ideology and the Sino-Soviet Alliance," *Moscow-Peking Axis; Strengths and Strains*, by H. L. Boorman *et al.* (New York, 1957), pp. 112–141.

———. "The Intelligentsia in Communist China—A Tentative Comparison," *Daedalus* (Summer, 1960), pp. 604–621.

———. "Marx and Lenin in China," *Far Eastern Survey*, XVIII:15 (July 27, 1949), 174–178.

————. "A Marxist Controversy in China," *Far Eastern Quarterly*, XIII (1953–1954), 143–153.

————. "New Trends in Maoism," *Problems of Communism*, VI:4 (July–August, 1957), 1–8.

————. "On the Originality of Mao Tse-tung," *Foreign Affairs*, XXXIV 1955), 67–76.

Snow, Edgar. *Red Star over China*, Black Cat ed. (New York, 1961).

Steiner, H. Arthur. *Chinese Communism in Action* (Los Angeles, 1953).

————. " 'On the Record' with Mao and His Regime," *Journal of Asian Studies*, XVII (1957–1958), 215–223.

Ting Shou-ho et al. *Shih-yüeh ke-ming tui Chung-kuo ke-ming ti ying-hsiang* (Peking, 1957).

Trotsky, L. *Problems of the Chinese Revolution* (New York, 1932).

Whiting, Allen S. *Soviet Policy in China, 1917–1924* (New York, 1954).

Wilbur, C. Martin, and Julie L. How, ed. *Documents on Communism, Nationalism and Soviet Advisers in China; 1918–1927* (New York, 1956).

Wittfogel, Karl A. "Some Remarks on Mao's Handling of Concepts and Problems of Dialectics," *Studies in Soviet Thought*, III:4 (December, 1963), 251–269.

————. and B. Schwartz. "The Legend of 'Maoism'," *China Quarterly*, No. 1 (January–March, 1960), pp. 72–86; No. 2 (April–June, 1960), pp. 16–42.

Zagoria, Donald S. *The Sino-Soviet Conflict, 1956–1961* (Princeton, 1962).

Index